T H A T ' S A
GREAT
QUESTION

THAT'S A GREAT QUESTION

WHAT TO SAY WHEN YOUR FAITH IS CHALLENGED

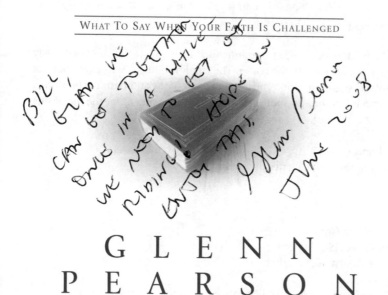

Bill,
Glenn we
can get together
once in a while so
we need to get to
[illegible]. Hope so
Enjoy this.
Glenn Pearson
June 2008

GLENN PEARSON

The Bible Teacher's Teacher

COOK COMMUNICATIONS MINISTRIES
Colorado Springs, Colorado • Paris, Ontario
KINGSWAY COMMUNICATIONS LTD
Eastbourne, England

Victor® is an imprint of
Cook Communications Ministries, Colorado Springs, CO 80918
Cook Communications, Paris, Ontario
Kingsway Communications, Eastbourne, England

THAT'S A GREAT QUESTION
© 2007 by Glenn Pearson

First Printing, 2007
Printed in the United States of America

1 2 3 4 5 6 7 8 9 10

Cover: Roark Creative
Cover Photo: iStockphoto
Interior Design: Karen Athen

ISBN 978-0-7814-4357-9
LCCN 2006933102

To Annette, Andy, and Stephanie—

*The three most important people
in my life*

CONTENTS

Appendixes and Readers' Guide at www.cookministries.com/GreatQuestion

ACKNOWLEDGMENTS

Sometimes a team working on a project is as effective as four people huddled around a jeweler's bench trying to fix a watch. At other times, it's like a NASCAR pit crew where each member plays a specific role designed to propel the driver on to victory. My experience writing this book was very much like the latter.

During the lengthy and sometimes torturous process of composing this work, many people assisted through offering words of encouragement, letting me test out ideas on them, lending me helpful material, providing insights into the publishing world, helping with the editing process, and/or praying for my success. To each of you, I offer hearty thanks.

In addition, I would like to offer three special notes of gratitude:

First, my deepest appreciation to the Wednesday morning Knuckleheads Anonymous and the Every-Other-Tuesday guys. Thanks so much for believing in this project and for encouraging me along the way.

Thanks to Duane Hanson for his words of support and helpful suggestions.

And finally, thanks to my good friend Rick Satterthwaite, who had the tenacity (or was it poor judgment?) to slog through an early draft, providing a much-needed reality check. Rick also suggested numerous excellent verbal images that helped bring many of my points to life. Some of the more colorful turns of phrase actually flowed from Rick's pen, not mine. Many thanks!

Author's Note

You will see that I use many real-life stories to illustrate my points. Although the characters often end up being heroes, that is not always the case. In some instances, I have changed selected details to protect the privacy of those involved.

INTRODUCTION

As we pulled around the corner onto Linwood Avenue, my wife, Annette, and I could hardly contain our excitement. The months of waiting were over and we were about to park the large yellow rental truck that contained all our earthly possessions in front of our very first house—modest though it was. Thankfully, it was early enough in the day that our clothing had not yet fused to the truck's "deluxe vinyl seats," but we knew we'd be plenty uncomfortable by the end of the day anyway because of all the lifting and hefting. But we didn't care. This was the beginning of a brand-new chapter in our lives.

I had just finished my grueling two-year master's degree program at Ohio State University that made the challenge of balancing the national budget seem like a simple Sunday afternoon task. Annette spent those two years working for an apartment management company whose ethical standards were only slightly higher than those of Hannibal Lecter from the movie *The Silence of the Lambs*. We went into the experience knowing that it would tax us to the max, but we figured we could "hold our breaths" for two years and make it through.

But all that was behind us now. We were moving from Columbus to its archrival city of Ann Arbor, Michigan, where I was to start my first job in my chosen field of health-care administration. Besides that, we were awaiting the arrival of our first child. And now we were about to join the ranks of weekend do-it-yourselfers. So the excitement meter in the Pearson family was at about 9.8!

We quickly settled into life in Ann Arbor, one of the truly great college towns in the country. Beyond the concerts, athletic events, special programs, and great restaurants, what we enjoyed the most was getting to know our neighbors and church friends in what was one of the first "adult" situations of our lives. We were no longer students, no longer transitioning from something. We were beginning a normal lifestyle in a great place to live.

We especially enjoyed becoming good friends with our next-door neighbors Steve and Jan Hamann, with whom we shared many interests. So we were disappointed a few years later when they announced that they would be moving to Chicago. Even though our friendship survives to this day, we knew then that things would inevitably change.

However, we were pleased to learn that the new family moving in was a young couple with a son, Tommy, who was almost exactly our son Andy's age. The Browns were the quintessential Ann Arbor family: Bill worked in the information technology center at the university, and Susan worked in one of the professional departments at a local hospital. They were well-educated and friendly professionals riding the growth curve of their respective careers. Both were devoted to Tommy, their only child, and they made sure he had only the best resources, as well as a stimulating environment in which his emerging curiosity could flourish. The Browns encouraged anything that furthered creativity and imagination: visits to the local hands-on museum, dozens of educational books, imaginative play activities, and anything else a wonderful city like Ann Arbor could offer. Andy and Tommy spent many afternoons doing typical boy things, and it was great to have a built-in playmate so readily available.

About the time Andy turned five, we invited Tommy to visit our church for the annual Christmas program. Because Andy was in the cast (playing, as I recall, the south end of a donkey), we had to arrive at the event early so all the children could rehearse their parts one more time. As typically happens in these settings, not every child was fully engaged in the activities on stage all the time. This allowed Andy and Tommy to exercise their God-given creativity by inventing a number of games to play in the pews, most of which involved rapid body motion.

Right in the middle of one of those games, Tommy suddenly stopped, picked up a Bible from the pew rack, and asked (rather loudly, I might add), "Hey! What's a dictionary doing in a church?"

Annette and I chuckled at the cuteness of his question. But the more I thought about it, the more I realized that this innocent five-year-old's question was an unwitting commentary on contemporary American culture when it comes to the Bible. Here was a bright, inquisitive boy, raised by two doting and well-educated parents in an incredibly enriched environment. Yet not only did he know nothing about the Bible; he didn't even recognize it. Instead, he mistook it for a dictionary.

Rather than seeking inspiration and meaning in life from the Bible, our culture has symbolically replaced it with the dictionary, a symbol of knowledge, learning, and enlightenment. I am committed to excellence in academics and intellectual pursuits, but this innocent mistake illustrates how so many people have replaced a vital relationship with their Creator (symbolized by the Bible) with a worship of knowledge and the mind (symbolized by the dictionary).

HARD TIMES FOR CONSERVATIVE RELIGION

It's safe to say that traditional religion has fallen into disfavor in contemporary American culture. Many people believe that religion is based in the dusty past and on worldviews that are no longer valid. If we were playing the old *$10,000 Pyramid* word-association TV game show, I suspect that the most popular matching words for *religion* would be *old, stuffy, formal, restricting,* and *outdated.* A close friend who does church work in Spain recently commented that some of the words that might appear in *$10,000 Pyramid Euro* would include: *dangerous, narrow-minded, bigoted,* and *irrelevant.*

Differing perspectives on the role of traditional religious ideas is a major point of debate between those we call theological conservatives and theological liberals. Conservatives believe that God's truth was delivered once for all and that, at its core, it is a never-changing set of beliefs that is relevant for all people in every age. They believe that, as history and cultures progress, its central message remains as reliable and relevant in the twenty-first-century as it was in the first.

Liberals disagree and argue that knowledge and understanding progress and evolve. If we take advantage of the latest thinking in such areas as science, medicine, and sociology, they argue, why shouldn't we recognize that religious concepts and thought advance as well? No one would suggest that the scientific knowledge of Jesus' day is superior to that of twenty-first century Western culture. Why, then, should we think their concepts of God would fare any better in the modern world?

Another blow to the reputation of traditional religion in contemporary life is the observation that intelligent and well-educated people often ignore or even ridicule conservative religious beliefs. Even though most of our nation's earliest colleges and universities were built on the foundational belief that all truth is God's truth, the number of contemporary university professors today who embrace the Christian faith and the Bible is disappointingly low. Committed Christian professors and students in today's academic environment have now been relegated to a second-class status.

Add to this the number of "cool" people in the media and entertainment industries who delight in scorning religion. It is easy to understand why Christianity is conspicuously absent from today's lists of hot youth culture trends.

THE PRESS WEIGHS IN

Much of contemporary American culture, and especially mainstream media, stereotypes anyone who believes the Bible. The media portray believers, at best, as undereducated or, at worst, as dangerous bigots who seek to impose a narrow, superstition-based worldview on everyone else. In an infamous *Washington Post* column published in 1993, staff writer Michael Weisskopf characterized followers of Jerry Falwell and Pat Robertson as "largely poor, uneducated, and easy to command."[1] Needless to say, his outrageous statement caused quite a stir among Christian intellectuals. Some evangelicals reportedly even began wearing lapel buttons that read, "Poor, Uneducated, and Easy to Command."

There was such an uproar that the *Post* printed a correction the following day, stating, "An article yesterday characterized followers of television evangelists Jerry Falwell and Pat Robertson as 'largely poor, uneducated, and easy to command.' There is no factual basis for that statement." According to reporter Terry Mattingly, Michael Weisskopf eventually "repented, sort of" by stating that he should have said that evangelicals are "'relatively' poor, uneducated, and easy to command."[2] Sadly, Weisskopf's comments reflect the view of many people who presumably consider themselves "well-off, educated, and not subject to manipulation." Imagine the howls of protest if a reporter described any other demographic group (Jewish people, Muslims, African Americans, Hispanics, senior citizens, southerners) as "largely poor, uneducated, and easy to command." That writer's career would experience a severe speed bump, if it survived at all.

More recently, Daniel C. Dennett penned an op-ed piece titled "The Bright Stuff" in the *New York Times* in which he promotes naturalism, the denial of any reality beyond what one can observe in nature. In it, Dennett suggests that we label the adherents of naturalism "brights." His definition of a "bright" is someone who doesn't

... BELIEVE IN GHOSTS OR ELVES OR THE EASTER BUNNY—OR GOD. WE DISAGREE ABOUT MANY THINGS AND HOLD A VARIETY OF VIEWS ABOUT MORALITY, POLITICS AND THE MEANING OF LIFE, BUT WE SHARE A DISBELIEF IN BLACK MAGIC—AND LIFE AFTER DEATH.[3]

According to Dennett, to say, "'I'm a bright' is not a boast, but a simple avowal of an inquisitive world view." Atheists, agnostics, and people with no religious preference are brights. He even identifies brights as "the moral backbone of the nation: brights take their civic duties seriously precisely because they don't trust God to save humanity from its follies."[4]

A month later, the *New York Times* ran another op-ed piece titled "Believe It, or Not" by Nicholas D. Kristof.[5] Kristof decried the fact that "American Christianity is becoming less intellectual and more mystical over time." A centerpiece of his argument is the statistic (for which he provides no source) that "Americans are three times as likely to believe in the Virgin Birth of Jesus (83 percent) as in evolution (28 percent)." He is concerned that, within Catholic and Protestant churches, the scholarly and religious worlds are "increasingly antagonistic." After opining that the Islamic world's current crisis is largely created by "a similar drift away from a rich intellectual tradition and toward the mystical," he concludes, "the heart is a wonderful organ, but so is the brain."

Did you catch that? If you believe in such "mystical" concepts as the virgin birth, you are thinking with your heart and not with your brain. And, of course, he implies that thinking with your heart is not thinking at all. Admittedly, a belief in the virgin birth requires elements outside the realm of what most "brights" would consider "admissible evidence," but to imply that the intellect has no role in supporting belief in the virgin birth smacks of unmitigated arrogance.

The aforementioned columns are examples of how skeptics typically view the Bible and anyone who takes it seriously. The implication (spoken or unspoken) is that intellectually curious people inevitably drift toward a rationalistic position that excludes anything supernatural. Anyone who believes in God probably also sets out fresh carrots on Easter Eve for the anticipated nocturnal visitor. To put it more bluntly, anyone who is smart will be a skeptic, and anyone who embraces traditional religious beliefs is intellectually suspect.

Any columnist, along with every other American, has the right to express his or her convictions about the ultimate questions of life and on the source or sources from which answers should be sought. Nevertheless, as I hope to demonstrate in this book, their declaration of victory in the battle for the intellectual high ground is premature.

MORE NEGATIVES

We immediately see that those who ascribe authority to the Bible face an uphill battle in academic and intellectual circles. We are the new counterculture. Our cause is made that much harder by the nagging public relations problem created by the misdeeds of groups and individuals who, in the name of Jesus, have committed serious and even dangerous acts. Church history unfortunately contains many dark chapters where zealous but misguided people acted in very unchristian ways. There were the medieval Crusades, the Spanish Inquisition, Galileo's heresy trial, and many other tragic acts.

In more recent times we have witnessed examples of fanatics whose misguided theology has resulted in deadly outcomes for themselves and/or others. A passionate young minister named Jim Jones formed a cult that relocated to Guyana in South America. In 1978, he ordered the suicides of 912 of his followers, making him the person responsible for the most number of murders in American history up to that point.[6] We have also seen egregious moral lapses committed by members of the religious establishment. During the 1980s, several prominent televangelists, by their sexual and financial indiscretions, smeared the very gospel they proclaimed. More recently the revelation and cover-up of sexual abuse and pedophilia has rocked the Catholic Church in America. And in late 2006, the evangelical world was shocked to learn that the Reverend Ted Haggard, president of the National Association of Evangelicals and pastor of a hugely influential Colorado church, admitted to a homosexual relationship.

The issue of "Christians behaving badly" is, of course, more than merely a public relations problem. It's indicative of a fundamental misunderstanding or misapplication of Jesus' message, and sometimes it's simply the result of sin.

Those who stand outside the walls of the church witness such behavior and conclude that, far from being the answer to life's ultimate questions, biblical Christianity often seems to be more the problem than the solution. It's not hard to see why Christianity and the Bible often receive as enthusiastic a welcome in today's popular culture as a Greenpeace activist would get at a Texas oil industry convention.

AM I CRAZY?

You might think it odd that I would introduce a book about the trustworthiness of the Bible with a litany of failures within the Christian faith. My purpose is to demonstrate that, far from being "largely poor, uneducated, and easy to command" or not particularly "bright," some Christians are willing to grapple with the intellectual and philosophical issues our position has generated. And despite these challenges, I am comfortable with the position held by Christians throughout the centuries that the Bible is God's inspired, inerrant, infallible, and historically reliable message for all people.

The purpose of this book, then, is to demonstrate that a commitment to academic excellence and intellectual integrity is consistent with belief in the Bible. I hope to equip you with valuable perspectives and insights that will help you identify and confidently respond to filters often used by those outside the historic Christian faith. Furthermore, I will arm you with practical principles that can clarify some tough challenges to Christian beliefs.

My book consists of two parts:

- Part 1—"The Filters"—goes behind the scenes to examine how our presuppositions can distort our perceptions of the Bible and Jesus.

- Part 2—"The Filter of Faith"—provides eighteen principles that help reconcile apparent contradictions in the New Testament Gospels.

THE TRUTH ABOUT ME

Before we launch into this discussion, however, here's a brief glimpse into my own academic and spiritual background to help you understand my perspective.

THE KID YOU LOVED TO HATE

Now, I have to tell you, I have mixed feelings about sharing the material that follows for two reasons. First, it is always at least a little uncomfortable to play up your own strengths and talk about your achievements. Second, I hesitate to go over this because I don't want you to think I was a total dork in high school (even though I have to admit that I probably was). I've been told that confession is good for the soul but bad for the reputation.

"Curve buster." "Teacher's pet." "Brownnose." Take your pick. Any of these terms would have fit me going through school. I was one of those rare kids who actually loved school. I even preferred standardized tests to Easter vacation, since that was where I could really shine! From very early in my elementary school career, I basked in the special attention and enriched learning opportunities that came my way.

As I moved into junior high school, I got into a friendly competition with a few of the other strong students, and we made a habit of (very publicly) sharing our terrific grades with each other (and anyone else who happened to be within fifty yards) to see who did the best. Disgusting, isn't it? And I was very proud of each letter of commendation from various junior high teachers.

By the end of my sophomore year of high school, I realized that I had one of the highest grade point averages in my class, and

I figured out that, with a lot of hard work and maybe just a little luck, I could probably graduate at the top of my class as either valedictorian or salutatorian. So I made it my goal to do just that. In fact, I even considered making a large sign to hang over the desk where I did my schoolwork that would read "V or S" as a daily reminder of my goal. You can imagine my pride as I delivered the valedictory address, which of course absolutely no one remembers, not even my mother.

OTHER ACADEMIC CREDENTIALS

My family was very pleased when Syracuse University, the State of New York, and a local foundation awarded me academic scholarships, which made my undergraduate education free. At Syracuse, I participated in the honors program all four years and graduated magna cum laude. I was also inducted into two national honor societies: Phi Beta Kappa and Phi Kappa Phi.

I also finished near the top of my graduate school program at Ohio State University, where I received two prestigious scholarships along with the Faculty Award for academic excellence. I am currently a fellow in the American College of Healthcare Executives and am board certified in health-care administration. My current employment is as executive vice president of a respected major health-care association.

My point is that, contrary to what the *Washington Post*'s Michael Weisskopf may think, not *all* Christians are "poor, uneducated, and easy to command."

SPIRITUAL BACKGROUND

All four of my grandparents were either born or raised in Hungary and came to the United States as part of the great Ellis Island immigration wave early last century. An interesting aspect of my upbringing is that, despite our thoroughly Eastern European roots, I didn't learn *anything* about religion from my family. I don't remember anyone from either my mom's or my dad's side ever once attending church. In retrospect, I realize how unusual this was. Many, if not most, immigrant families brought strong religious beliefs and practices with them from the Old Country. To have two families so totally irreligious is unusual.

When I was eight years old, my dad decided we would attend a Unitarian fellowship. Unitarians tend to reject the beliefs and creeds of the more traditional church, including belief in the Trinity (that is, that Jesus and the Holy Spirit are equally God with the Father). To put it another way, they deny the deity of Jesus and the Holy Spirit, so they are left with a "unified" view of God. Hence, the term *Unitarians*.

Many Unitarians hold tolerance and sound reasoning as primary values. Some do not even consider themselves particularly Christian at all. Besides Jewish and Christian teachings, Unitarians also draw "wisdom from the world's religions which inspires us in our ethical and spiritual life" and "humanist teachings which counsel us to heed the guidance of reason and the results of science."[7]

In recent years, some Unitarian churches have moved even further away from conventional Christianity. In June 2004, the Thomas Jefferson Memorial Church in Charlottesville, Virginia (a Unitarian Universalist church named after one of the movement's heroes), hosted a meeting called "Exopolitics: Implications of Extraterrestrial Contact." This is how its promotional material described the meeting:

LEARN MORE ABOUT HOW OFF PLANET CULTURES HAVE IMPACTED HUMANITY IN THE PAST, HOW THEIR PRESENCE IS CURRENTLY BEING DEALT WITH, AND WHAT ARE POSSIBLE IMPLICATIONS OF THIS CONTACT FOR OUR FUTURE.... EXOPOLITICS CONCERNS ITSELF WITH THE POLITICAL, SOCIAL, ECONOMIC, TECHNOLOGICAL, ENVIRONMENTAL, SPIRITUAL, MILITARY, SCIENTIFIC AND PERSONAL IMPLICATIONS OF OFF PLANET CULTURES INTERACTING WITH HUMANITY.[8]

I suspect the Unitarian Universalist Association doesn't officially embrace these views, but the fact that such a meeting took place in one of its churches shows at least an openness to such topics.

Unitarians aren't exactly religious conservatives or fundamentalists. They typically reject many of the beliefs of the historic Christian church.

In a lot of ways, the "brand" of Unitarianism that I was raised in was more of a philosophy than a religion. It was a creed that stressed humanitarianism and humanism. Our activities and lessons probably had more in common with a comparative religion or anthropology course than the formal religious training offered by most churches. We placed great value on studying and learning about the belief systems of other groups.

Early in my experience as a Unitarian I researched the Greek philosopher Socrates in order to write a speech about his life that I delivered to my class. We also devoted several weeks to studying the ancient Egyptians, and we built a pyramid measuring eighteen inches square out of sugar cubes. We also studied Australian Aborigines and crafted copies of their boomerangs. Our teacher then provided our class of ten-year-old boys with the time to try them out. Right. In a church that follows the "guidance of reason."

So it wasn't exactly the *Old Time Gospel Hour*. The supreme value taught through our fellowship was to understand others so all humanity will get along. This emphasis is both the blessing and the bane of Unitarianism. Unitarians are absolutely right about the need to be respectful of other cultures and to be tolerant of ideas with which we disagree. However, if we take this view to the extreme, all ideas become equally valid; and, conversely, nothing is ultimately or absolutely right. This leaves us adrift in a sea of relativism.

Even though we left the Unitarian Fellowship when I was thirteen, Unitarian thought clearly left its mark on me. Part of its appeal was the sense that somehow we Unitarians were "brighter" (a familiar term?) and intellectually superior to our religiously narrow friends who attended more "limiting" churches.

NEW CHURCH, SIMILAR MESSAGE

After a religious hiatus of several years, I attended during high school another theologically liberal church. This was primarily because I developed a friendship with the minister's son (who also happened to have two knockout gorgeous sisters). Part of the process for joining this new church included a personal interview with the pastor. To be honest, even though I knew him well from visits at his house, I was a bit apprehensive because I was afraid he might try to talk me into a lot of "religious stuff" that I really didn't believe. As it turned out, I had nothing to worry about. We had a friendly chat and talked about God in vague ways, but I certainly didn't feel like he was trying to convert me. He merely impressed me as a wonderful and sincere person. Even though he and the church members talked about Jesus more than the Unitarians did, the underlying message was much the same: tolerance, understanding, and peace.

The bottom line: I was totally outside the realm of traditional biblical Christianity and very proud of it. I had little use for the common churchgoer who, I felt, was trapped in religious bondage and superstition. Religion was largely an intellectual exercise. I had almost no sense of God and certainly didn't feel the need for him. I was in many ways a teenage version of our Ann Arbor next-door neighbors' son, Tommy, who confused the Bible with a dictionary.

THE PROFESSORS HAVE THEIR SAY

What was my view of the Bible at this point in my life? It reflected that of the academic world. I simply revered and respected the Scriptures as an assortment of the thoughts and beliefs of ancient philosophers and spiritual visionaries.

It isn't difficult to argue that academia regards the Bible as simply a collection of stories, rooted in truth somewhere in the distant past, but so encrusted with myths, fairy tales, contradictions, and wishful thinking that it is difficult to determine what is valuable and what is nonsense.

As an "aspiring intellectual," I adopted this same view in order to show I belonged. My position was bolstered by the fact that I didn't know a single person who I respected intellectually who held anything close to a high regard for Scripture. On the contrary, it was fashionable to consider anyone who really believed the Bible as uneducated, mindless, and narrow-minded.

If you had asked me to point to some of the contradictions that I claimed plagued the Bible, however, my response would have been embarrassingly brief. I had never seriously read the Bible and had no idea what it contained. I was so uninformed that I didn't even know there was an Old Testament and a New Testament. I must have missed that week in the Unitarian Fellowship's "comparative religions" series.

Despite all my pretenses about academic superiority, I was more dedicated to proving my intellectual prowess than studying philosophy and religion or truly searching for personal meaning. I was too smart for my own good. I was your classic pseudointellectual.

Yet here I am today, author of a book that defends the Bible as God's inspired, inerrant, and infallible message for all people. At the same time, I maintain an unshakable commitment to intellectual integrity. Obviously, something has changed. Two events transformed my perspective:

1. During my sophomore year of college, God touched my life and established a relationship with me that has grown and flourished for several decades.

2. When I finally sat down and examined the evidence for the validity and authority of the Bible, I discovered there really are

people with academic integrity who considered the Bible reliable and who could rationally defend their positions.

Today I stand convinced that the Bible is completely accurate and trustworthy. In this book, I hope to debunk anti-Christian misinformation similar to the prejudices I once held. Also, I wish to demonstrate that we can maintain intellectual integrity as we pursue the resolution of apparent problems in the New Testament Gospels.

Journey with me as we look into the issues that surround the trustworthiness of the Gospels. I think you will see that not all Christians are "poor, uneducated, and easy to command."

PART 1

THE FILTERS

F I L T E R S

D on't you love those group exercises that conference speakers use as illustrations? You know what I mean. You're at a seminar, counting the lightbulbs in the chandelier, and the presenter interrupts your daydreaming with a group assignment. This is not a bad tactic because it draws you in and keeps your attention. It also provides a memorable object lesson and drives home the speaker's point, so it sticks with you longer than her brilliantly crafted four-point outline ever could.

These group exercises often contain a hook or some kind of twist to trick you. Being the smart aleck I am, I always try to anticipate where the speaker is going. Let me give you an example.

I was recently in a session on interpersonal communications. It addressed why physicians and hospital administrative staff sometimes approach issues from opposite perspectives. About fifteen minutes into the session, the speaker told us he would display a list of ten words on the overhead. We would have forty-five seconds to memorize the entire list. Then, he would come back to test us on how many words we could recall. His list included *slumber, snore, pillow, nap,* and *pajamas,* all of which made me want to reach for the NoDoz. Actually, they brought out the competitive student in me. I was going memorize that list perfectly!

Forty-five seconds later, the instructor turned the projector off and asked us to raise our hands if we recalled seeing each of the words he would mention. The first was "pajamas," to which about 95 percent of the hands went up. Next came "slumber." Again nearly everyone raised their hands. He got a similar response to the word "sleep." The only problem was that *sleep* did not appear on his over-head. He proved it by flipping on the projector again, revealing the "sleep-less" list. The point of the illustration was that, given a list of ten words, all of which relate in one way or another to the concept of sleeping, if we're not careful, we'll begin to see things that aren't there—like the word *sleep*.

Toward the end of the session, our presenter gave us the chance to redeem ourselves. He announced that he wanted us to take the next sixty seconds to observe every item in the conference room that was red. He had gotten me with the first example, so I was not about to be "had" again. I sat there trying simultaneously to observe every red object in the room and to figure out what the trick would be with this example. While noting the obvious items, I wondered if the trick had to do with the definition of red. Would he consider the mauvish, purplish color in the carpet red? What about the pink cover sheet of the handouts?

At the end of the minute, he asked that all eyes be fixated on his nose. "Now," he announced, "I want you to list for me every *green* object in this room." Of course, the only green items we could come up with were the ones that happened to be directly behind his head. We were so obsessed with looking for red that we had completely fil-tered out the green.

The obvious purpose of both speaker tricks was to demonstrate that we can reach erroneous or incomplete conclusions if we allow filters to limit our perceptions.

ODE TO FILTERS

Presuppositions. Prejudices. Preconceived ideas. Assumptions. Opinions. Filters. It is impossible to go through life without developing views that help us navigate life. Some of the terms seem negative, and they can be. But in a real sense, our filters make it possible for us to survive in an environment that barrages us with millions of impressions each day. We need a quick way to eliminate obvious trash and free up the random-access memory in our brains to spend time dealing with the relevant stuff.

As part of my English major in college, I had to take a creative writing class. Now let me tell you, to see a thoroughly left-brained guy take creative writing was amusing at best and pathetic at worst. We used a typical early 1970s textbook that reflected the prevailing cultural mood of the day. It included psychedelic graphics, text printed upside down or in relief, random thoughts splattered throughout, and other trappings of that groovy era. One day we spent a full ten minutes in class discussing the last time we felt a doorknob. I mean *really felt* a doorknob! I felt chided because I hadn't fondled a doorknob in the last week. The goal was to help us see that, with the countless stimuli we face each day, we often overlook things that are potentially significant. We were encouraged to open ourselves up—through heightened sensitivities—to some of the messages we might be missing.

Even TV news is in the bombardment business. We used to turn on the news and watch visual images of the story while the announcer did a voice-over describing the particular scene. Every few seconds, there might be a change of visual shot, sometimes returning to the in-studio announcer or sometimes going to some kind of graphic. A few years ago, though, one of the cable stations hit the twenty-first-century communications mother lode. They began to crawl messages across the bottom of the screen—messages that conveyed information about items totally unrelated to the featured story. Now when I watch the local morning news, I can either watch the featured story, check last night's baseball scores, view the current temperature and forecast, or synchronize my watch with an atomic clock. I can even try to do all of them simultaneously, which is, of course, impossible!

The point is, we can't possibly deal with every stimulus that comes our way. We have to be selective. It is impossible to process every single physical sensation, every visual cue, and every advertising message that assaults us. We develop filters to help us concentrate on what we perceive to be important at the moment.

A GOOD THING

Chris Argyris noted the positive role of filters and presuppositions in an article in *Harvard Business Review*:

> IT IS IMPOSSIBLE TO REASON ANEW IN EVERY SITUATION. IF WE HAD TO THINK THROUGH ALL THE POSSIBLE RESPONSES EVERY TIME SOMEONE ASKED, "HOW ARE YOU?" THE WORLD WOULD PASS US BY. THEREFORE, EVERYONE DEVELOPS A THEORY OF ACTION—A SET OF RULES THAT INDIVIDUALS USE TO DESIGN AND IMPLEMENT THEIR OWN BEHAVIOR AS WELL AS TO UNDERSTAND THE BEHAVIOR OF OTHERS. USUALLY, THESE THEORIES OF ACTIONS BECOME SO TAKEN FOR GRANTED THAT PEOPLE DON'T EVEN RECOGNIZE THEY ARE USING THEM.[1]

We learn early in life to focus on what we think is important to the task at hand, so filters can be a good thing. Over time, we learn some of the harder truths of life:

- Being on the "up" side of the seesaw and having the person on the "down" side suddenly bail out is not fun (although being the "bailer" on the down side can be).
- Not every doggy you meet is friendly.
- Not every teacher you have in school is necessarily going to appreciate your sense of humor.
- Not every girl you are attracted to will feel the same way about you.

These life events lead us to develop thought and behavioral

patterns consistent with our experiences and may influence our future attitudes and actions:

- If I am dumped from the top of the seesaw enough times, I may learn to laugh it off. Perhaps I will become timid and avoid seesaws. Or I might become hostile and aggressive toward playmates and become the "dumper" before I become the "dumpee."

- If I repeatedly experience another type of dumping, specifically by every girl I date, I can either erroneously conclude that all women hate men or decide that I'm a social dud and give up entirely.

- If I have been badly bitten by a dog, I may develop a prejudice against dogs and instead become a cat person.

Beyond such practical navigational skills, we also develop a philosophy of living that shapes our worldview. Some worldviews are deeply religious, and others are decidedly not. As long as they conform to standard norms of courtesy and legality, society permits us to pursue our lives as we see fit. And since we live in a country that values free speech, we often engage in healthy debates with others who don't share our views.

Filters turn negative, though, when we inappropriately screen out valid information. As Chris Argyris noted, our theories can become so well ingrained that we no longer recognize them as presuppositions and just assume that they (and we) are automatically right. When we review the opinions of others without an awareness of the filters they have in place, we may erroneously conclude that they are objective in their conclusions.

What Is This Section About?

Part 1 of this book will investigate the issue of filters: how they develop; how they shape our current attitudes; and, more specifically, how they can interfere with our reading of the Bible and our view of Jesus. We will examine two types of filters employed by people outside the historic Christian faith:

1. Filters that add to the basis of authority, where information beyond the biblical texts takes on more weight than the texts themselves. There are two filters in this category:
    * The Filter of New Revelation reinterprets the Bible and Jesus in light of what some claim to be new information from God.
    * The Filter of Outlandish Speculation gives credence to all kinds of wild theories about Jesus.

2. Filters that subtract from or reduce the authority of the Bible. There are three filters in this category:
    * The Filter of Atheism views belief in God as a reflection of an unmet psychological need.
    * The Filter of Antisupernaturalism assumes that all events in life are explainable through science and reasoning and treats God (if he exists at all) as essentially irrelevant.
    * The Filter of Selective Christian Theology rigidly defines what God is like and how he must act, to the point that Scripture no longer means what it clearly says.

The main point is this: *Each of us* operates with presuppositions that affect our conclusions about the Bible, God, and Jesus. In fact, I would assert the following: The conclusions that some people reach may be more a reflection of their presuppositions than of the evidence they consider.

This is a variation of the old saw "Don't confuse me with the facts; I've already made up my mind."

Skeptics also bring presuppositions to their reading of the Bible, and although some are willing to admit their prejudices, many are not. They may hide behind the cloak of academic objectivity.

Throughout this book, I refer to those who view the Bible as inspired, inerrant, infallible, and historically reliable as "Bible advocates" and those who don't as "skeptics."

It is also important to recognize that there are not just two stances on biblical authority and reliability. There are all sorts of intermediate positions and shades of views. Some believe that every word in the Bible is accurate. Some believe that the Bible is reliable in all matters except when it deals with scientific topics. Although I would consider both positions to reflect a relatively high view of the Bible, I will not attempt to define where a high view stops and a skeptical view begins.

WHICH CAME FIRST: THE PRESUPPOSITION OR THE RESEARCH?

Every book about Jesus or the Christian faith was written by someone with opinions about who Jesus was. By the time an author sits down to write a book about Jesus, he has come to hold some pretty well-defined opinions about who he was: a revolutionary, a peacemaker, a philosopher, the Son of God, or something else. He examines and evaluates every bit of information through the filters he has developed over his lifetime. That is true of anyone who writes about the Bible, including me. This is a fact the reader must consider as he casually picks up a book about Jesus to read while he sips a tall café mocha at his favorite bookstore.

This phenomenon works both ways. Since I have a high view of the Bible, I assume the stories it relates are historically reliable, and I interpret them through the Filter of Faith. Others assume the stories are unreliable and develop explanations consistent with that assumption. The preconceptions of each writer influence the conclusions each of them will reach.

Let's say I meet with my good friend Phil once a month for lunch at La Parilla Mexican restaurant. I have learned that Phil is reliable;

he has never missed an appointment. One day, however, he doesn't show up at the normal time. I'm firmly planted in our regular booth and am already working on the second basket of chips. But where is Phil? He's twenty minutes late.

What do you think I conclude? Something has happened: There was a problem at work; he had an accident; he got sick; there was a family emergency. I give Phil, based on my past experiences with him, the benefit of the doubt. There must be a legitimate reason why he didn't come.

Consider another scenario. My coworker Ralph and I have a strained relationship. We have a history of conflict. Since I consider him disloyal and unreliable, I don't trust him.

Ralph and I are to meet for lunch to discuss a job-related joint project. We decide to meet at La Parilla, the place Phil and I always eat. Guess what? Ralph doesn't show up. What am I likely to conclude? He's showing a lack of respect for my time; he's trying to insult me; he's playing some type of power game. "That's just like Ralph," I sputter.

So I have two lunch appointments at the same place and two no-shows. But I have two opposite reactions. In the first case, I am very forgiving of Phil and even worried about his well-being. In the second, I feel anger and resentment toward Ralph. Why the difference? I have filtered the available information through my presuppositions and my previous experiences with my lunch partners. And, of course, my conclusions may be wrong. Perhaps it was Phil who was forgetful this one time and Ralph who had the legitimate excuse.

SELF-FULFILLING PROPHECY

There is a specialty area within the discipline of business management called "organizational behavior," which, in its simplest form, is the study of how people act within the context of an organization. A basic theory of organizational behavior is the "self-fulfilling prophecy." In a famous research project conducted in 1968 by psychologists Robert Rosenthal and Lenore Jacobsen, elementary school teachers in a lower-class neighborhood were asked to administer a nonverbal intelligence test to identify students who they expected to exhibit a sudden surge in intelligence. The researchers then identified the 20 percent of the students who would be future intellectual late bloomers.

The problem with the experiment was that the list of likely late bloomers was randomly generated and had absolutely nothing to do with the intelligence test or any other characteristics of the children. The real purpose of the research was to study the impact of teachers' expectations on pupils' performance.

Eight months later, when the researchers readministered the intelligence test, they discovered that the 20 percent in the late-bloomer group showed an overall average gain in IQ of four points, while the children in the control group showed no change.[2] The conclusion: The teachers' expectations about their students somehow worked themselves out in the lives of the students. That's the self-fulfilling prophecy.

The discipline of organizational behavior also describes a sister phenomenon called the "Pygmalion effect," named after George Bernard Shaw's play titled *Pygmalion*. It spins the tale of a Professor Henry Higgins, whose efforts transform the lowly street dweller Eliza Doolittle into a sophisticated society lady. The premise of the play is that the way one person treats another has a transforming impact on that person.

J. Sterling Livingston describes how this principle operates in the work setting in "Pygmalion in Management," published in *Harvard Business Review*. He states,

THE WAY MANAGERS TREAT THEIR SUBORDINATES IS SUBTLY INFLUENCED BY WHAT THEY EXPECT OF THEM. IF MANAGERS' EXPECTATIONS ARE HIGH, PRODUCTIVITY IS LIKELY TO BE

EXCELLENT. IF THEIR EXPECTATIONS ARE LOW, PRODUCTIVITY IS LIKELY TO BE POOR. IT IS AS THOUGH THERE WAS A LAW THAT CAUSED SUBORDINATES' PERFORMANCE TO RISE OR FALL TO MEET MANAGERS' EXPECTATIONS.[3]

Stated in other terms, you get what you expect. If you expect good performance, you tend to get it, and vice versa.

This phenomenon carries over to the way we see the Bible. If your history and experience with the Bible have been positive, when you encounter difficult passages, you are more likely to give it the benefit of the doubt. Similarly, if you are predisposed to skepticism, you will probably view it through critical eyes.

THE LONG AND WINDING CONSPIRACY THEORY

Anybody born during or before the *Leave It to Beaver* era and who was into rock music in the late 1960s undoubtedly remembers the stunning rumor that swept the music scene in late 1969. The rumor was that one of the Beatles, Paul McCartney, had been killed in a car accident on November 9, 1966, and was replaced by a look-alike. College students across the country scrutinized the artwork, graphics, lyrics, and music on all the Beatles albums produced since 1966. They found amazing clues everywhere.

In one photo on the *Magical Mystery Tour* album, Paul's bandmates wear red carnations, while "Paul" mysteriously wears a black one, an alleged reference to his death.

The *Abbey Road* cover has the Beatles solemnly walking single file as if they were in a funeral procession. John Lennon leads the pack, dressed in white, symbolizing God; Ringo Starr is next, wearing black as a pallbearer would; Paul is barefoot, a symbol of his death; and George Harrison brings up the rear, dressed in working-class clothes to represent the grave digger. Paul is also out of step with the others and is the only Beatle carrying a cigarette (a "coffin nail").

Also visible on the *Abbey Road* cover is an automobile with the license plate "28 IF," a reference to the fact that Paul would have been twenty-eight years old when this album was released *if* he had not died.

Even the Beatles' songs themselves yielded intriguing clues, including the following:

- The famous repeated spoken line, "number 9, number 9, number 9, ..." at the end of "Revolution Number 9" on the *White Album,* when played backward, sounds like, "Turn me on, dead man" (but only if the listener has pulled two consecutive all-nighters during finals week). I would like to know who first decided to look for clues by playing songs backward!
- At the very end of the song "Strawberry Fields Forever," John speaks words that could be "cranberry sauce," "I'm very slow," or more likely (according to the conspiracy theorists), "I buried Paul," proof positive that Paul had, indeed, graduated to the great rock band in the sky.

There are dozens of other clues buried throughout the various late '60s Beatles albums. They all purportedly point to one thing: Paul truly was dead. The only problem: He wasn't. But that didn't matter. We *knew* it was true, even if it wasn't.

What a great example of self-fulfilling prophecy. Once I decide that something is true, I can find all kinds of substantiating proof. If I decide that Paul is dead, I can find ample evidence.

If my presupposition filter is calibrated to discern contradictions and problems with Bible texts, I'll probably find them. If problems aren't that evident, I might even get creative and invent some that are invisible to most readers. When we get to the chapter on the Filter of Selective Christian Theology, you'll notice the creative lengths to which some skeptics will go to find issues.

J E S U S U N F I L T E R E D

The December 28, 2003, edition of the *Atlanta Journal Constitution* featured a story titled "Ideas That Mattered in 2003."[1] As I scanned this top ten list, I was amazed to see that the issue that created the most stir in 2003 was an item called "Rethinking Jesus: Decoding the Divine." It was a reference to Dan Brown's astoundingly successful novel *The Da Vinci Code.*

Who could have predicted that the question of Jesus' identity would beat out such other major trends as

- the rift between the United States and Europe in the wake of the war in Iraq,
- the debate over gay marriage,
- the seismic shift in the world of music downloads that required pay for play,
- the explosion in digital camera sales, and
- China's first successful manned space mission?

Brown's book swept the nation in late 2003 and became a publishing phenomenon. As I waited to board a flight from Tampa to Atlanta right after the book came out, I spied *three* different people from my flight reading *The Da Vinci Code* in the waiting area. The subsequent 2006 movie also attracted millions of viewers worldwide.

Both *Time* and *US News and World Report* ran cover stories in their December 22, 2003, issues that addressed the topic of "rethinking

Jesus." And in February 2004, the airwaves were abuzz with the controversy over Mel Gibson's film *The Passion of the Christ*, which dramatized the last twelve hours of Jesus' earthly life. So Jesus continues to generate media buzz nearly two thousand years after his time on earth.

PICK A JESUS, ANY JESUS

I am a book junkie. When I am on a business trip and have time to kill, I cruise a bookstore for the latest hot sellers and for bargains. I always tell myself that I will *not* buy anything, but this promise is just as effective as telling Maddie, our overweight dog, not to break into the refrigerator when we leave the house. I have the bulging bookshelves and Maddie has the bulging waistline to prove that neither of us is very good at resisting temptation.

One of my typical stops is the religion department. Next time you visit a bookstore, check out this section. You should find at least a dozen titles (more if it's a larger store) that deal with some aspect of Jesus' life or ministry. Depending on which book you pick up, you will learn that Jesus was

- the Son of God, the second person of the Trinity, and the only way to salvation,
- Israel's anticipated Messiah,
- a prophet,
- a political activist,
- a revolutionary,
- a brilliant teacher,
- a confused teacher who wasn't really sure who he was,
- an honorable man who was transformed into something divine by his followers after his death,
- a deistic, rationalistic thinker,
- an enlightened seeker of truth,

- the original flower child,
- a mystic,
- a divine healer who tapped into the creative essence of the universe,
- a magician,
- a hypnotist,
- the prototype of the new spiritual humanity to come,
- the eternal essence of universal goodness sublimely manifested in a human personage,
- gay,
- any one of several other versions, or
- some combination of the above.

How do we explain this phenomenon? How could Jesus be both brilliant and confused? How could he be the Son of God *and* a personage his followers invented? Could these authors have read the same gospel accounts?

Debate about Jesus' identity has been a hot topic for nearly two thousand years, and it actually began during Jesus' own lifetime. One day, Jesus asked his disciples,

> "WHO DO PEOPLE SAY I AM?"
>
> THEY REPLIED, "SOME SAY JOHN THE BAPTIST; OTHERS SAY ELIJAH; AND STILL OTHERS, ONE OF THE PROPHETS."
>
> "BUT WHAT ABOUT YOU?" HE ASKED. "WHO DO YOU SAY I AM?" (MARK 8:27–29)

From the very beginning, while Jesus still walked the earth, there was debate about his true identity.

It seems everybody has a pet theory concerning Jesus. Many publishers have become wealthy churning out book after book about him. The range of speculation is incredible. My high school English teacher always taught us that, in a debate, we should never present an argument that is simplistically obvious. With apologies to Mr.

Presby, I need to point out that everyone who writes a book about Jesus has an opinion about who he was. Each author, through his research, has reached certain conclusions about Jesus' true identity. And every author claims that his or her Jesus is the "real Jesus." The problem, of course, is that one author's "real Jesus" directly contradicts another researcher's "real Jesus."

Jesus' biographers range from learned religion professors to professional clergy to individuals who discovered the latest secret that will unlock the truth about Jesus. Charlotte Allen wrote a fascinating book called *The Human Christ: The Search for the Historical Jesus,* which amounts to a "study of the study" of Jesus. Listen to this noteworthy excerpt from the book's dust jacket:

> MANY BOOKS HAVE CLAIMED TO IDENTIFY WHO THE "HISTORICAL" JESUS REALLY WAS, BUT THIS IS THE FIRST TO EXPOSE WHAT THE QUEST FOR THE HISTORICAL JESUS HAS REALLY BEEN ABOUT. FOR GENERATIONS, SCHOLARS, INTELLECTUALS, NOVELISTS, AND FILMMAKERS HAVE SET OUT TO FIND THE "REAL" JESUS AND HAVE COME UP WITH MIRROR IMAGES OF THEMSELVES. THEIR EFFORTS AMOUNT TO AN EXERCISE IN THEOLOGY RATHER THAN HISTORY AND ONE THAT TELLS MORE ABOUT THE INTELLECTUAL AND POPULAR FADS OF THEIR TIME THAN IT DOES ABOUT JESUS.[2]

Allen absolutely nails it! Many of the authors of "Jesus books" already "know" what he was like and then proceed simply to validate their conclusions. Their views have taken shape as they have passed through one or more of the filters we will discuss in the chapters that follow. As a result, their conclusions are more the outgrowth of their presuppositions than from objective evidence. Allen astutely recognizes that many who write about Jesus attempt to reshape him in their own image. And *everyone* has an opinion about Jesus, even those who would not necessarily consider themselves Christians. Who is right? Which is the "real Jesus"? Was he God in the flesh or a confused teacher?

JESUS UNPLUGGED

MTV got its start in the 1980s as the purveyor of glitzy rock videos replete with high-tech images and special effects. Each video tried to outdo the previous one in total bombastic tonnage. In the 1990s, though, MTV added a new aspect to its programming: the "unplugged" concerts. These are performances by rock megastars in a more intimate, acoustic setting. Instead of electrified music, laser light shows, and dry-ice-induced fog, these concerts feature musicianship, plain and simple.

When it comes to Jesus, many authors attempt to reinterpret or rediscover him. The cover blurbs often proclaim newly discovered documents (many of which the early church supposedly suppressed), or they offer "fresh" interpretations of who Jesus really was. But before we look at the "new" Jesus, let's take a look at the "original" Jesus, "Jesus Unplugged," if you will, Jesus as the New Testament gospel accounts present him: undiluted, unadulterated, straight up. Before we modify or reject the biblical portrait of Jesus, let's try to understand what that original portrait looks like.

I've heard that the process of training Treasury Department officials to spot counterfeit currency focuses almost entirely on studying genuine bills. The objective is to have agents so familiar with each swirl of President Jackson's hair, each dot and curlicue on the border, and each stripe in the flag on the twenty-dollar bill that the trained expert will immediately recognize any variations. Rather than study deviations, they study the real thing, so they can instantly spot the fake.

That is what we must do with Jesus. We need to start with the primary source about Jesus: the New Testament Gospels. In any trial, the defendant has the opportunity to speak for himself. Let's look at the Gospels to see the "unplugged" and "unfiltered" Jesus.

By the Book

If I were to pick up the New Testament and read about Jesus, what conclusions would I reach about who he thought he was and who others thought he was? Whether that is an accurate reflection of reality or not is not under discussion for now. As I said, the question is, "What do the Gospels tell us about Jesus? If all I had to go on were these four accounts, what would I conclude about Jesus?"

Below are a number of verses from the Gospels that record Jesus' words and actions.

1. Jesus Asserted His Identity with the Father

Jesus had the habit of performing miracles on Saturday (the Jewish Sabbath), which caused smoke to come out of the ears of the hyper-religious leaders of his day.

> So, because Jesus was doing these things on the Sabbath, the Jews persecuted him. Jesus said to them, "My Father is always at his work to this very day, and I, too, am working." For this reason the Jews tried all the harder to kill him; not only was he breaking the Sabbath, but he was even calling God his own Father, making himself equal with God. (John 5:16–18)

On another occasion, Jesus made the following claim in front of the religious authorities:

> "My sheep listen to my voice; I know them, and they follow me. I give them eternal life, and they shall never perish; no one can snatch them out of my hand. My Father, who has given them to me, is greater than all; no one can snatch them out of my Father's hand. I and the Father are one."
>
> Again the Jews picked up stones to stone him, but Jesus said to them, "I have shown you many great

MIRACLES FROM THE FATHER. FOR WHICH OF THESE DO YOU
STONE ME?"

"WE ARE NOT STONING YOU FOR ANY OF THESE," REPLIED
THE JEWS, "BUT FOR BLASPHEMY, BECAUSE YOU, A MERE MAN,
CLAIM TO BE GOD." (JOHN 10:27–33)

What could be clearer? This traveling teacher from Nazareth
stated that he was God. Whoa!

He also claimed to be the only way to God.

JESUS ANSWERED, "I AM THE WAY AND THE TRUTH AND THE
LIFE. NO ONE COMES TO THE FATHER EXCEPT THROUGH ME."
(JOHN 14:6)

PHILIP SAID, "LORD, SHOW US THE FATHER AND THAT WILL
BE ENOUGH FOR US."

JESUS ANSWERED: "DON'T YOU KNOW ME, PHILIP, EVEN
AFTER I HAVE BEEN AMONG YOU SUCH A LONG TIME? ANYONE
WHO HAS SEEN ME HAS SEEN THE FATHER." (JOHN 14:8–9)

[JESUS SPEAKING] "AND NOW, FATHER, GLORIFY ME IN YOUR
PRESENCE WITH THE GLORY I HAD WITH YOU BEFORE THE
WORLD BEGAN." (JOHN 17:5)

Some will object that all these references come from the gospel
of John, which most skeptical scholars consider historical rubbish.
John's gospel clearly presents Jesus' deity, but Jesus' references to his
divine nature are by no means limited to that one gospel. The examples that follow are nearly all from Matthew, Mark, and Luke.

2. JESUS EXERCISED A CHIEF PREROGATIVE OF GOD: FORGIVING SINS

Consider the story of one of Jesus' earliest miracles.

A FEW DAYS LATER, WHEN JESUS AGAIN ENTERED CAPERNAUM,
THE PEOPLE HEARD THAT HE HAD COME HOME. SO MANY

GATHERED THAT THERE WAS NO ROOM LEFT, NOT EVEN OUT-
SIDE THE DOOR, AND HE PREACHED THE WORD TO THEM.
SOME MEN CAME, BRINGING TO HIM A PARALYTIC, CARRIED BY
FOUR OF THEM. SINCE THEY COULD NOT GET HIM TO JESUS
BECAUSE OF THE CROWD, THEY MADE AN OPENING IN THE
ROOF ABOVE JESUS AND, AFTER DIGGING THROUGH IT, LOW-
ERED THE MAT THE PARALYZED MAN WAS LYING ON. WHEN
JESUS SAW THEIR FAITH, HE SAID TO THE PARALYTIC, "SON,
YOUR SINS ARE FORGIVEN."

NOW SOME TEACHERS OF THE LAW WERE SITTING THERE,
THINKING TO THEMSELVES, "WHY DOES THIS FELLOW TALK
LIKE THAT? HE'S BLASPHEMING! WHO CAN FORGIVE SINS BUT
GOD ALONE?"

IMMEDIATELY JESUS KNEW IN HIS SPIRIT THAT THIS WAS
WHAT THEY WERE THINKING IN THEIR HEARTS, AND HE SAID TO
THEM, "WHY ARE YOU THINKING THESE THINGS? WHICH IS
EASIER: TO SAY TO THE PARALYTIC, 'YOUR SINS ARE FORGIVEN,'
OR TO SAY, 'GET UP, TAKE YOUR MAT AND WALK'? BUT THAT
YOU MAY KNOW THAT THE SON OF MAN HAS AUTHORITY ON
EARTH TO FORGIVE SINS...." HE SAID TO THE PARALYTIC, "I
TELL YOU, GET UP, TAKE YOUR MAT AND GO HOME." HE GOT
UP, TOOK HIS MAT AND WALKED OUT IN FULL VIEW OF THEM
ALL. THIS AMAZED EVERYONE AND THEY PRAISED GOD, SAYING,
"WE HAVE NEVER SEEN ANYTHING LIKE THIS!" (MARK 2:1-12)

Luke 7:36–50 tells the story of another person whose sins Jesus forgave. According to *The NIV Study Bible* notes, "Jesus' forgiveness of sin was a claim to deity."[3]

3. JESUS ASSERTED HIS OMNIPRESENCE, THAT HE COULD BE EVERYWHERE SIMULTANEOUSLY

Two great examples of Jesus' claim not to be "geographically challenged" are found in Matthew:

For where two or three come together in my name, there am I with them. (Matt. 18:20)

This seems to transcend all boundaries of time and space.

Then Jesus came to them and said, "All authority in heaven and on earth has been given to me. Therefore go and make disciples of all nations, baptizing them in the name of the Father and of the Son and of the Holy Spirit, and teaching them to obey everything I have commanded you. And surely I am with you always, to the very end of the age." (Matt. 28:18–20)

By way of clarification, during his earthly ministry Jesus chose to limit his physical location. It was not until after his ascent to be with God the Father that he reinstated his attribute of omnipresence.

Like a CD with hidden tracks, the last example from Matthew 28 also contains a bonus claim. Besides Jesus' assertion that he will always be with us, it also clearly presents his claim to have "all authority in heaven and on earth."

4. He Demonstrated His Omniscience, That He Supernaturally Knew All Things, Including the Future

He knew what his personal future held:

From that time on Jesus began to explain to his disciples that he must go to Jerusalem and suffer many things at the hands of the elders, chief priests and teachers of the law, and that he must be killed and on the third day be raised to life. (Matt. 16:21)

He also accurately predicted that Peter would deny him. When Jesus told his followers that they would all desert him, Peter cockily claimed,

"Even if all fall away, I will not."

"I TELL YOU THE TRUTH," JESUS ANSWERED, "TODAY—YES, TONIGHT—BEFORE THE ROOSTER CROWS TWICE YOU YOURSELF WILL DISOWN ME THREE TIMES."

BUT PETER INSISTED EMPHATICALLY, "EVEN IF I HAVE TO DIE WITH YOU, I WILL NEVER DISOWN YOU." AND ALL THE OTHERS SAID THE SAME. (MARK 14:29–31)

Of course, Jesus was correct. See Mark 14:66–72 for the account of Peter's failure.

In one last example, John states,

JESUS HAD KNOWN FROM THE BEGINNING WHICH OF THEM [I.E., THE DISCIPLES] DID NOT BELIEVE AND WHO WOULD BETRAY HIM. (JOHN 6:64)

As with the previous trait, Jesus voluntarily limited this attribute during his time on earth.

5. HE ASSERTED HIS OMNIPOTENCE

We already read Matthew 28:18, where Jesus claimed all authority in heaven and on earth. He made another strong assertion during his trial before the Jewish authorities:

AGAIN THE HIGH PRIEST ASKED HIM, "ARE YOU THE CHRIST, THE SON OF THE BLESSED ONE?"

"I AM," SAID JESUS. "AND YOU WILL SEE THE SON OF MAN SITTING AT THE RIGHT HAND OF THE MIGHTY ONE AND COMING ON THE CLOUDS OF HEAVEN."

THE HIGH PRIEST TORE HIS CLOTHES. "WHY DO WE NEED ANY MORE WITNESSES?" HE ASKED. "YOU HAVE HEARD THE BLASPHEMY. WHAT DO YOU THINK?" (MARK 14:61–64)

This reference to the Son of Man hearkens back to a passage in the Old Testament book of Daniel that was familiar to Jesus' contemporaries and that describes God's coming judgment:

IN MY VISION AT NIGHT I LOOKED, AND THERE BEFORE ME WAS
ONE LIKE A SON OF MAN, COMING WITH THE CLOUDS OF
HEAVEN. HE APPROACHED THE ANCIENT OF DAYS AND WAS LED
INTO HIS PRESENCE. HE WAS GIVEN AUTHORITY, GLORY AND
SOVEREIGN POWER; ALL PEOPLES, NATIONS AND MEN OF EVERY
LANGUAGE WORSHIPED HIM. HIS DOMINION IS AN EVERLAST-
ING DOMINION THAT WILL NOT PASS AWAY, AND HIS KINGDOM
IS ONE THAT WILL NEVER BE DESTROYED. (DAN. 7:13–14)

The Mark passage also provides the additional tidbit that clearly identified Jesus as the Jewish Messiah or Christ. In another, Luke 7:11–15, Jesus brought back to life the dead son of a widow. And in John 5:21–23 he claimed the ability to give life to whomever he pleases and that he will be the judge of all.

Anyone who claims to be the Christ, the Son of the Blessed One; who will have a kingdom that will never be destroyed; who could bring dead people back to life; and who will be the judge of all humanity would, in my opinion, be a front-runner in the "Mr. Omnipotent" contest.

6. HE RECEIVED AND APPROVED OF HUMAN WORSHIP OF HIMSELF

There are three separate occasions in the gospel of Matthew where the writer specifically mentions that people worshipped Jesus.

Jesus once sent his disciples on ahead by boat in the Sea of Galilee. A few hours later, Jesus himself came walking on the water in order to join them in the boat. Peter asked to join Jesus on the water, but once Peter saw the waves, he became afraid and began to sink and had to be rescued by Jesus.

AND WHEN THEY CLIMBED INTO THE BOAT, THE WIND DIED
DOWN. THEN THOSE WHO WERE IN THE BOAT WORSHIPED
HIM, SAYING, "TRULY YOU ARE THE SON OF GOD." (MATT.
14:32–33)

Matthew goes on to the next incident without recording any disapproval from Jesus. Jesus did not chastise them for what, if it were not true, would certainly have been blasphemy.

We observe in Matthew 28:8–9 a second incident when some women saw the resurrected Savior:

SO THE WOMEN HURRIED AWAY FROM THE TOMB, AFRAID YET FILLED WITH JOY, AND RAN TO TELL HIS DISCIPLES. SUDDENLY JESUS MET THEM. "GREETINGS," HE SAID. THEY CAME TO HIM, CLASPED HIS FEET AND WORSHIPED HIM.

The third time occurs just a few verses later, right before Matthew's account of Jesus' miraculous ascension into heaven:

THEN THE ELEVEN DISCIPLES WENT TO GALILEE, TO THE MOUNTAIN WHERE JESUS HAD TOLD THEM TO GO. WHEN THEY SAW HIM, THEY WORSHIPED HIM; BUT SOME DOUBTED. (MATT. 28:16–17)

Do you detect a theme in Matthew?

You might think, *What's the big deal about letting someone worship you? Aren't there a million love songs where a love-struck guy croons his worship of his beloved girlfriend?* But that would be reading the Bible with twenty-first-century eyes. In the context of the Jewish faith of Jesus' day, worship was something reserved for God alone. Period. One of the recurring themes of the Old Testament is that God punished the Jewish people precisely because of their lack of faithfulness to him and their worship of pagan gods. Remember, the first commandment reads, "I am the LORD your God.... You shall have no other gods before me" (Ex. 20:2–3).

Jesus himself taught that God alone is to receive worship. One of Satan's three temptations of Jesus in Matthew 4 was the enticement to worship him (Satan). Jesus responded by quoting Deuteronomy 6:13: "Away from me, Satan! For it is written: 'Worship the Lord your God, and serve him only'" (Matt. 4:10). So when Jesus accepted the worship of others, it was a shocking claim to deity that his critics did not miss.

By way of contrast, there are two incidents in the New Testament where someone tried to worship someone other than God. The first occurred after Jesus' resurrection and in the early days of the church when the apostle Paul and his group were preaching to a crowd in the town of Lystra. Through God's miraculous power, Paul healed a man who had been lame from birth. Acts 14:11–16 records what happened next. The crowd thought Barnabas and Paul were gods and tried to worship them. "But when the apostles Barnabas and Paul heard of this, they tore their clothes and rushed out into the crowd, shouting: 'Men, why are you doing this? We too are only men, human like you'" (vv. 14–15).

The second event takes place in the very last book, Revelation. This time a person (the apostle John) falls down at the feet of an angel to worship him. The angel rebukes him, saying, "Do not do it! I am a fellow servant with you and with your brothers who hold to the testimony of Jesus. Worship God!" (19:10).

The Bible consistently teaches that we are to worship God alone. To revere any other created being, whether it be a person or even an angel, is strictly off-limits. The fact that Jesus accepted and approved of his followers' worship clearly reinforces his claims to deity. (For further evidence of Jesus' deity, go to www.cookministries. com/GreatQuestion and read appendix entry 2.1.)

JESUS COULDN'T HAVE BEEN AN "INVENTION"

Skeptics have a basic problem when it comes to explaining Jesus' message. They claim that the Jesus of the Gospels was a remarkable but mortal man whom his followers elevated to divinity. But they never seem able to explain adequately just who did the extreme image makeover or who wrote his amazing speeches. Jesus' disciples consistently confused his message even to the point that, late in his ministry, they argued among themselves about which of them was the greatest (see Mark 9:33–37). When the other disciples learned that James and John wanted special seats of honor in Jesus' kingdom, they became indignant at their audacity (see Mark 10:35–41). Even moments before Jesus ascended to heaven after his resurrection, they didn't understand the true nature of his ministry and still expected him to immediately crush Israel's Roman occupiers (see Acts 1:6).

Who could have invented Jesus or penned "divine wisdom" into his message? He introduced the unheard-of concept of grace into religious thought. His message was that God accepts us, not on the basis of our merit, but because he loves us. Despite our rejection of him, he took the initiative to welcome us back into a relationship with him.

One of my favorite parables of Jesus is the one about the workers hired to work various lengths of time, all of whom were paid the same amount whether they worked twelve hours or one (see Matt. 20:1–16). Those who labored all day were paid a fair wage, exactly the amount they were promised. The fact that the vineyard's owner lavished the same amount on those who only worked one hour is a picture of God's generosity. Grace is free to bestow gifts however, to whomever, and whenever it chooses to.

Perhaps the most famous story in all of ancient literature is Jesus' parable of the prodigal son (see Luke 15:11–32), whom a loving father welcomed back despite the son's foolishness and impropriety. The "righteous" older brother who never strayed from the straight and narrow clearly resented the grace his father bestowed on his younger sibling.

Author Philip Yancey observes,

THE GOSPEL IS NOT AT ALL WHAT WE WOULD COME UP WITH ON OUR OWN. I, FOR ONE, WOULD EXPECT TO HONOR THE VIRTUOUS OVER THE PROFLIGATE. I WOULD EXPECT TO HAVE

TO CLEAN UP MY ACT BEFORE EVEN APPLYING FOR AN AUDI-
ENCE WITH A HOLY GOD. BUT JESUS TOLD OF GOD
IGNORING A FANCY RELIGIOUS TEACHER AND TURNING
INSTEAD TO AN ORDINARY SINNER WHO PLEADS, "GOD HAVE
MERCY."[4]

There is not another major world religion whose central message is that God longs to embrace humanity despite its sin.

THE NOTION OF GOD'S LOVE COMING TO US FREE OF
CHARGE, NO STRINGS ATTACHED, SEEMS TO GO AGAINST EVERY
INSTINCT OF HUMANITY. THE BUDDHIST EIGHTFOLD PATH,
THE HINDU DOCTRINE OF KARMA, THE JEWISH COVENANT,
AND THE MUSLIM CODE OF LAW—EACH OF THESE OFFERS A
WAY TO EARN APPROVAL. ONLY CHRISTIANITY DARES TO MAKE
GOD'S LOVE UNCONDITIONAL.[5]

Who could have made this up? The fact that Jesus' message defies every human expectation points to its divine origin.

WHAT ARE OUR CHOICES?

There is no doubt that the Jesus of the Bible claimed for himself pre-rogatives that belong only to God: the ability to forgive sins, a supernatural knowledge of events he could not know through normal means, his power and authority over others, plus many other attributes. He claimed to be God, and he actually behaved like God.

Perhaps the most famous paragraph a Christian has written to demonstrate the deity of Jesus was penned by C. S. Lewis in one of the best-selling Christian books of all time, *Mere Christianity*. After noting that Jesus clearly claimed to be God, Lewis writes,

I AM TRYING HERE TO PREVENT ANYONE SAYING THE REALLY
FOOLISH THING THAT PEOPLE OFTEN SAY ABOUT HIM: "I'M

READY TO ACCEPT JESUS AS A GREAT MORAL TEACHER, BUT I DON'T ACCEPT HIS CLAIM TO BE GOD." THAT IS THE ONE THING WE MUST NOT SAY. A MAN WHO WAS MERELY A MAN AND SAID THE SORT OF THINGS JESUS SAID WOULD NOT BE A GREAT MORAL TEACHER. HE WOULD EITHER BE A LUNATIC— ON A LEVEL WITH THE MAN WHO SAYS HE IS A POACHED EGG—OR ELSE HE WOULD BE THE DEVIL OF HELL. YOU MUST MAKE YOUR CHOICE. EITHER THIS MAN WAS, AND IS, THE SON OF GOD: OR ELSE A MADMAN OR SOMETHING WORSE. YOU CAN SHUT HIM UP FOR A FOOL, YOU CAN SPIT AT HIM AND KILL HIM AS A DEMON; OR YOU CAN FALL AT HIS FEET AND CALL HIM LORD AND GOD. BUT LET US NOT COME UP WITH ANY PATRONISING NONSENSE ABOUT HIS BEING A GREAT HUMAN TEACHER. HE HAS NOT LEFT THAT OPEN TO US. HE DID NOT INTEND TO.[6]

How many times have you heard someone assert what Lewis said we are *not* free to assert? I myself uttered such words many times during my former pseudointellectual days.

According to C. S. Lewis's challenge above, we must decide who we think Jesus really was. The inescapable conclusion? The New Testament teaches that Jesus was and is God himself.

Those who admire Jesus' philosophy and moral teachings but don't accept Jesus' statements about his identity have a fundamental problem. How do they decide which portions of Jesus' teachings to believe? Most simply pick out the warm, fuzzy statements about love for my neighbor, God's promises to meet my needs, and the like. Sorry. Such selective reasoning is not allowable. I'll have much more to say about this "wishful thinking" approach in the Filter of Selective Christian Theology chapter.

Of course, skeptics have a handy escape hatch. If they can undercut the authority of the Bible, they can develop theories that allow them to keep just those portions they like and discard the parts they don't. Most skeptics jettison the parts where Jesus claims to be the only way to know God. They also discount Jesus' teaching that all who reject him will be separated from God for all eternity. Could this be why the Bible is such a lightning rod? If I accept the Bible as God's principal vehicle for the revelation of truth, I have to submit myself to *all* he teaches in it, including those parts that are difficult to understand and which I may not particularly like. If I can demonstrate, though, that the Bible is not really authoritative (i.e., is "recommended reading" only), I am free to pick and choose which of its lessons I will believe and which I will pitch. The latter view is much more comfortable.

Why is that? One of the main reasons is that, for at least *some* skeptics, their conclusions have been shaped more by their presuppositions than by what they read in the Gospels. The motivation perhaps for *some* may be a desire to escape the behavioral mandates of the Bible. This approach amounts to viewing Jesus through one or more filters, which results in a distorted portrait of Jesus. Some people, out of negative past experiences with authority figures, may use filters as a way to escape a God they fear or distrust. It might surprise them to learn that the "unfiltered" Jesus loves them enough to lay down his life for them (see John 15:13).

Let's consider, in the next four chapters, each of the following filters:

- The Filter of New Revelation
- The Filter of Outlandish Speculation
- The Filter of Atheism
- The Filter of Antisupernaturalism
- The Filter of Selective Christian Theology

FILTERS THAT ADD

Not everyone is equally gifted in every area. Since I was 5'8" tall and 148 pounds in high school, I knew I would never have to face the agony of choosing among several colleges that offered me either a basketball or football scholarship. As I explained in the introduction, I pinned my hopes more to my academic prowess.

Along the way, though, I decided I also wanted to develop my artistic skills. Mind you, any expectation for me to master small motor skills for activities like drawing or sculpting would be as realistic as encouraging the towering Shaquille O'Neal to become a jockey. Even longhand writing is a chore for me. Just last year, I mailed a handwritten postcard to a friend, and the next time I saw him he told me that he had to study it for almost a minute to determine if it had been written in English or in some foreign language! He marveled that the post office was able to decipher the address well enough to deliver it and said that the only person he knows who has worse handwriting than I do had survived a stroke. Annette wonders how many sweepstakes and lotteries I have actually won without realizing it because the sponsors couldn't figure out who held the winning ticket. So, for me, the hobby of pencil sketching was definitely out.

But several years ago I thought photography might work, the main attraction being that it doesn't require any manual dexterity beyond clicking the shutter button. One day I met Rick Satterthwaite—

one of my best friends—in New York City and went to one of the Midtown photography super-discount stores to buy my first "real" camera, a 35 mm Pentax. Rick and I decided to do some sightseeing, and one of our stops was the World Trade Center in Lower Manhattan. It was from the observation deck atop what at the time was the world's tallest building that I shot my first roll of 35 mm pictures.

Imagine my delight when that first go-round yielded several spectacular images of New York City from over thirteen hundred feet above street level! Conditions were ideal that day, and the color and lighting were absolutely perfect. In fact, I have behind my desk at work a framed twenty-by-thirty-inch print of the East River and the Brooklyn Bridge from that very first roll of film. People often comment on what a great picture it is and are surprised that it isn't a professional shot when I "just happen" to mention that I took it. It's that good!

I thought, *Man, why did I wait so long to start into this photography thing? I'm so good that maybe I can turn this into a career or at least a nice little side business.* I was living in a fool's paradise, though. *Nothing* I tried after that first roll has come close to the quality of those first few shots. Thank goodness I have a stable career that pays the bills.

Perhaps the reason for my ongoing photography failure is the complex interaction among the factors that go into making a great photograph: composition, lighting, weather conditions, shutter speed, f-stop, and a host of other considerations. Plus, back in the old days (that is, before 2001) when people used film to take pictures, camera filters played a large role in picture outcomes. The correct filter could make for a great picture.

But today, digital photography has changed everything. It allows even rank amateurs to add colors, adjust lighting levels, delete unwanted background features, and do all sorts of neat things after clicking the shutter. Gone are the days of the home darkroom with cancer-inducing chemicals and exotic treatments to modify your prints. Electronic wizardry has replaced all of that.

Early in my 35 mm days, I learned that there are two types of filters:

- Filters that add (such as starburst filters that turn points of light into starlike patterns, multiple image filters that replicate a portion of the image throughout the photograph, color filters that enhance hues, diffraction filters that add rainbow colors, and others)
- Filters that subtract (such as polarizing filters that reduce reflected glare, and UV or haze filters that absorb ultraviolet radiation, resulting in truer colors)

If we leave the world of photography, we see other types of filters designed to add or subtract items from their environments. "White noise" filters, for example, add sound that masks unwanted background sounds. Oil filters remove impurities from the lubricant in our cars. We have come to accept filters as part of our everyday lives because of the useful role they play, so much so that we rarely stop to think about them.

Filters of a different sort affect how we read the Bible, as well as the conclusions we reach about its central figure, Jesus. Just like some of the filters described above, we often experience the effects of theological filters without even realizing they are in place.

In this chapter, I discuss two types of filters that add to the Bible:

- The Filter of New Revelation
- The Filter of Outlandish Speculation

Just like the photographic filters that add effects to an image that were not in the original, both of these filters add material, thereby altering the concepts the Bible teaches, as well as the picture of Jesus that emerges.

I will later present three filters that cause the reader to subtract from, rather than add to, the Bible.

- The Filter of Atheism
- The Filter of Antisupernaturalism
- The Filter of Selective Christian Theology

Each of these is built on a rationale that allows the rejection of all or part of the Bible as a reliable source of information about Jesus.

Every filter contributes to a picture of Jesus that varies considerably from the image of Jesus "Unfiltered," as I described in chapter 2. Every one of the wildly divergent conclusions about Jesus that I listed at the beginning of that chapter (i.e., the confused revolutionary, the "flower child," etc.) results from the respective author's view of the Bible and Jesus through one of these five filters.

THE FILTER OF NEW REVELATION

The basic idea behind the Filter of New Revelation is that God has chosen a special person through whom he has provided an "update" of his prior messages. Those who embrace these new sources inevitably claim that they don't contradict, but complement, the Bible. Let's consider three groups that champion new revelations.

ISLAM

Islam's seventh-century founder was Muhammad. He was born in Mecca, in what is today the modern-day country of Saudi Arabia. When he was about twenty-five years old, he married an older widow whose wealth allowed him to devote significant time to the pursuit of spiritual matters. When he was about forty years old in AD 610, Muhammad began to receive a series of revelations from God, so he thought, that lasted until his death in AD 632. The prophet wrote these messages down, resulting in the Qur'an, Islam's holy book, which Muslims consider to be "God's direct and inalterable word."[1] Muslims, furthermore, consider the Qur'an "the extension of the divine into the earthly realm, the embodiment on earth of God's mercy, power, and mystery."[2] Disagreement with the Qur'an is, therefore, disagreement with God.

One of the foundational teachings of Islam is the need to honor all the prophets of God, of whom there are more than one hundred thousand. Twenty-five of this group are worthy of special honor and receive specific mention in the Qur'an. Most of these are from the Old Testament, with only three from the New Testament: Zechariah (the father of John the Baptist), John the Baptist, and Jesus.[3]

The portrait of Jesus the Qur'an paints varies significantly from that of the Gospels. Consider the following teachings from Islam's holy book:

THEY DO BLASPHEME WHO SAY: "ALLAH IS CHRIST, THE SON OF MARY." BUT SAID CHRIST: "O CHILDREN OF ISRAEL! WORSHIP ALLAH, MY LORD AND YOUR LORD." (SURAH 5:72)

CHRIST, THE SON OF MARY WAS NO MORE THAN A MESSENGER; MANY WERE THE MESSENGERS THAT PASSED AWAY BEFORE HIM. (SURAH 5:75)

THE CHRISTIANS CALL CHRIST THE SON OF GOD.... ALLAH'S CURSE BE ON THEM: HOW THEY ARE DELUDED AWAY FROM THE TRUTH. (SURAH 9:30)[4]

Not only does Islam deny that Jesus was the unique Son of God who died to pay for the sins of the entire world, but they even deny that he was crucified at all.

THE QUR'AN MAKES IT VERY CLEAR THAT JESUS NEVER DIED ON THE CROSS. HOWEVER, IT WAS MADE TO APPEAR TO PEOPLE AS IF JESUS HAD BEEN CRUCIFIED. THUS, GOD WAS INVOLVED IN SOME KIND OF DECEIT TO SAVE THE GREAT HON-ORED PROPHET JESUS.[5]

According to Islamic teaching,

AFTER THE JEWS FINALLY REJECTED HIM, JESUS SIMPLY DISAP-
PEARED FROM VIEW AND SOMEONE ELSE WAS CRUCIFIED IN
HIS PLACE. IN THE WAKE OF THAT SPIRITUAL DEBACLE,
MOHAMMED WAS SENT FROM GOD TO FULFILL THE MISSION
JESUS COULDN'T ACCOMPLISH.[6]

The Qur'an has altered the image of Jesus. Instead of God in human form (as the unfiltered Gospels clearly teach), he is only one of many prophets. Furthermore, since to Muslims, the Qur'an is God's final revelation, what it says about Jesus supersedes the Bible's teaching.

MORMONISM

Mormonism traces its roots back to the early nineteenth century when, between 1820 and 1830, a young man named Joseph Smith allegedly received numerous visitations from various heavenly beings. Among them were the Father, the Son, and an angel named Moroni. Moroni told him where he could find a book written on thin golden plates, which contained information written by Moroni's father, a prophet named Mormon. It is from this prophet that the Book of Mormon derives its name.[7] The Book of Mormon communicates the "true gospel" and tells the story of Jesus' supposed visitation to North America after his resurrection.

The church Joseph Smith founded is officially known as the Church of Jesus Christ of Latter-day Saints (LDS). Mormonism denies the traditional doctrine of the Trinity and believes instead that the Father, Son, and Holy Spirit are separate personages and three separate gods. Essentially, the LDS Church teaches polytheism, the belief in multiple gods, each of whom has taken wives in heaven.

Mormons further believe that the Father in heaven has a physical body and that he used to be a man who subsequently achieved "exaltation." And just like the Father, Jesus worked his way up to godhood. He was a preexistent spirit who in the incarnation took on a physical body. According to Mormonism, another name for Jesus is Jehovah, the firstborn of the spirit children of a different god, Elohim.[8] Mormonism thus teaches a confusing maze of doctrines that are dramatically different from the simple statement about Jesus in John 1:1: "In the beginning was the Word, and the Word was with God, and the Word was God."

Mormons believe that

> ... THE BOOK OF MORMON IS FAR SUPERIOR TO THE BIBLE BECAUSE IT CONTAINS THE "PURE" WORDS OF CHRIST. THE BIBLE, THEY CHARGE, HAS BEEN ALTERED BY WICKED PRIESTS. MORMON APOSTLE LEGRAND RICHARDS CLAIMS THAT "THE 'EVERLASTING GOSPEL' COULD NOT BE DISCOVERED THROUGH READING THE BIBLE ALONE."[9]

Can you spell F-I-L-T-E-R?

I was recently working around the house late on a Saturday afternoon when the doorbell rang. As I opened the door, I immediately recognized the well-groomed, white-shirt-clad young men on my doorstep as Mormon missionaries. I'm never one to turn down a good debate, but Annette and I were to leave for a dinner party in about an hour. If I went looking like I did at the moment I opened the door, that might have been our last dinner invitation for quite some time.

I told those young men that I was short on time and that I doubted I could persuade them of my position, and I knew they couldn't persuade me of theirs. There was probably no point to any conversation we could have. But they were insistent in a friendly way, so I relented and invited them in for a few minutes. I knew we had a very limited time, so I got straight to the point and asked them who they thought Jesus was. Despite the fact that they used words that sounded pretty "Christian," I knew they were not talking about the same "unfiltered Jesus" as I was. As we saw in chapter 2, the unfiltered Jesus of the gospel accounts is uniquely God the Son.

When they insisted that they believe in the Bible just like I do, I remarked that they may pay homage to the Bible, but they had to be interpreting it through the filter of the Book of Mormon and other Mormon teachings because of the conclusions they reached about, among other things, Jesus' identity. The doctrines of the LDS Church just don't match what the Bible clearly teaches. I never did get them to admit that the Jesus they believe in does not match the Jesus of the New Testament, but we had a pleasant conversation.

The LDS Church has much going for it. Its members tend to be model citizens and people of great moral character. It is tempting to think someone's actions and behavior should outweigh his or her specific beliefs when we evaluate the attractiveness of a religious faith. This is especially true when we see such well-mannered, well-trained, and committed young men who believe in their faith so much that they willingly devote two years of their lives to spreading their message.

However, the apostle Paul makes it clear that preaching the gospel message accurately is of paramount importance. He chides the Galatian Christians:

> I AM ASTONISHED THAT YOU ARE SO QUICKLY DESERTING THE ONE WHO CALLED YOU BY THE GRACE OF CHRIST AND ARE TURNING TO A DIFFERENT GOSPEL—WHICH IS REALLY NO GOSPEL AT ALL. EVIDENTLY SOME PEOPLE ARE THROWING YOU INTO CONFUSION AND ARE TRYING TO PERVERT THE GOSPEL OF CHRIST. BUT EVEN IF WE OR AN ANGEL FROM HEAVEN SHOULD PREACH A GOSPEL OTHER THAN THE ONE WE PREACHED TO YOU, LET HIM BE ETERNALLY CONDEMNED! AS WE HAVE ALREADY SAID, SO NOW I SAY AGAIN: IF ANYBODY IS PREACHING TO YOU A GOSPEL OTHER THAN WHAT YOU ACCEPTED, LET HIM BE ETERNALLY CONDEMNED! (1:6–9)

I can't read this passage, which refers to an angel appearing and preaching a different gospel, without thinking of the Mormon Church. It traces its roots to an angelic appearance, by which Joseph Smith supposedly received his message from God. Isn't the Mormons' "different gospel" a perfect example, right down to the delivery mechanism through an angel, of what Paul condemned so vehemently? Mormons assert that their gospel isn't a different message at all, but a comparison of Mormon teaching and the New Testament shows that it clearly is.

So, like Muslims, Mormons read Jesus through the filter of a newer revelation.

THE BAHÁ'Í FAITH

The last belief system we will consider is the Bahá'í faith, which was founded in 1863 by Persian-born Bahá'u'lláh. Bahá'ís consider him "the Messenger of God for this age, the latest in a series of founders of great world religions sent by God to humanity."[10] Among Bahá'í's teachings are the oneness of God, the oneness of religion, the oneness of humanity, and the belief that God continues to reveal himself to succeeding generations.

> ALL RELIGIONS CONTAIN TRUTH.... RELIGIONS ARE NOT ALTERNATIVE PATHWAYS TO GOD, HOWEVER. THEY ARE GOD'S MESSAGE SENT AT DIFFERENT TIMES TO DIFFERENT PLACES.... THIS COMMON FAITH IS TRANSMITTED BY GOD TO HUMANITY THROUGH A SERIES OF MESSENGERS HOLDING IDENTICAL DIVINE STATIONS, INCLUDING KRISHNA, BUDDHA, MOSES, JESUS, MUHAMMAD AND OTHERS. THE MESSENGER FOR THIS DAY IS BAHÁ'U'LLÁH.[11]

Jesus, then, is the founder of a great world religion, but not unique as the "one mediator between God and men" as Paul taught in 1 Timothy 2:5. Rather, he holds an "identical divine station" as many other religious founders. The Bahá'ís' Jesus is certainly not the same "Jesus Unfiltered" that we discussed in the last chapter.

I mentioned to my Mormon visitors that the Bahá'í faith and that of Latter-day Saints seem to share an important similarity. They both stake their claims on a new and updated revelation that they believe came directly from God. If the Mormons believe that God continues to reveal himself, I asked, why didn't they take the next leap forward from Mormonism to the Bahá'í faith, since the latter came after Mormonism? Wouldn't Bahá'u'lláh be the next logical car on the revelation train? They had no answer to my question.

OTHER PROPHETS

History is replete with many other prophets who all claim to speak for God and who almost always disagree with each other. In my lifetime I have seen the likes of the Reverend Sun Myung Moon (founder of the Unification Church), Jim Jones (leader of the People's Temple that eventually self-destructed in Guyana), and David Koresh (prophet of the Branch Davidians in Waco, Texas). In each of these cases, followers are convinced "their man" speaks for God himself and, therefore, commands unquestioning obedience.

The bottom line on the Filter of New Revelation is that it trumps all other versions of the truth. Since these new revelations are seen as God's latest word to humankind, they are, by definition, beyond dispute.

THE FILTER OF OUTLANDISH SPECULATION

Back in the late 1980s, right after I finished my two-year stint at the University of Michigan Medical Center postgraduate training program, I took a job in a hospital in one of the Detroit suburbs. This involved a thirty-eight-mile commute twice a day. If you've never had the pleasure of an extended commute, let me clue you in that on a daily basis it can get quite monotonous.

People resort to all sorts of interesting ways to pass the drive time, including reading the newspaper while driving (not recommended). The most interesting thing I ever saw, though, occurred one day as I passed a car that was in the right lane on the freeway. As I glanced to my right, I saw my fellow commuter playing a French horn as he drove his car! Seriously.

I never got as exotic as that brassy gentleman. My mainstay activity to pass the time was listening to a variety of recorded messages and radio stations. As I drove home one day, I heard on National Public Radio about a historian who espoused a new theory about Jesus. According to this researcher, Mary, the mother of Jesus, was one of the first feminists in history. She was sick of the male-dominated religious establishment of her day, and she devised a way to allow women to infiltrate that oppressive structure. According to this theory, she was so well versed in Jewish religious thought that she recognized that the circumstances surrounding the birth of her child bore some resemblance to Old Testament prophecies concerning the coming Messiah. She was also creative enough to orchestrate other events to build the impression that Jesus was truly the Messiah.

This view wasn't necessarily the invention of that historian. Others have suggested variations on the same theme. They assert that Jesus and/or those surrounding him successfully manipulated circumstances to portray him as the Christ. But here is where this new theory got especially imaginative. Remember, this scholar said that Mary was really a feminist at heart. She thought the ultimate coup would be for a female to play a pivotal role in the religious life of Israel. Here's how it happened: Her child, Jesus, *was really a girl*; and Mary managed to disguise her as a boy and fool everyone into thinking she was a "he" and was Israel's Messiah!

I nearly drove off the road. What kind of evidence could possibly exist for this absurd theory except a fertile imagination and creative interpretations that are not at all supported by reliable sources? Nothing in the New Testament gospel accounts even remotely supports such a ludicrous theory.

The originator of this theory faces another insurmountable problem. The accounts of the crucifixion in the Gospels include a description of Jesus' flogging by the Roman soldiers in which they would have stripped him of his clothing. The gospel of John mentions that his *undergarment* was seamless, woven in a single piece.

Rather than tear it into pieces, the soldiers decided to award it to the winner of a gambling game. Presumably, the winner took home the spoils, which meant that Jesus was left wearing nothing. The victims of Roman crucifixion were naked. That was part of the humiliation.

First-century Roman soldiers and Jewish citizens may not be as sophisticated as twentieth-century biblical scholars, but I suspect that they knew enough about human anatomy to rule out this scholar's theory. I am amazed that such an outrageous theory could even warrant coverage on a national news program!

E.T., PHONE HOME

As I recounted this story to Annette that night at dinner, she commented that the next thing you know, someone will say that Jesus was really an alien from outer space. Guess what? A couple of years later, someone sent me a book that claims the following:

- Jesus' true father was Gabriel, who was not an angel but an extraterrestrial being from the Pleiades star cluster. (I guess that would make Jesus "Son of E.T.")
- The star of Bethlehem, which "traveled" to the stable in Bethlehem; the spirit that descended onto Jesus at his baptism; and Jesus' ascent to heaven are all explained by the extraterrestrial Gabriel's UFO-like vehicle.
- Instead of being in the desert for forty days during his temptation, Jesus actually spent those forty days in the Pleiadeseans' UFO learning cosmological truth.
- Jesus was probably married, and Mary Magdalene was the most likely candidate.
- Jesus really taught reincarnation instead of resurrection.
- Jesus didn't really die on the cross.
- After he was resuscitated—not resurrected, since he never really died—Jesus moved to India with his mother, Mary, and his brother Thomas to live out his life.[12]

The sources of this wealth of new information, according to author James Deardorff, were Aramaic scrolls encased in resin for over nineteen hundred years and discovered in 1963. The discoverer was assassinated, and (conveniently) the original documents were burned in 1974, so we cannot examine them. A large section of the manuscript had already been translated, however, so we have a partial record.[13]

MARY MAGDALENE RISING

During one of my frequent visits to the local bookstore, I came across a book by Lynn Picknett and Clive Prince called *The Templar Revelation*. It is a fascinating study in speculation. Among the theories the authors postulate are the following:

- Jesus was not the Son of God. And even though he might have been ethnically Jewish, he did not adhere to the Jewish religion. He instead taught the beliefs of the ancient Egyptian Isis/Osiris cult.

- Jesus' miracles find explanation in the fact that he was actually a sorcerer trained in the art of Egyptian magic.

- John the Baptist did not believe that Jesus was the Messiah. The reason he baptized Jesus may have been that Jesus was actually one of John's disciples. Unfortunately for John, Jesus ultimately upstaged him.

- Mary Magdalene was a priestess, a powerful preacher, and the "Apostle of the Apostles." She was also probably Jesus' wife.

- Mary, not Peter, was really Jesus' intended spiritual successor, and because Peter hated her, Mary fled to France after the crucifixion out of fear of what Peter might do to her.[14]

The authors also tie in such disparate strands as the search for the Holy Grail, the medieval Knights Templar, the Shroud of Turin, Leonardo da Vinci, the Freemasons, and others. About the only "traditions" that do not appear in the book seem to be the Loch Ness Monster and Bigfoot.

This is just another in the long line of books that speculate about censored truths and elevate the role of Mary Magdalene. Others include *Holy Blood, Holy Grail* by Michael Baigent, *The Gospel of Mary Magdalene* by Jean-Yves Leloup, and *The Goddess in the Gospels: Reclaiming the Sacred Feminine* by Margaret Starbird. Of course, the best-known in this tradition is Dan Brown's phenomenally success-ful 2003 novel, *The Da Vinci Code,* which introduced millions of readers to these theories. For supporting evidence, these writers point to a variety of traditions, manuscripts, and books that they claim have been long suppressed by the church establishment and others.

COMMON THREADS

Is it possible that Jesus was a girl? Is it possible that Jesus' father was an alien from the constellation Pleiades? Is it possible that Jesus was really an Egyptian magician who married Mary Magdalene? Sure it's *possible*. It's also possible that I might sprout wings and flutter around my living room, but it's highly unlikely.

All these speculative studies and books share two common traits. They assume the existence of

- some newly discovered truths, secret documents, or new insights and
- suppressed truths and conspiracies by "the establishment" in order maintain the status quo.

One of the interesting things about conspiracy theories is that their adherents interpret any evidence contradictory to their theory as part of the "cover-up." Those who would debunk the theory are either coconspirators or unknowing dupes of the "established church." In either case, the counterevidence presented by those who dismiss the conspiracy theory is seen as further evidence of the plot.

All of these are examples of the Filter of Outlandish Speculation. In each case (Jesus the girl, Jesus the E.T., or Jesus the married), we learn the "truth" about Jesus through some documentation or theory beyond the scope of the biblical text. The adherents go back to the New Testament Gospels and simply read into them the clues that make sense to the initiated as the texts are viewed through the lens of the new theory. Makes me wonder if Paul McCartney really *did* die.

My favorite example of this retrospective revisionism is the E.T. filter theory that claims the star of Bethlehem was really Gabriel's spaceship. If you start with the assumption that aliens visited this planet at the time surrounding Jesus' birth, it is easy to inject that interpretation into the description of the star of Bethlehem as "moving over the stable." Once postulated, these theories take on a life of their own and become more important than the legitimate evidence presented in the Bible.

So the first two filters (the Filter of New Revelation and the Filter of Outlandish Speculation) add an overlay through which revisionists reinterpret the Bible and reinvent Jesus. God continues, of course, to speak to people today, but not in the same way as when Jesus was here in person. The ultimate purpose of the Bible is to teach us how Jesus bridged the chasm that opened when Adam and Eve made their fateful dietary decision. Once Jesus died and physically rose, and once the age of the apostles came to an end, the need for additional special revelation ended. The Bible clearly teaches that Jesus' death to address our sin problem was "once for all" (Heb. 10:10) and that this message was entrusted to God's people "once for all" (Jude v. 3). We don't need additional revelation, and certainly none that contradicts what God has already made plain.

We are, of course, to continue our diligent study of the New Testament and to consider material from various sources. No one can claim to fully comprehend the depths of all the Bible teaches, and extrabiblical sources can provide rich insights into the biblical texts. The sources to which we refer, however, should be both credible and supportive of the historicity of the Bible instead of wildly hypothetical or sensationalistic and scandalous in their theories about Jesus.

In the next three chapters, we will consider other filters that detract from the authority of the Bible and deconstruct a biblical view of Jesus.

FILTERS THAT
SUBTRACT — ATHEISM

In the last chapter, we considered two filters that add to the Bible. Both types—allegedly new revelation from God and outlandish speculation—result in a Bible that is subordinate to a higher authority with which it is virtually impossible to argue. If there is a conflict between the new authority and the Bible, guess who wins?

There are also filters that chip away at the Bible's authority, with the result that they compromise it as an authoritative source.

- The Filter of Atheism
- The Filter of Antisupernaturalism
- The Filter of Selective Christian Theology

Each of these approaches the Bible and, therefore, Jesus with varying degrees of skepticism about the historicity of the accounts. There is a continuum that ranges between two extremes: from the position that some, but not all, of the Bible is accurate to the view that precious little is reliable and that most of it was the fabrication of Jesus' followers. Nearly everyone who employs one of these filters would agree that the New Testament was probably rooted in the historical reality of a human teacher named Jesus. But the early church embellished his reputation in the centuries that followed his tragic (but rather unremarkable) death. Well-meaning and perhaps deceptive followers manufactured or exaggerated stories of Jesus' miracles and thereby applied a veneer of divinity to a good but merely mortal man.

Many writers fall into more than one of the "filter categories." It can, therefore, be difficult to determine which of their filters is operating at any given time.

- Atheism, by definition, rejects any concept of God.
- Antisupernaturalism seeks to explain Bible stories in terms of normal human events that overzealous followers have spun into the tales of the miraculous.
- Selective Christian theology is a little harder to define. This position covers a broad range of views from nearly orthodox (i.e., sort of believing the Bible) to a total rejection of all major Christian doctrines. It is difficult to draw hard and fast lines, and I want to be careful not to "condemn" the spirituality of all those who view the Bible less positively than I do. Consequently, I will focus on the more radical end of selective Christian theology in order to show what its tendencies look like when taken to an extreme.

In some cases, it's hard to pinpoint the individual positions of various thinkers. Some antisupernaturalists could also be atheistic. Or they could fall into the selective Christian theology category. Many in the latter group employ some of the same approaches and have the same attitudes toward the Bible as those who fall into the antisupernaturalist or atheistic categories.

To try to bring some order to this discussion, I will organize the next three chapters as follows:

- The atheism chapter discusses self-described atheists.
- The antisupernaturalism section focuses primarily on those involved in the so-called Quest for the Historical Jesus.
- The chapter on selective Christian theology utilizes examples

where a preconceived theological position (usually by someone who considers himself or herself Christian) leads to a
seriously distorted reading or application of Scripture.

GOD ISN'T

The word *atheism* comes from the Greek word *theos* (which means
"god") with the prefix "a-" (which means "not"). This position
denies the existence of God. One of the classic charges atheists bring
against their believing comrades is that theists—those who believe
in God—have created God out of a psychological need for a higher
power or to provide a sense of order to an otherwise chaotic and
fear-provoking universe.

Presbyterian theologian R. C. Sproul paints an overview of four
foundational thinkers of modern nineteenth-century atheism:
Sigmund Freud, Ludwig Feuerbach, Karl Marx, and Friedrich
Nietzsche. These four attribute the emergence of religion to several
types of human fears. According to these atheists,

> ... FEAR OF NATURE, WISH-PROJECTION, RELIEF FROM GUILT
> AND ANXIETY, FEAR OF ECONOMIC REVOLUTION, AND FEAR OF
> NOTHINGNESS ARE ALL LABELS FOR VARIOUS PSYCHOLOGICAL
> STATES THAT MAKE RELIGION APPEALING. TO BE LEFT ALONE
> AND UNPROTECTED IN A HOSTILE OR INDIFFERENT UNIVERSE
> IS A TERRIFYING THOUGHT. THE PROVERBIAL MAXIM "NECES-
> SITY IS THE MOTHER OF INVENTION" IS APPLIED TO
> RELIGION....[1]

In other words, theism represents a human response to deep psychological fears that find some degree of relief through the creation
of a deity or deities to help people cope with the traumas and difficulties of life.

Sproul astutely observes that all the arguments brought forth by
these renowned atheists have nothing to do with the issue of

whether or not God exists. Rather than trying to disprove the existence of God, they start with the presupposition that God is fictitious. As a result, instead of probing the existence of God, "they were dealing with the question, Since there is no God, why is there religion?"[2]

Elsewhere, Sproul observes,

EMOTIONAL PREJUDICE IS NOT LIMITED TO THE DULL-WITTED, THE ILLITERATE, AND THE POORLY EDUCATED. IT IS EXCEEDINGLY DIFFICULT FOR THE MOST BRILLIANT OF MEN TO BE FREE OF IT. PHILOSOPHERS AND THEOLOGIANS ARE NOT FREE FROM VESTED INTERESTS AND PSYCHOLOGICAL PREJUDICE THAT DISTORT THINKING....

THE QUESTION OF THE EXISTENCE OF GOD IS A QUESTION THAT PROVOKES DEEP EMOTIONAL AND PSYCHOLOGICAL PREJUDICE. IN THE ARENA OF THEOLOGICAL-PSYCHOLOGICAL DEBATE THE STANDS ARE CROWDED WITH VESTED INTERESTS.[3]

Sproul charges that, rather than approach the issue of the existence of God with the "blank slate" of objectivity, many atheists allow their prejudices to color their study of religion.

BLAME IT ON THE DAD

In a fascinating book called *Faith of the Fatherless: The Psychology of Atheism*, NYU professor of psychology Paul C. Vitz conducts an analysis of patterns that distinguish atheists from theists. He observes that the intellectual community almost universally assumes that "belief in God is based on all kinds of irrational, immature needs and wishes, whereas atheism or skepticism flows from a rational, grown-up, no-nonsense view of things as they really are."[4] The thesis of his book is a reversal of the typical charge that religious believers have created God to fulfill a psychological need. On the contrary, he posits "that atheism of the strong or intense types is to a substantial degree generated by the peculiar psychological needs of its advocates."[5]

Vitz, a Stanford-trained PhD, looks at atheists who grew up under two types of less-than-ideal fathers: the dead father (six atheists including Friedrich Nietzsche, Bertrand Russell, Jean-Paul Sartre, and Albert Camus) and the abusive and weak father (nine atheists including Voltaire, Sigmund Freud, and H. G. Wells). In the formation of his conclusions, he relies on these thinkers' writings, documented facts from their biographies, and comments by their contemporaries.

He concludes that, in virtually every case, each of these well-known atheists had poor or nonexistent relationships with his father. As a seasoned researcher, he recognizes that there might be a confounding variable that explains the nearly universal correlation between poor paternal relationships and atheism. All these atheists grew up in roughly the same period of history in Western culture. Perhaps their atheism merely reflected the social conditions of their age.

To provide a control group, Vitz examines the early lives of twenty-one theists (including Blaise Pascal, William Wilberforce, Alexis de Tocqueville, and Dietrich Bonhoeffer) who lived in the same general historical period. His conclusion: In every case, the theists had basically positive paternal relationships.

> ALL TOLD, THE EARLY CHILDHOODS OF THESE TWENTY-ONE IMPORTANT THINKERS ARE REMARKABLE FOR THEIR SUPPORT OF MY HYPOTHESIS: THERE IS NO EARLY DEATH OF A FATHER, NO ABANDONMENT, NO DRAMATIC REJECTION BY THE FATHER.... THIS PICTURE IS IN MARKED CONTRAST WITH THE ATHEIST SAMPLE.[6]

Vitz presents a somewhat surprising conclusion concerning the role of psychology in the study of the existence of God:

> SINCE *BOTH* BELIEVERS AND NONBELIEVERS IN GOD HAVE

PSYCHOLOGICAL REASONS FOR THEIR POSITIONS, ONE IMPOR-
TANT CONCLUSION IS THAT IN ANY DEBATE AS TO THE TRUTH
OF THE EXISTENCE OF GOD, PSYCHOLOGY SHOULD BE IRREL-
EVANT. A GENUINE SEARCH FOR EVIDENCE SUPPORTING, OR
OPPOSING, THE EXISTENCE OF GOD SHOULD BE BASED ON
THE EVIDENCE AND ARGUMENTS FOUND IN PHILOSOPHY, THE-
OLOGY, SCIENCE, HISTORY, AND OTHER RELEVANT
DISCIPLINES.[7]

As an interesting side note, Vitz tucks in toward the end of his
book an intriguing chapter called "Superficial Atheism: A Personal
Account." It reminds me of my own journey.

ON REFLECTION, I HAVE SEEN THAT MY REASONS FOR BECOM-
ING, AND REMAINING, AN ATHEIST-SKEPTIC FROM AGE
EIGHTEEN TO AGE THIRTY-EIGHT WERE, ON THE WHOLE,
SUPERFICIAL AND LACKING IN SERIOUS INTELLECTUAL AND
MORAL FOUNDATION. FURTHERMORE, I AM CONVINCED THAT
THESE REASONS ARE COMMON AMONG AMERICANS, ESPE-
CIALLY IN INTELLECTUAL, ACADEMIC, AND ARTISTIC
COMMUNITIES AND IN THE MEDIA.[8]

He enumerates several factors that led to his atheistic worldview:

- General Socialization—Vitz describes his sense of embarrassment over his Ohio-based, "terribly middle class," vague,
  mixed German-English-Swiss background. He also recalls a
  graduate school seminar in which all four members (a
  Southern Baptist, a small-town Mormon, a Brooklyn Jewish
  ghetto resident, and Vitz) were trying to distance themselves
  from their nonglamorous or "nonmodern" pasts.
- Specific Socialization—In order to make a name for himself
  professionally, Vitz felt he had to embrace the "culture" of academic research psychology. He observes that even though his
  Stanford professors disagreed on many things professionally,

they were "united in two things: their intense career ambitions and their rejection of religion."

- Personal Independence—One of the overriding attributes of Western society is the "chip on the shoulder, 'no-one-tells-me-what-to-do' mentality that has been widely admired and has become a cliché of modern culture.... For me, as presumably for many, becoming an atheist was part of a personal infatuation with the 'romance of the autonomous self.'"

- Personal Convenience—He observes that serious religious faith, with its lifestyle demands of personal holiness, high levels of time commitment for church services and religious studies, and obligations to perform good deeds, is not convenient in a secularized society.[9]

He summarizes his "pre-theistic life" this way: "The intellectual basis for my atheism, like that of countless others, appears in retrospect to be much more of a shallow rationalization than an objective rationale."[10] Vitz reports that he rediscovered Christianity in his late thirties "in the very secular environment of academic psychology in New York City."[11]

BERTRAND RUSSELL

One of Professor Vitz's subjects is atheist Bertrand Russell, perhaps best known for his collection of essays titled *Why I Am Not a Christian*. Russell was born into an aristocratic family in 1872, two years before his mother's death and four years before his father's. After these tragedies, he went to live with his grandparents, but his grandfather died just two years later. This left his grandmother as his greatest childhood influence. Unfortunately, her morbid temperament and "mournful Christian humility" earned her the less-than-complimentary nickname "Deadly Nightshade."[12] Russell's only other parental figures were a string of nannies to whom he often got emotionally attached and whose eventual departures caused him great distress.

Russell rejected the religion of his grandmother rather early in life. However, he demonstrated an abiding desire for certainty in his life and once commented, "I wanted certainty in the kind of way in which people want religious faith."[13] He has been described as a loner with no close friends and who retreated into "a distant and increasingly abstract world."[14] Russell is a good example of the atheist who fits Vitz's model, an intelligent young man with an absent father whose personal psychological needs later translated into his philosophical and theological views.

THE IMPACT OF RUSSELL'S FILTERS

How did Russell's atheism play out in his views about Jesus? In 1927, he gave a talk titled "Why I Am Not a Christian," which became the anchor essay in his later book of the same name. In that address he stated that "it is quite doubtful whether Christ ever existed at all" and also included a section called "Defects in Christ's Teachings" in which he charges the New Testament Jesus with promulgating deficient and unwise teachings.[15]

His first complaint is that Jesus apparently believed that his second coming would occur during the lifetimes of those who were alive at that time.

> I AM CONCERNED WITH CHRIST AS HE APPEARS IN THE GOSPELS, TAKING THE GOSPEL NARRATIVE AS IT STANDS, AND THERE ONE DOES FIND SOME THINGS THAT DO NOT SEEM TO BE VERY WISE. FOR ONE THING, HE CERTAINLY THOUGHT THAT HIS SECOND COMING WOULD OCCUR IN CLOUDS OF GLORY BEFORE THE DEATH OF ALL THE PEOPLE WHO WERE LIVING AT THE TIME.[16]

He cites two passages as evidence, the first of which is, "Ye shall not have gone over the cities of Israel, till the Son of Man be come."

He does not identify this verse, but a quick check of your Bible will show that it is the last half of Matthew 10:23 taken word for word from the King James Version.

Russell takes this passage to mean that Jesus believed that his second coming would happen before his hearers all died. That certainly is one way to interpret this verse. However, as Leon Morris points out in his commentary *The Gospel according to Matthew*, there are many other interpretations that could be equally valid. For example, the "coming" to which Jesus referred could be his coming to the Father in heaven, indicating the successful conclusion of his earthly mission. Or it could refer to Jesus' coming in the triumph of his resurrection to his disciples. Or it could be as simple as Jesus' saying that he himself would follow along right after them in their mission and would catch up with them. Or it could mean that Jesus "came," in a manner of speaking, to bring judgment on the city of Jerusalem in AD 70 when the Roman army destroyed it.[17] The abundance of interpretations clearly indicates that this is one of those Bible passages that are not entirely clear. There are various different interpretations that preserve the integrity of Jesus' teaching. Russell, however, takes one of the least "supportive" interpretations and turns it into a problem passage. Is it because of his atheistic presuppositions?

The second verse Russell uses is Matthew 16:28: "There are some standing here which shall not taste death till the Son of Man comes into His kingdom." But he misquotes it. The King James Version reads, "There be some standing here, which shall not taste of death, till *they see* the Son of man coming in his kingdom." Russell omitted the reference to those who were there and *saw* the kingdom of God.

Stick with me as we examine the precision of Russell's charges against the texts. I checked various translations to see if Russell perhaps quoted a version that omits the idea of *seeing*. A helpful reference is *The New Testament from 26 Translations*,[18] which reports significant differences in the ways that twenty-six different versions of the Bible translate New Testament verses. None of the twenty-six delete the word *see*. A check of the Greek text, the original language of the New Testament, reveals that the word *see* is definitely in the text.[19]

The rationale for Russell's omission is a mystery. It clearly leads to a misinterpretation. Russell claims that Jesus taught that he would come in his kingdom before all those in his hearing died, but that is not what the verse really says. It says that some of those in his hearing would *see* the Son of Man coming in his kingdom. This is a significant difference.

Three different gospels (Matthew, Mark, and Luke) report what Jesus said about seeing him come in his kingdom. In all three accounts, this story appears at the end of a lesson Jesus gave his disciples about the demands of being his follower. All three gospel writers then *immediately* present the story of what we call the transfiguration. Jesus, in this amazing event, took his three closest disciples high on a mountain, and there Jesus was miraculously transformed, or transfigured, before their eyes so that his face shone like the sun and his clothing became a brilliant white. Moses and Elijah, both of whom had been gone from the earth for at least a thousand years, appeared and spoke with Jesus about his impending death in Jerusalem. This was not your typical Bible study meeting.

Most Bible advocates see a divinely purposeful juxtaposition of prediction and fulfillment. After all, seeing your teacher and leader start to glow like the sun while he talks with two Old Testament characters who were old enough to be your "great, great, great, great, etc. something" would certainly qualify as something you might see in the kingdom of God. Many scholars assert that some of his disciples did, indeed, see Jesus come in the power of the kingdom of God.

The gospels of Matthew, Mark, and Luke take a similar approach to covering Jesus' life and are referred to as the Synoptic Gospels, while John's gospel offers a unique perspective. The chronology of stories in Matthew, Mark, and Luke often varies. There are only a few times that two stories are presented in exactly the same order in the Synoptics. Whenever all these Gospels report two events in the same order, it is likely that the stories are intended to be linked and seen as a unit. Keep in mind as well that chapter divisions were added centuries after the writing of the texts. The fact that all three writers present the stories together probably indicates that they intended the saying and the story to be a unit. The supposed problem concerning Jesus' prediction that some of his followers would not die until he comes in his kingdom finds an easy explanation when we accurately quote the verse and recognize that there is significant evidence that his prediction saw its fulfillment in the transfiguration.

It seems that Russell's filter of atheism is firmly in place and that he interprets these teachings of Jesus in a way so as both to magnify the problems and undercut the veracity of the teaching. His position is based on a combination of bad scholarship and what could probably be considered a bias against the text.

This preceding discussion may seem like splitting hairs to you. Does it really matter if Jesus said that some standing there wouldn't taste death until the Son of Man comes or until *they see* the Son of Man coming? It does. If you are "taking on Jesus," it's important to be precise in the way you handle the evidence. Russell's sloppiness in his reading of the text leads him to create a false rendition of what Jesus taught. He then proceeds to shoot down an easy target of his own creation.

More to Complain About

Russell's next criticisms are what he calls Jesus' "serious defect" of belief in hell and of a "vindictive fury against those people who would not listen to His preaching."[20] He characterizes the Jesus of the Gospels as one who takes "a certain pleasure in contemplating wailing and gnashing of teeth, or else it would not occur so often."[21]

Russell, at least in this instance, views Jesus through both the Filter of Atheism and the Filter of Selective Christian Theology, which we will discuss further in chapter 6. He decides, based on his own sense of right and wrong, what the "correct" moral position should be and declares inappropriate anything in the gospel accounts that contradicts his presuppositions. Russell's view is valid if you buy his assumptions, that the punishment for rejection of Jesus' teaching does not fit the crime. However, if you take the gospel accounts at face value and accept Jesus as the Son of God as he claimed to be, then it is Jesus' duty to reveal the truth and to warn us about judgment and hell.

Russell also complains about Jesus' exorcism of evil spirits from a demon-possessed man. Mark 5:1–20 describes the confrontation of Jesus by a wild man who lived in a cemetery. Jesus knew he was demon possessed and asked the demon's name. "My name is Legion … for we are many," replied the man (v. 9). Legion was the Roman army's designation for a company of five to six thousand soldiers,[22] so the evil spirits must have done some serious inhaling to all fit in. When Jesus commanded them to leave the man, they requested that he send them into a herd of swine. Jesus acquiesced, and the pigs, apparently panicky when they sensed their new "houseguests," stampeded off a cliff to their deaths.

Russell takes issue with Jesus' solution and criticizes that "it certainly was not very kind to the pigs"[23] for Jesus to have solved one problem by creating another. "You must remember that He was omnipotent, and He could have made the devils simply go away; but He chose to send them into the pigs."[24] Russell feigns respect for Jesus' omnipotence but then undercuts it with criticism of his judgment. Isn't this the craziest objection? The demons asked to go into the pigs. If Jesus had denied the demons' request, I wonder whether

Russell and others like him would complain that Jesus was very kind to the demons.

Russell is not the only skeptic to find fault with Jesus for this incident. Others have taken the side of the poor swineherd who lost his livelihood and charged Jesus with a certain level of cruelty for thrusting this unfortunate man into poverty.

But is this story about the death of pigs or about Jesus' liberation of a man who had been bound up and tormented by demons? Beyond the rescue of a precious human being, Jesus also wanted the onlookers to see the nature of demons and what their intent is: Even pigs can't stand them, and the goal of demons is to destroy their hosts. For Jesus, the death of a herd of swine was worthwhile if it meant all who would read this story would recognize demons' evil nature.

Perhaps Russell serves as a good example of a theological glass that is half-empty. His logic is reminiscent of the Pharisees' objection to Jesus' habit of healing people on the Jewish Sabbath, a day when no work was to be done. On one occasion they rebuked him for healing a crippled woman on the wrong day. He responded:

> YOU HYPOCRITES! DOESN'T EACH OF YOU ON THE SABBATH UNTIE HIS OX OR DONKEY FROM THE STALL AND LEAD IT OUT TO GIVE IT WATER? THEN SHOULD NOT THIS WOMAN, A DAUGHTER OF ABRAHAM, WHOM SATAN HAS KEPT BOUND FOR EIGHTEEN LONG YEARS, BE SET FREE ON THE SABBATH DAY FROM WHAT BOUND HER? (LUKE 13:15–16)

Russell's philosophical biases cause him to focus on the relatively minor loss to the swineherd, instead of the tremendous liberation of a demon-possessed man, as well as the spectacular demonstration of Jesus' authority.

Russell's rejection of the deity of Jesus, as well as the existence of God, leads him to read the biblical texts through the Filter of Atheism, which leads to a skewed exposition of the text and which

ultimately reinforces his predetermined skepticism. Rather than trying to see how some problematic passages might find satisfactory
resolution, Russell seems to *look* for problems. This is characteristic
of all three of the filters that subtract. (For more examples of atheistic filtering, go to www.cookministries.com/GreatQuestion and read
appendix entry 4.1.)

BOTTOM LINE

Bertrand Russell allows his atheistic presuppositions to interfere
with an objective reading of the New Testament texts. He is so committed to the position that God doesn't exist and his belief that Jesus
could not be God that he actually misreads the text, inventing a nonexistent problem in the process, and imposes his presuppositions
onto the stories. Russell provides one brief example of how someone
who reads the Bible through lenses of unbelief can miss the big picture and concoct problems that either don't exist or are readily
explainable. Just like I "knew" that the word *sleep* was on the conference speaker's list of words to remember, Bertrand Russell "knew"
that there are problems with Jesus' teachings. Remember, one of my
themes in this part of the book is that a person's presuppositions
may be more important than the evidence.

FILTERS THAT SUBTRACT — ANTISUPERNATURALISM

Atheists are not the only ones who embrace a skeptical filter. Since antisupernaturalists contend that miracles are impossible, their filters also blind them to any evidence to the contrary. With a little creative reasoning, they believe allegedly supernatural actions have a purely natural explanation. Apparent miracles are natural events that believers have either misinterpreted or intentionally exaggerated.

To antisupernaturalists, whether or not there is a God is less important than the belief that man is the locus of knowledge and wisdom. God, if he exists at all, is removed from human affairs and is largely irrelevant. An outcome of this philosophy is that all phenomena can be explained within the framework of the natural world. Hence, the allegedly supernatural is either an illusion, a misunderstanding, the product of superstition, or an intentional deception. Like everyone else, adherents of antisupernaturalism develop their own "versions" of Jesus that are consistent with their presuppositions.

THE QUEST

Of course, there have always been a variety of notions about Jesus that date back to his own day. Even before the crucifixion many considered him an important but merely mortal man. And from the earliest days of church history there have been many who portrayed Jesus differently from the "Unfiltered Jesus" of the New Testament. But the new worldview the eighteenth-century Enlightenment ushered in turbocharged the critical study of Jesus. Its influence continues to this day. As Michael J. Wilkins and J. P. Moreland observe about the new mind-set embraced in the "scientific age,"

> THE ADVENT OF HISTORICAL REASON IN THE MODERN ERA MEANS THAT WE ARE OBLIGATED TO DISTINGUISH BETWEEN FACTUAL AND FICTIONAL ACCOUNTS OF THE PAST. JUST AS SCIENTIFIC ADVANCES IN MEDICINE, ASTRONOMY, AGRICULTURE, AND PHYSICS SWEPT AWAY OLD SUPERSTITIONS AND MYTHS, SO THE APPLICATION OF SCIENTIFIC METHODS OF INVESTIGATION TO JESUS OF NAZARETH IS BOUND TO SWEEP AWAY ARCHAIC RELIGIOUS BELIEFS. THE CHRIST OF CREED AND DOGMA IN THE MIDDLE AGES IS THUS SAID TO BE VIABLE NO LONGER FOR PEOPLE WHO HAVE WITNESSED THE SCIENTIFIC REVOLUTION.[1]

Charlotte Allen elaborates on the impact of this sea change in thinking prompted by the Age of Enlightenment:

> WE LIVE IN AN AGE WHEN SCIENCE AND SCHOLARLY RESEARCH ARE SUPPOSED TO SUPPLY ANSWERS TO ALL OUR QUESTIONS.... THE SEARCH FOR THE "HISTORICAL" JESUS—THE HUMAN BEING WHO WALKED THE ROADS OF GALILEE 2,000 YEARS AGO—HAS THUS BECOME A HALLMARK OF MODERNITY, AN OBSESSION THAT HAS GRIPPED THE MINDS OF INTELLECTUALS FOR NEARLY THREE CENTURIES.[2]

The quest for the "historical Jesus" is now well entrenched among both New Testament academicians and popular culture. It attempts to strip away the exaggerations, myths, and superstitions thought to have been laminated onto the simple carpenter from

Galilee by his disciples and the early church who literally deified him. The goal is to recapture the kernel of the "pure" teachings and personhood of this first-century teacher.

THE QUEST GOES HOLLYWOOD

The media-savvy Jesus Seminar was organized in 1985 by Guggenheim Fellow and Senior Fulbright Scholar Robert Funk. To produce the volume *The Five Gospels: The Search for the Authentic Words of Jesus*, seventy-four Jesus Seminar scholars, called "fellows," gathered twice a year for several years to debate matters of theology. At the close of the debates, the fellows used colored beads to cast their votes regarding the authenticity of various words and actions that the Gospels attributed to Jesus. Their voting code was as follows:

- Red—"Jesus undoubtedly said this or something very like it."
- Pink—"Jesus probably said something like this."
- Gray—"Jesus did not say this, but the ideas contained in it are close to his own."
- Black—"Jesus did not say this; it represents the perspective or content of a later or different tradition."[3]

According to the Jesus Seminar's criteria, only about 20 percent of the words attributed to Jesus "make the cut" and end up in red or pink. Shockingly, the Jesus Seminar determined that only one verse from the entire gospel of Mark—which is almost universally considered by skeptical critics to be the oldest and most reliable—survives. That verse is Mark 12:17: "Give to Caesar what is Caesar's and to God what is God's." To no one's surprise, the seminar relegates the entire gospel of John to uncertainty.[4] Many skeptics have long dismissed that gospel as historically useless.

The Jesus Seminar eliminates anything that smacks of the supernatural. Why? One look at the backgrounds of the seminar's participants betrays their presuppositions and, therefore, their conclusions. Despite the claim that the Jesus Seminar represents a consensus of modern scholarship, forty of the seventy-four scholars are relative unknowns in the world of New Testament study. Many had only recently earned their PhDs, and eighteen of them had apparently not published any books or articles on New Testament studies. Almost all were Americans, and thirty-six of the seventy-four (or nearly half) either hold a degree from or were at the time teaching at Harvard, Claremont, or Vanderbilt—schools that have some of the most liberal departments of New Testament studies anywhere.[5]

So the jury has been tampered with to exclude scholars who are more supportive of the New Testament. Is it any wonder that the conclusions are as skeptical as they are? A surefire way to guarantee a desired outcome is to handpick participants who you know will support the conclusion you seek, and *voilà*, the group of experts endorses your view. This is exactly what the Jesus Seminar has done. As I stated earlier, a person's presuppositions, rather than the evidence, may have the greatest impact on his or her conclusions.

This approach of "stuffing the ballot box" is the very same one that most network television programs follow when they consider Christian topics. They typically interview several scholars, but the ones who receive the most airtime are the ones with the most provocative and least "conventional" theories. This makes for great TV but results in slanted presentations. Sometimes there are no Bible advocates at all, but even when there are they get little airtime.

A prime example of this was the February 20, 2004, edition of NBC's *Dateline* called "The Last Days of Jesus." The stimulus for this edition was the unprecedented media attention Mel Gibson's movie *The Passion of the Christ* received. One skeptic charged that it was extremely unlikely that the crowds in Jerusalem who hailed Jesus on Palm Sunday would demand his execution just a few days later. Another claimed that the ruthless Pontius Pilate known to history would not have been as willing to forgive Jesus as the Pilate portrayed in some of the Gospels. A final scholar opined that Judas may not even have been a historical figure, but instead may have been a symbolic embodiment of betrayal. The bottom line of the program was that, when it comes to trustworthiness, the gospel accounts strike out.

There were few orthodox scholars to balance these headline-grabbing allegations from the liberal skeptics. Typical. I cannot recall a single network television program that has provided equal time to Bible advocates.

IT CAN'T HAPPEN

This approach that screens everything through the "Quest for the Historical Jesus" mind-set is what I have dubbed the "Filter of Antisupernaturalism." It is the tendency to assume that supernatural phenomena are impossible; therefore, all of life, including all purported supernatural phenomena, really occurs by purely natural processes.

For example, the miracle where Jesus fed five thousand men with five loaves and two fish (John 6:6–13) is recast to teach that the young boy who gave his food to Jesus simply inspired others to share their food. The miracle, therefore, is in the human heart and not a supernatural creation of overwhelming plenty from a couple of sack lunches.

The resurrection is also foundational to a divine Jesus and therefore has become one of the prime victims of the Filter of Antisupernaturalism. Early in the last century, Percival Gardner-Smith suggested an ingenious rewrite of Matthew 28:5–7 to reinterpret the resurrection stories in purely naturalistic terms. These verses appear in the unedited gospel as follows:

THE ANGEL SAID TO THE WOMEN, "DO NOT BE AFRAID, FOR I KNOW THAT YOU ARE LOOKING FOR JESUS, WHO WAS CRUCI-FIED. HE IS NOT HERE; HE HAS RISEN, JUST AS HE SAID.

COME AND SEE THE PLACE WHERE HE LAY. THEN GO QUICKLY
AND TELL HIS DISCIPLES: 'HE HAS RISEN FROM THE DEAD AND
IS GOING AHEAD OF YOU INTO GALILEE. THERE YOU WILL SEE
HIM.'"

Gardner-Smith applies "white out" to a few lines to make the verses read as follows:

THE ANGEL SAID TO THE WOMEN, "DO NOT BE AFRAID, FOR I
KNOW THAT YOU ARE LOOKING FOR JESUS, WHO WAS CRUCI-
FIED. HE IS NOT HERE; ~~HE HAS RISEN, JUST AS HE SAID~~.
COME AND SEE THE PLACE WHERE HE LAY. ~~THEN GO QUICKLY
AND TELL HIS DISCIPLES 'HE HAS RISEN FROM THE DEAD AND
IS GOING AHEAD OF YOU INTO GALILEE. THERE YOU WILL SEE
HIM.'"~~ [6]

According to Gardner-Smith, the women apparently went to the wrong tomb, and the angel merely reoriented them to the correct spot. Maybe they should have used MapQuest. What justification could there be for the deletion of these verses except the presupposition that the resurrection didn't happen and that the supernatural aspects were later overlays?

THE DATING GAME

Dating the gospel accounts is also a hotbed of controversy. Since antisupernaturalists believe that no one can know the future, any time the Bible predicts a historical event of record, it has to be the result of hindsight. Jesus had a lot to say about the end of time, his future return to earth, and the coming destruction of the city of Jerusalem (Matt. 24—25 and Mark 13). Such a prediction goes beyond the realm of nature and presents a problem for the skeptics. Here is their filtered logic about Jerusalem's destruction:

- No one can accurately predict the future.

- The Gospels say that Jesus predicted the destruction of Jerusalem (Luke 19:41–44).
- Jesus died around AD 30.
- Jerusalem was destroyed by the Romans in AD 70.
- Therefore, Jesus could not have uttered the predictions about Jerusalem's destruction, since his death predated the event by four decades.

Matthew and Mark, therefore, couldn't have been written before AD 70, the year in which the city was demolished. This creates a significant gap between the events and their written record, which would allow plenty of time for legend and myth to creep in. Furthermore, there would be few if any eyewitnesses left to verify or contradict the accounts.

All this is based on the presupposition that Jesus could not have predicted the future. But this argument melts faster than the Wicked Witch of the West did when doused with water if the "Unfiltered Jesus" was really who he said he was. It seems that skeptics conclude Jesus couldn't have predicted the future because they have already decided he was a mere mortal man, incapable of such an accomplishment.

SYRACUSE CLASS

In the introduction I described my "thin-soup" spiritual background that lasted through my first year of college. In November of my sophomore year, my entire view of Christianity began to change dramatically. The following fall, I took a course about the New Testament Gospels, and I'm happy to report that by then I did understand the difference between the Old Testament and the New Testament.

On the first day of class, Professor Jackson identified himself as an ordained minister from one of the mainline denominations, but he assured us that he was not there to convert anyone. "That's the job of the chapel," he said. Then he added with a smile, "They still do that over there, don't they?" The class laughed, but I had had a couple of encounters with the campus chaplain, and I wasn't so sure.

He assured us that his would be an "objective" class. Now, I may have been naive, but my concept of objective meant to present both sides of an argument with as little bias as possible in a way that would allow us to reach our own conclusions. This was apparently not Professor Jackson's concept, though, because throughout the course he constantly pointed out problems, controversies, and supposed contradictions in the gospel stories. He almost never presented any evidence or discussion concerning the Gospels' historical accuracy and certainly no evidence that they were divinely inspired. We considered the traditional specialized areas of New Testament study including historical criticism, form criticism, and higher criticism, most of which presuppose a nondivine Bible.

One thing I appreciated about the class was that even though Professor Jackson didn't really present the material objectively, he was at least respectful of the text. Horror stories circulated among the Christian students about other professors who reportedly delighted in shredding the Gospels and anyone naive enough to take them seriously.

Nevertheless, Dr. Jackson, in the tradition of the Quest for the Historical Jesus, clearly employed the Filter of Antisupernaturalism. He tended to discount the divine aspects of Jesus' ministry by raising issues that undercut the veracity of the accounts:

- Why did Jesus submit to John the Baptist's baptism, since it was clearly for "sinners"? How do we reconcile this with the Christian concept that Jesus was sinless?
- Were the stories of Jesus' miracles merely a retelling of his parables recast to make them seem like historical events?
- Could it be that Jesus was slightly hypocritical, since he taught

forgiveness yet was so hard on the Pharisees? Why don't we have any accounts of his forgiving a Pharisee?

- Since early believers felt they had the "mind of Christ" and the Holy Spirit to guide them, could it be that they unconsciously produced teachings that they then attributed to Jesus?

The professor's attitude was that, because we can't definitively prove whether the miracle stories happened or not, we should not view them as terribly important. He also had the habit of implying that differences in reports of the same events in various gospels equal contradictions. There were at least two instances where the professor allowed his presuppositions to grossly distort the evidence, which resulted in lapses of intellectual integrity. Let's look.

ONCE AGAIN, THE AGE-OLD QUESTION

"Who do you say I am?" Jesus asked his disciples in Matthew 16:15. As we saw in the chapter on the Unfiltered Jesus, that is *the* question at the heart of Jesus' life and ministry. Of course, our class dove headlong into this issue. Professor Jackson took an approach I had not heard of before. He noticed that Jesus, along with others, called himself by various titles. He wanted to determine which titles Jesus really applied to himself and which were used only by others. The question wasn't so much "Who do others say he was?" but "What did Jesus think of himself?"

I looked forward to that lecture in particular because it tackled the pivotal question of the New Testament. At the beginning of class, the professor wrote on the blackboard the following six titles that are sometimes applied to Jesus:

1. Son of David
2. Son of God
3. Lord (Greek—*kyrios*; Hebrew—*Adonai*)
4. Servant (of the Lord)

5. The Christ (Anointed One, Messiah)
6. Son of Man

Then he asked, "Which of these, if any, did Jesus apply to himself?"

The first thing I noticed was that many terms were missing from the list. Among them were

- the Way, the Truth, and the Life;
- the Resurrection and the Life;
- the Good Shepherd;
- the Bread of Life; and
- the Light of the World.

We were far enough into the semester that I knew why these names were missing in action. They all appear in the gospel of John, which Professor Jackson considered totally unreliable. There *are* challenges involved with reconciling John's gospel and the other three gospels. But Professor Jackson's course assumed John had no historical credibility whatsoever. We could simply scrap John.

If the question is "What did Jesus think of himself?" the outcome is already largely "rigged" by only admitting partial evidence. *But that's okay,* I thought. *There's still plenty of "good stuff" in the six titles left on the blackboard.*

So which of six titles did Jesus actually use? Professor Jackson covered each title to see where the evidence led.

SON OF DAVID

"Son of David" is a Jewish title that obviously referred back to Israel's greatest king, David. Jesus' use of this name is somewhat dubious, Dr. Jackson claimed. Jesus seemed to reject it in the story of healing two blind men. Here is the account as reported in Matthew 9:27–31.

AS JESUS WENT ON FROM THERE, TWO BLIND MEN FOLLOWED HIM, CALLING OUT, "HAVE MERCY ON US, SON OF DAVID!"

WHEN HE HAD GONE INDOORS, THE BLIND MEN CAME TO HIM, AND HE ASKED THEM, "DO YOU BELIEVE THAT I AM ABLE TO DO THIS?"

"YES, LORD," THEY REPLIED.

THEN HE TOUCHED THEIR EYES AND SAID, "ACCORDING TO YOUR FAITH WILL IT BE DONE TO YOU"; AND THEIR SIGHT WAS RESTORED. JESUS WARNED THEM STERNLY, "SEE THAT NO ONE KNOWS ABOUT THIS." BUT THEY WENT OUT AND SPREAD THE NEWS ABOUT HIM ALL OVER THAT REGION.

The professor interpreted Jesus' instruction not to tell anyone as a denial of that title. In other words, Professor Jackson's take on why Jesus told the men to be quiet is that they were wrong in calling Jesus the "Son of David." So Dr. Jackson picked up his chalk and drew a line through the words "Son of David."

Does this explanation make sense, or could there be another reason behind Jesus' instruction about keeping a low profile? First of all, I'm not sure Professor Jackson even interpreted Jesus' instructions to the men correctly. He said, "See that no one knows about this." My take on what "this" means is the whole healing event, not necessarily the fact that the men called Jesus the Son of David. In fact, the "Son of David" aspect is somewhat peripheral to the whole story. The most natural way to interpret "this" in the context of the story is the healing.

But even if Professor Jackson was right, we must remember that "Son of David" was very much a loaded term in first-century Jerusalem. Everyone who heard it knew that it was closely linked to the expected Messiah who, it was thought, would come to deliver the Jewish people from politically oppressive Rome. So the Romans would hardly roll out the red carpet for anyone claiming this title. To introduce yourself as the Son of David in that context would generate about the same reaction as a presidential candidate at the Republican National Convention announcing that he was the "Gun Control Candidate."

The event Matthew 9 records took place early in Jesus ministry, and it is likely that if the Roman authorities thought that Jesus believed he was the political Messiah, his ministry would have been prematurely at risk. In fact, one of the main reasons Pontius Pilate ultimately ordered Jesus' execution a few years later was precisely because he considered him a political threat. Because of this sensitivity, Jesus wanted to fly below the radar. It does not require Professor Jackson's interpretation to understand why Jesus told the blind men not to refer to him as the Son of David.

SON OF GOD

Next we tackled the title "Son of God." Although others may have called him this, according to the professor, there is no evidence that these words ever came out of Jesus' lips when referring to himself. As evidence of this, he referenced Mark 3:11–12 and read the following:

> WHENEVER THE EVIL SPIRITS SAW HIM, THEY FELL DOWN BEFORE HIM AND CRIED OUT, "YOU ARE THE SON OF GOD." BUT HE GAVE THEM STRICT ORDERS NOT TO TELL WHO HE WAS.

Professor Jackson pointed out that it was the evil spirits who called Jesus the "Son of God," not Jesus. Was his instruction a denial of that title? Yes, according to Dr. Jackson. So out came the chalk, and out went "Son of God."

But read Jesus' words again. He doesn't say that the evil spirits are wrong, only that they shouldn't *reveal* who he was. That's a big difference. And what were they revealing about him? That he was the Son of God. His directive is actually tantamount to a *claim* to be the Son of God. They said, "You are the Son of God." Jesus said, "Don't tell anybody." That would be like Lois Lane saying to Clark Kent, "I know that you're really Superman" and Clark responds, saying, "Don't tell anyone." Would that be a denial or simply a request for confidentiality?

By this point of the class, I began to worry.

LORD

Next up was the title "Lord." This term, according to the professor, is problematic, since it can have multiple meanings. The Greek word we translate as "Lord" is *kyrios*, which can mean "mister," "sir," "master" (of a slave), or "king." Since it has such a broad array of meanings, even if Jesus did apply this term to himself, we really can't be exactly sure what he meant.

But not to worry. Once again, according to Professor Jackson, there is "no evidence" that Jesus ever called himself "Lord." Really? What about the incident recorded in Matthew 21:1–3 where Jesus sent his disciples into the village to prepare for the Passover dinner right before his crucifixion? As part of his instructions he says, "If anyone says anything to you, tell him that the Lord needs them." Admittedly it is not crystal clear which of the multiple meanings he would have been assuming. But how could Professor Jackson say Jesus never applied that title to himself?

SERVANT

Did Jesus ever call himself the "Servant of the Lord"? Perhaps, according to my professor, but he did so only indirectly. Jesus said in Mark 10:45 that he came to serve and to give his life as a ransom for many. According to Jackson, this may relate back to Isaiah chapter 53, which is the well-known "Suffering Servant" passage in the Old Testament that carries strong messianic overtones. Since Jesus never clearly called himself "Servant of the Lord," however, this title is likewise a little fuzzy. We were down to only two titles: "Christ/Messiah" and "Son of Man."

CHRIST/MESSIAH

Christ is the Greek equivalent of the Hebrew word *Messiah*, which means God's chosen and anointed one who was to deliver Israel. Professor Jackson stated that Jesus never unambiguously claimed to be the Messiah. In fact, the only time that Jesus affirmatively applied this term to himself was during his trial in front of the high priest. But, Jackson said, there are some issues surrounding the reliability of that story. (I will cover those challenges in online appendix 5.1.) So there goes "Christ."

But Professor Jackson's conclusion is plainly wrong. What about the well-known account of Jesus when he asked the disciples who people thought he was? Here is Matthew's record of that event.

WHEN JESUS CAME TO THE REGION OF CAESAREA PHILIPPI, HE ASKED HIS DISCIPLES, "WHO DO PEOPLE SAY THE SON OF MAN IS?"

THEY REPLIED, "SOME SAY JOHN THE BAPTIST; OTHERS SAY ELIJAH; AND STILL OTHERS, JEREMIAH OR ONE OF THE PROPHETS."

"BUT WHAT ABOUT YOU?" HE ASKED. "WHO DO YOU SAY I AM?"

SIMON PETER ANSWERED, "YOU ARE THE CHRIST, THE SON OF THE LIVING GOD."

JESUS REPLIED, "BLESSED ARE YOU, SIMON SON OF JONAH, FOR THIS WAS NOT REVEALED TO YOU BY MAN, BUT BY MY FATHER IN HEAVEN. AND I TELL YOU THAT YOU ARE PETER, AND ON THIS ROCK I WILL BUILD MY CHURCH, AND THE GATES OF HADES WILL NOT OVERCOME IT. I WILL GIVE YOU THE KEYS OF THE KINGDOM OF HEAVEN; WHATEVER YOU BIND ON EARTH WILL BE BOUND IN HEAVEN, AND WHATEVER YOU LOOSE ON EARTH WILL BE LOOSED IN HEAVEN." THEN HE WARNED HIS DISCIPLES NOT TO TELL ANYONE THAT HE WAS THE CHRIST. (16:13–20)

Is there anything here that even remotely resembles a denial of himself as Messiah? He calls Peter "blessed" because he recognizes this truth, then goes on to state that this insight was from the Father himself. What could be more obvious?

SON OF MAN

"Son of Man" was the last name standing, so to speak. There is no doubt that Jesus called himself this many times. However, according to Professor Jackson, we can't really be sure exactly what he meant by this since the term is somewhat unclear. It could mean

- "I" or "me"—referring to himself,
- "He"—pointing to someone else, or
- "It"—meaning some collective group of people (perhaps the church).

So even though Jesus called himself "Son of Man," we can't know what he intended by that term.

With all due respect to my professor, that conclusion is a cop-out. Any Jew of Jesus' day would have immediately recognized it as a reference to the Old Testament book of Daniel. The prophet Daniel says,

> IN MY VISION AT NIGHT I LOOKED, AND THERE BEFORE ME WAS ONE LIKE A SON OF MAN, COMING WITH THE CLOUDS OF HEAVEN. HE APPROACHED THE ANCIENT OF DAYS AND WAS LED INTO HIS PRESENCE. HE WAS GIVEN AUTHORITY, GLORY AND SOVEREIGN POWER; ALL PEOPLES, NATIONS AND MEN OF EVERY LANGUAGE WORSHIPED HIM. HIS DOMINION IS AN EVERLASTING DOMINION THAT WILL NOT PASS AWAY, AND HIS KINGDOM IS ONE THAT WILL NEVER BE DESTROYED. (7:13–14)

Let's go through Daniel 7:13–14, one phrase at a time, and observe who this "son of man" is:

- He comes with the clouds of heaven.
- He approaches the Ancient of Days (clearly God) and is led into his presence.
- He is given authority, glory, and sovereign power.

- All people, nations, and men of every language worship him.
- He has an everlasting dominion that will not pass away, and his kingdom will never be destroyed.

The "one like a son of man" clearly possesses divine attributes. Of how many people can we say, "All peoples, nations, and men of every language worship him"? The Bible unmistakably teaches that we are to worship God alone. My list of candidates consists of just one name. His name is Jesus, the Son of Man who Daniel saw in his vision.

The following table is a partial summary of how Jesus used the phrase "Son of Man":

JESUS' USE OF THE TERM "SON OF MAN"

Mark 2:10	Has authority on earth to forgive sins
Mark 2:28	Is Lord even of the Sabbath
Mark 8:31	Must suffer many things; be rejected by the elders, chief priests, and teachers of the law; be killed; and after three days rise again
Mark 8:38	Will be ashamed of anyone who is ashamed of him and his words when he comes in the Father's glory with the holy angels
Mark 9:9	Will rise from the dead
Mark 9:12	Must suffer much and be rejected
Mark 10:33–34	Will be betrayed to the chief priests and teachers of the law; be condemned to death; and be handed over to the Gentiles, who will mock him, spit on him, flog him, and kill him; will rise three days later
Mark 10:45	Did not come to be served but to serve and to give his life as a ransom for many
Mark 13:26–27	Will come in the clouds with great power and glory; will send his angels to gather his elect from the four winds, from the ends of the earth to the ends of the heavens

Mark 14:41	Will be betrayed into the hands of sinners
Mark 14:62	Will be visible sitting at the right hand of the Mighty One and coming on the clouds of heaven
Matthew 8:20	Has no place to lay his head
Matthew 11:19	Came eating and drinking and was accused of gluttony and drunkenness and of being a friend of tax collectors and sinners
Matthew 12:40	Will be three days and three nights in the heart of the earth just as Jonah was three days and three nights in the belly of a huge fish
Matthew 13:37	Is the sower of the good seed (in the parable of the wheat and the weeds)
Matthew 13:41	Will send out his angels to weed out of his kingdom everything that causes sin and all who do evil
Matthew 16:27	Is going to come in his Father's glory with his angels and will reward each person according to what he has done

This representative list shows that when Jesus talked about the Son of Man, he was referring to himself. There is no way to miss the first-person meaning (i.e., "I") in Jesus' words. Skeptics would like to attribute the more supernatural aspects of the Son of Man to someone or something else, but this artificial distinction seems more the result of their filters than of the plain meaning of Jesus' teaching.

"In Conclusion ..."

What was the point of this class session? Who did Jesus think he was? According to Dr. Jackson, we really can't be sure. Others may have attributed various divine titles to him, but these words never came out of Jesus' mouth. Even those statements that seem to indicate that Jesus thought he was divine could have a variety of interpretations. The only name we know for sure he called himself was "Son of Man," and who knows what that means? This is an alarmingly convenient conclusion for the skeptic.

Since I was rather new in my faith at the time, I could not properly articulate my disagreement with his conclusions. Furthermore, it would not have been prudent to attempt to take on in hand-to-hand combat a full professor who had taught this course for many years. As I've grown in my understanding of the Christian life and the intellectual basis for our beliefs, the fallacies of his logic have become increasingly apparent and distressing.

Even if we were unsure by which names Jesus actually called himself and believe that when other people called him "Son of God" or "Son of David" (meaning Messiah or Christ) Jesus rejected those designations, there are several incidents where he acted in a manner in which only God would behave. As I pointed out in chapter 2, the gospel of Matthew presents three occasions on which Jesus allowed people to worship him.

1. After Jesus got into the disciples' boat and calmed the storm (Matt. 14:22–33)
2. Immediately after the resurrection, when the women first saw Jesus outside the tomb (Matt. 28:9)
3. Just before Matthew's account of Jesus' miraculous ascent into heaven (Matt. 28:16–17)

If these events were recorded in the gospel of John, skeptics would not even bother to discuss them since they consider John's stories clearly spurious. But these accounts appear in Matthew, which is considered older and more reliable.

Dr. Jackson ignored these events when Jesus allowed others to worship him. My professor didn't technically violate his stated objective of considering the names that Jesus applied to himself. Jesus never said the words, "Worship me." But he clearly accepted these acts of worship and refused to chastise his followers for what would otherwise have been a violation of the first commandment. If we take the texts at face value, the Jesus the Gospels portray undoubtedly claimed to be God. (For a discussion of an outlandish example of how Professor Jackson rewrote the facts to fit his theory about who Jesus was, go to www.cookministries.com/GreatQuestion and read appendix entry 5.1.)

LOOKING BACK

As I've reflected on that college course over the intervening years, I have recognized several points of questionable scholarship:

1. First and foremost, despite the claim to be "objective," it clearly focused primarily on a historical methodology (in the tradition of the Quest for the Historic Jesus) that assumes the supernatural stories the Bible records were embellishments the early church added to the text. Such an approach cannot be objective, since it fails to present the multiple sides of the issue in a fair manner.

2. It ignored a whole body of evidence (the gospel of John), presupposing it to be historically unreliable. If this were a truly objective class, we would have considered the evidence for the historical reliability of John along with the problems that gospel presents.

3. We consistently jumped to obscure conclusions about the supernatural elements of Jesus' life. For example, when Jesus told the blind men who called him "Son of David" not to tell anyone about the healing, and when he told the evil spirits who called him "Son of God" to be silent, the professor assumed that Jesus was denying their labels. As we saw above, Jesus' reason for keeping a low profile could have been due to the charged political climate and what the consequences would have been of his publicly accepting that designation so

early in his ministry. I don't recall any discussion of that possibility in class.

4. He ignored the fact that Jesus accepted worship from his disciples, which was clearly an acknowledgment of his own deity.

5. When the professor said that there was "no evidence" that Jesus applied the term "Lord" to himself, he ignored the incident with the donkey before his triumphal entry (Matt. 21:1–3). Similarly, he ignored Jesus' commendation of Peter for calling him "the Christ" (Matt. 16:17).

6. He explained away Jesus' clear application of the term "Christ" to himself in answer to the high priest's question. (For more information, go to www.cookministries.com/GreatQuestion and read appendix entry 5.1.)

7. In that same incident, the professor went to great lengths to debunk any supernatural significance associated with Jesus' use of "Son of Man" (i.e., his sitting at the right hand of power and coming on the clouds of heaven). All this, despite the fact that those who were present on these occasions clearly "got" what he meant.

WILL THE CIRCLE BE UNBROKEN?

When it comes to the Filter of Antisupernaturalism as it is demonstrated by the Quest for the Historical Jesus, I detect circular reasoning. Adherents presuppose that the miraculous doesn't happen. They'll start by saying, "If you see an account that records an allegedly supernatural event, you can know it's not reliable."

"Why not?" I ask in response.

"Because we know that the miraculous doesn't happen. There is no evidence for it."

"There isn't?" I counter. "What about this story we are looking at that includes supernatural aspects? Isn't that evidence?"

"Perhaps, but it's inadmissible," they answer. "Since miracles don't take place, those who recorded the events have to be guilty of filtering the events through supernatural, religious, or superstitious worldviews."

I don't think they're the only ones who could be charged with filtering. Within the closed system they have defined, the skeptics are consistent. But their approach is like a refusal to allow valuable evidence in a court case, something like, "I know the accused person is guilty, so I won't allow any information that might prove his innocence."

As I reviewed my class notes and the textbook we used, I relived the vague sense of spiritual confusion that permeated Dr. Jackson's class. The prevailing mood was one of ambiguity. There was so much uncertainty about every aspect of Jesus' life that we couldn't really be sure about anything. The Filter of Antisupernaturalism tainted *everything*. I am not opposed to honest questions, even the hard ones, but there is a difference between a question that seeks to gain a better understanding and a question designed to intentionally undermine the credibility of the source.

As my friend and Sunday school teacher Les Saunders often says, there are two reasons to read the Bible:

- To prove that you are right
- To get to know God better

The questions that emerge from the antisupernatural skeptics clearly fall into the first category. They filter out what they don't like and then claim to be objective.

FILTERS THAT SUBTRACT — SELECTIVE CHRISTIAN THEOLOGY

In 1985 Doubleday publishers stirred up a minor tempest within the literary world with their release of a new edition of Mark Twain's classic book *The Adventures of Huckleberry Finn*. To create this new version, a writer named Charles Neider took it upon himself to "edit" Twain's work in order to create, as Doubleday put it, "a masterful novel truer to its spirit and vision than ever before."[1] Neider added five thousand seven hundred words that were Twain's own words, but were in a different book, and eliminated eight thousand three hundred words that Twain included in his own original version of *Huck Finn*.

Columnist Jonathan Yardley wryly observes,

> IT SEEMS THAT CHARLES NEIDER AND DOUBLEDAY HAVE A CLEARER VIEW OF THE NOVEL'S "SPIRIT AND VISION" THAN DID ITS AUTHOR, SO WE SHOULD BE GRATEFUL TO BOTH FOR DOING HIM, AND US, THE FAVOR OF EDITING THE BOOK INTO A FORM THAT MARK TWAIN HIMSELF DOUBTLESS WOULD PREFER TO THE ORIGINAL IF ONLY HE WERE AROUND TO READ IT.

Yardley continues,

HE [NEIDER] HAS CUT ... 8,300 WORDS FROM TWAIN'S GREAT NOVEL NOT BECAUSE THEY WERE ORIGINALLY WRITTEN AGAINST TWAIN'S WILL, OR BECAUSE HE HAS DISCOVERED A NOTE IN TWAIN'S HANDWRITING EXPRESSING DISSATISFACTION WITH THEM; CHARLES NEIDER HAS CUT THESE 8,300 WORDS FROM "HUCKLEBERRY FINN" FOR THE SIMPLE AND SINGLE REASON THAT CHARLES NEIDER DOES NOT LIKE THEM....

IT QUITE TAKES ONE'S BREATH AWAY, DOESN'T IT? IN THIS BIZARRE VIEW OF LITERATURE, READERS AND CRITICS ARE FREE NOT MERELY TO EXPRESS THEIR OPINIONS, BUT TO TINKER WITH BOOKS TO THEIR OWN SATISFACTION.[2]

I once had a boss who was in the habit of rewriting minutes of a meeting so they would reflect an outcome different than what actually happened. There were times when I did not even recognize his report as a description of the meetings I had personally attended. A coworker and I used to joke that our boss's minutes weren't what really happened but what he wished had happened.

As preposterous as these examples may seem, they match a trend that goes on every day in the world of theology.

A RELIGIOUS PARALLEL

Every so often, an event triggers another skirmish in what I call the "Gay Wars." Courts or legislators make controversial decisions to expand the rights of homosexuals. Or a church denomination either sanctions or condemns same-sex unions. Passionate letters to editors land like Molotov cocktails for about a week, and each side fans the flames of controversy.

I remember that several years ago, the *Grand Rapids Press* in Michigan hosted such a melee. One hand grenade a mainline minister lobbed invoked the account from the gospel of John where Jesus prevents the stoning of a woman who had been caught in the act of adultery. You probably know the story. The religious leaders are ready to kill this woman for her sin, but Jesus changes the dynamic when he grants permission to stone her *only* to those who themselves were without sin. Of course, as they reflect on the state of their own hearts, each of the would-be vigilantes recognizes his own sin. One by one, they depart until only Jesus and the woman are left.

Jesus asks the woman where her accusers are.

> "HAS NO ONE CONDEMNED YOU?"
>
> "NO ONE, SIR," SHE SAID.
>
> "THEN NEITHER DO I CONDEMN YOU," JESUS DECLARED.
> (JOHN 8:10–11)

The pastor, who supported gay rights, held up this story as an example of how we should not judge others. After all, if Jesus did not judge the woman because of her sexual activity, how can we?

The only problem with this conclusion is that it commits the same type of textual tampering with Jesus' words that Charles Neider did with Mark Twain's. The pastor's letter retains the vast majority of the text but omits one very important sentence: the last one. The entirety of Jesus' response reads,

> "THEN NEITHER DO I CONDEMN YOU," JESUS DECLARED. "GO NOW AND LEAVE YOUR LIFE OF SIN."

Thus, the full thrust of Jesus' teaching is twofold: the woman is forgiven, and she is to leave her life of sexual sin. The author of this letter, however, distorts Jesus' teaching by ignoring his last statement. This allowed him to conclude that, since Jesus did not condemn the woman's adulterous activity, neither should we judge homosexual behavior. In fact, a correct application of this text to the Gay Wars issue is twofold:

- Just as Jesus forgave the woman of her sexual indiscretion, so too, repentant homosexuals are to be forgiven.

- Both the woman caught in adultery and practicing homosexuals should leave their lives of sin.

This letter to the editor is a perfect example of reading the Bible through the Filter of Selective Christian Theology. It happens when we conveniently rewrite or selectively ignore Scripture to support our position, even if it completely contradicts the clear teaching of the Bible.

In a real sense, this is most insidious filter of all. It results in a message that includes some elements of truth, but with distortions. C. S. Lewis has a great analogy for this phenomenon. If someone's objective is to obtain gold, brass is more "dangerous" than clay. It is far more likely that I will mistake brass for gold than I will clay for gold, thereby being deceived in my quest.[3]

In November 2001, *Christianity Today* magazine ran a fascinating story called "meetingGod@beliefnet.com" by one of the contributing editors, Lauren F. Winner.[4] She described a position she held as a book reviewer at a Web site devoted to spiritual but not necessarily Christian topics. Among the books she reviewed were *If the Buddha Dated* and a vegetarian Wiccan cookbook. So the gate was very wide on this one. As a committed Christian who prayed through her assignments, she never felt God tell her not to review a book about Hinduism. But she did occasionally feel prompted to avoid books that preached, as she called it, "heterodox Christianity." She continued, saying,

ON REFLECTION, THIS MAKES SENSE TO ME: I MAY REALLY HAVE SOMETHING TO LEARN FROM A DEVOUT HINDU—MORE THAN I HAVE TO LEARN FROM A WISHY-WASHY LIBERAL EPISCOPALIAN WHO HAS SACRIFICED THE CORE OF HIS FAITH IN THE NAME OF INCLUSIVITY. I THINK I AM CAPABLE OF RECOGNIZING HINDUISM AS HINDUISM. BUT I'M STILL YOUNG IN THIS CHRISTIAN LIFE, AND I MAY NOT BE ABLE TO RECOGNIZE SOME OF THE PERSUASIVE-SOUNDING PSEUDO-CHRISTIAN ARGUMENTS FOR WHAT THEY ARE: HERESY.[5]

It is important in this world where brass resembles gold to have our sensors activated so we can legitimately learn from sources whose fundamental beliefs are different from ours. We must, nevertheless, beware the danger of quasi-Christian beliefs that pose as orthodoxy.

Most people who read atheistic material recognize it as such and evaluate it accordingly. Many who read material produced by people with the Filter of Antisupernaturalism may buy in to some of the arguments. Many more, I'm afraid, listen to teachers so firmly committed to the Filter of Selective Christian Theology that the student considers the teachings authoritative because of their veneer of Christianity. Unfortunately, these teachers often deny the very core of the New Testament's message.

I have labeled this mental grid the "Filter of Selective Christian Theology." Technically, there is a broader general theological filter employed by adherents of Judaism, Hinduism, and Buddhism, among others. Since historically most theological books that subtract from the Unfiltered Jesus are written by people within the walls of Christendom, often by denominational leaders and seminary professors, I am focusing on the selective Christian filter.

THE JEFFERSON BIBLE

I admitted earlier that I am a book junkie. A few years ago I had a conference in Williamsburg, Virginia, one of the best-preserved historic cities in our country. During an afternoon break, I decided to stroll through the little downtown village area. As I walked along brick sidewalks amid golden and red leaves gently tumbling to the pavement, I noticed a quaint little independent bookstore. I couldn't resist!

There in the religion section, I came across a small volume called *The Jefferson Bible*, written by Thomas Jefferson, the third president of the United States. I had heard about this book for years but had never seen it. *How appropriate, I thought, to buy a book by this renowned scholar and giant of American history in one of the most historically rich cities in the country. Who knows? Maybe old Thomas himself walked down the very street I was on. And, just maybe, he even stopped at the same Starbucks from which I had just come.*

According to Jefferson, this volume consists of only the "legitimate" teaching of Jesus. As I read on, I learned that *only* Jesus' teachings on morality and ethics make the cut. Jefferson excludes anything remotely supernatural, including the following:

- Jesus' virgin birth
- The angelic announcement of his birth to the shepherds
- All of Jesus' miracles
- His physical resurrection

Why would Jefferson excise these aspects of Jesus' life? It's simple. Jefferson was a Unitarian. In fact, my copy of *The Jefferson Bible* was published by Beacon Press, an affiliate of the Unitarian Universalist Association of Congregations. You probably remember from the introduction that intellect and sound reasoning are among the Unitarians' highest values. A supernatural Jesus who is the only means of salvation violated Jefferson's rationalistic grid, so whenever he came upon a passage that referenced anything supernatural, he just hit the delete button.

In Jefferson's mind, Jesus' teachings in the Gospels had several disadvantages to overcome, having not

... BEEN COMMITTED TO WRITING BY HIMSELF, BUT BY THE MOST UNLETTERED OF MEN, BY MEMORY, LONG AFTER THEY HAD HEARD THEM FROM HIM, WHEN MUCH WAS FORGOTTEN, MUCH MISUNDERSTOOD, AND PRESENTED IN EVERY PARADOXICAL SHAPE. YET SUCH ARE THE FRAGMENTS REMAINING AS TO SHOW A MASTER WORKMAN.[6]

In a personal letter to Benjamin Rush, a prominent Philadelphia physician with whom he had many theological conversations, Jefferson wrote, "To the corruptions of Christianity, I am indeed opposed; but not to the genuine precepts of Jesus himself."[7] In other words, the Gospels are not trustworthy, and his objective was to cull the false teachings from the true ones.

Jefferson described the process by which he selected "the very words only of Jesus" in a letter to John Adams dated October 13, 1813:

> I HAVE PERFORMED THIS OPERATION FOR MY OWN USE, BY CUTTING VERSE BY VERSE OUT OF THE PRINTED BOOK, AND BY ARRANGING THE MATTER WHICH IS EVIDENTLY HIS, AND WHICH IS AS DISTINGUISHABLE AS DIAMONDS IN A DUNGHILL. THE RESULT IS AN OCTAVO OF FORTY-SIX PAGES, OF PURE AND UNSOPHISTICATED DOCTRINES, SUCH AS WERE PROFESSED AND ACTED ON BY THE UNLETTERED APOSTLES, THE APOS-TOLIC FATHERS, AND THE CHRISTIANS OF THE FIRST CENTURY.[8]

Jefferson assumed that the apostles and later Christians added to and corrupted Jesus' "pure" teachings. How does he know? Was he there to hear what Jesus actually said? Does he cite any objective textual evidence that indicates the disciples twisted earlier versions of Jesus' words as they created the Gospels that we know today?

In a letter to Francis Adrian van der Kemp, a Dutch scholar and Unitarian minister, Jefferson describes Jesus as "a great Reformer of the Hebrew code of religion" but indicates that he disagrees with Jesus in some of his doctrines. "I am a Materialist; He takes the side of Spiritualism. He preaches the efficacy of repentance toward forgiveness of sin; I require a counterpoise of good works to redeem it, etc."[9]

He then adds,

> AMONG THE SAYINGS AND DISCOURSE IMPUTED TO HIM BY HIS BIOGRAPHERS, I FIND MANY PASSAGES OF FINE IMAGINATION,

CORRECT MORALITY, AND OF THE MOST LOVELY BENEVO-
LENCE; AND OTHERS, AGAIN, OF SO MUCH IGNORANCE, SO
MUCH ABSURDITY, SO MUCH UNTRUTH, CHARLATANISM AND
IMPOSTURE, AS TO PRONOUNCE IT IMPOSSIBLE THAT SUCH
CONTRADICTIONS SHOULD HAVE PROCEEDED FROM THE SAME
BEING. I SEPARATE, THEREFORE, THE GOLD FROM THE DROSS;
RESTORE TO HIM THE FORMER, AND LEAVE THE LATTER TO
THE STUPIDITY OF SOME, AND ROGUERY OF OTHERS OF HIS
DISCIPLES. [10]

The introductory chapter to the copy of *The Jefferson Bible* that I bought that day in Williamsburg was written by F. Forrester Church. He chose to call this chapter "The Gospel according to Thomas Jefferson." He said Jefferson "carved out a Gospel for himself, one whose witness he could respect and whose message he could understand." [11]

Did you catch that? What was Jefferson's criterion for including "authentic" teaching?

According to Church, it was whether or not he could respect and understand it. We read Jefferson's own words where he argues with Jesus over what is required for salvation. Jesus accepts repentance alone, but Jefferson adds good works. He sat as judge over Jesus' teaching, calling parts of it "charlatanism" and "dross." I'd say that's a bit arrogant. Jefferson apparently claimed to know the truth better than Jesus did—or at least better than the Jesus who he alleges was invented by his followers.

This is a great example of a writer's reinterpretation of Jesus based on his own theological bias. He boldly admits that he deliberately screens Jesus' teachings, which he presupposes were tainted by the early church, according to his personal conclusions about what is theologically acceptable. Perhaps Charles Neider drew some of his inspiration for editing *Huckleberry Finn* from Thomas Jefferson.

SPONGED

Let's move now to a more contemporary example of a Christian thinker whose filters serve as blinders. Retired Episcopal Bishop John Shelby Spong was one of the most controversial popular theological writers of the late twentieth century. He is an outspoken liberal clergyman who would disagree with almost everything in this book. Spong has written a number of best-selling books that attack traditional and orthodox Christian beliefs. Perhaps his most provocative work is *Rescuing the Bible from Fundamentalism*.

Spong states that his objective is to liberate the Bible "from the clutches of mindless literalism" while asserting its continued relevance to us today.[12] In his introduction, Spong decries the fact that there are many scholarly books available for professional clergy, but there are few for the average church member in the pew that reflect what he considers the state of the art of biblical research. Spong's view of the state of the art reflects a theological position that abandons the concept of a reliable Bible. He wishes that there were more volumes that would bring this enlightened viewpoint to the masses.

"Most Christians," he says, "who are generally unaware of this scholarship seem to believe that they must either be biblical literalists or admit that the Bible contains nothing of value for them." Fortunately, though, he sees another way: "that intelligence does not have to be a casualty of church life, that God can be worshiped with our minds."[13]

In other words, most Christians think they have to choose between mindlessly believing the Bible or rejecting it altogether. If this dichotomy sounds familiar, it's because it's a first cousin to the argument presented by Nicholas Kristof, to whom I referred in the introduction, who strongly implies that you can't be a Christian and intelligent at the same time. Spong's solution to this dilemma? Study the same type of material he has apparently studied, and you will see that you can then worship God with your mind.

The greatest commandment, according to Jesus, is "Hear, O Israel, the Lord our God, the Lord is one. Love the Lord your God with all your heart and with all your soul and with all your mind and with all your strength" (Mark 12:29–30). The four aspects of our being with which we are to worship God are our

- heart,
- soul,
- mind, and
- strength.

Notice that Jesus includes the mind.

Now, consider again Spong's comment "that intelligence does not have to be a casualty of church life, that God can be worshiped with our minds."[14] Isn't that what Jesus just said? Believe it or not, I agree with Spong's statement as listed above. I disagree completely, however, with the way Spong applies his assertion. Let's look at his logic, one thought at a time.

His first statement is that most Christians are not aware of current scholarly research on the Bible. This is probably true. His second statement is that many Christians who don't know about contemporary biblical scholarship conclude that they have to believe the whole Bible literally or else reject it entirely. This also may be true. He then asserts that it is possible to be a faithful church member and maintain your intellectual integrity. Of course, I agree with this position. I also agree with his stated goal of rescuing the Bible from "mindless literalism."

So if I agree with everything Spong says, why am I taking him on? Because he bases his arguments and statements on assumptions that are fundamentally flawed. He assumes that anyone with intellectual integrity and who studies the evidence will conclude that the Bible is not inspired, reliable, or accurate. In other words, Spong believes that knowledge leads to skepticism about the Bible.

One well-known but nonlegitimate technique of debate is to

create what is called a "straw man" argument, where I develop a position that falsely purports to accurately represent my opponent's beliefs. I then proceed to decimate it. This makes for great entertainment when I turn my straw man over to the Wicked Witch of the West and her flaming broomstick. It's a resounding "win" for the shredder but is unfair to the "shredee." I may cleverly convince the reader that I have accurately represented the other's position, when I really have not.

Spong begins *Rescuing the Bible from Fundamentalism* with a section titled "Proof Texting and Prejudice" in which he describes growing up in the South, where he heard the Bible quoted to justify segregation, racism, corporal punishment, standing against "secular modernists," and opposing "God-denying modernists."[15] He also devotes several paragraphs to railing against Christians who use Scripture to limit the role of women in church and oppose the homosexual lifestyle.[16]

With the ease of an Olympic gymnast, Spong makes a huge leap of logic. His argument appears to be that anyone who is a "literalist" buys in to the list of sins he named above. Despite his implied commitment to wrestle with nuances of tough theological challenges, he does not appear to make allowances for differing shades of interpretation. Stated another way, Spong seems to adopt an "all or nothing" view. "Because I don't believe *all* these things," he seems to be saying, "I can't take the Bible literally."

I would counter by stating, "I don't believe *all* these things either, and I *do* take the Bible literally, in the sense that I consider the Bible inspired, inerrant, and infallible." In other words, there is not necessarily an inextricable link between people who hold racist, sexist, and other similar views and people who believe the Bible is historically reliable and accurate.

One of the classes I had at Syracuse University as part of my English education curriculum dealt with teaching others how to engage in active reading. We learned that there are three steps involved in the active reading of any literary passage:

1. Observation—What does it say?
2. Interpretation—What does it mean?
3. Application—What does it mean *to me*? Or how does it apply to me?

Of course, the New Testament is literature, so these steps apply to the Bible as much as to any other writing.

Since Spong doesn't agree with some of the *applications* a few have made for these passages, he concludes that the Bible can't be authoritative or true. That would be like saying that because terrorists hijacked planes and flew them into the World Trade Center we should declare the airline industry a failure. The fact that some people seized a technology and used it for evil purposes doesn't render the technology invalid. But because some misuse the Bible, Spong concludes that the Bible can't be literally true.

THEOLOGICAL FILTERING

Let's see if we can discern why Spong holds his particular views. The bishop complains that he has major problems with the picture of God painted by the Old Testament:

*   God rejoiced over the Egyptians' drowning in the Red Sea (see Ex. 15). *Wasn't Israel's God also the Egyptian's God?* he wonders.
*   God instructed Israel to dash the heads of children against the rocks (see Ps. 137:7–9).
*   God is called a "man of war" in Exodus 15:3 (KJV). "A concept," he says, "far removed from the one I had come to call the 'Prince of Peace.'"[17]

He continues with a litany of quarrels he has with God's Old Testament laws, including

*   Exodus 22:20's commandment that anyone who sacrifices to a god other than Israel's God "shall be utterly destroyed" (KJV);

- Leviticus 21:16–22's prevention of anyone who was blind or lame, a hunchback or dwarf, or who had certain other physical deformities from becoming a priest; and
- Leviticus 24:16's requirement that blasphemers be executed.[18]

He then states, "This list of objectionable passages could be expanded almost endlessly." He objects to verses used as recently as the eighteenth century to justify murdering "countless women" suspected of being witches and mediums, he states that parts of the Bible were used as rationale for burning at the stake actual or suspected homosexuals (even if they were really "living a responsible gay or lesbian life"), and he claims that some passages have been used to glorify war so that many political leaders could justify their national ambitions and use war to amass great wealth.[19]

Isn't he guilty of the very error I mentioned above? Isn't he rejecting the validity of the source because he doesn't like the way some people have interpreted it? For the record, I don't advocate the execution of suspected witches or homosexuals; neither do I believe in the glorification of war so that some people can build a fortune. My question to Spong is "What does this have to do with whether or not I believe in an authoritative Bible?" I do believe that the Bible is God's inspired, inerrant, infallible, and historically reliable Word. But I, too, reject the same abusive applications of the Bible that Spong also decries.

Unfortunately, under Bishop Spong's pen, the New Testament doesn't fare much better. Of this portion of Scripture, he says, "There are passages in the gospels that portray Jesus of Nazareth as narrow-minded, vindictive, and even hypocritical." For example, Jesus told us to love our enemies and pray for our persecutors (Matt. 5:44) and not to call others by harsh names (Matt. 5:22). And yet Jesus himself called his enemies "a brood of vipers" (Matt. 12:34), "snakes" (Matt. 23:33), and "blind fools" (Matt. 23:17). He also applied the derogatory name "dogs" to Gentiles (Matt. 15:26).

Furthermore, even though he taught us to honor our parents, he disowned his immediate family (Matt. 12:46–50) and said he had come to set a man against his father and a daughter against her mother (Matt. 10:35).[20]

Does this logic ring a bell? To me, it sounds a lot like Thomas Jefferson's quarrel with Jesus over his teachings. Because both Jefferson and Spong read the Bible through their lenses of a preconceived theological bias, they can't conceive of a "legitimate" Jesus who would say the words attributed to him. According to Spong,

> IF THE BIBLE IS READ LITERALLY, IT MUST BE SAID THAT JESUS SEEMS TO HAVE ACCEPTED WITHOUT QUESTION THE LANGUAGE OF HELL EMPLOYED BY HIS RELIGIOUS CONTEMPORARIES. IS ETERNAL PUNISHMENT THE PLAN OF THE ALL-MERCIFUL GOD? WAS JESUS MISTAKEN?[21]

We may infer that, when Spong reads Jesus' teachings, he sees only two choices:

- Jesus truly was narrow-minded and hypocritical, or
- He never really said all those things and others inserted the "troubling" sayings into his mouth.

But there is a third option: He really said these things, and it is possible to reconcile them in a way that is both spiritually satisfying and intellectually acceptable.

Let's look at a final objection raised by Spong:

> A LITERAL BIBLE PRESENTS ME WITH FAR MORE PROBLEMS THAN ASSETS. IT OFFERS ME A GOD I CANNOT RESPECT, MUCH LESS WORSHIP; A DEITY WHOSE NEEDS AND PREJUDICES ARE AT LEAST AS LARGE AS MY OWN. I MEET IN THE LITERAL UNDERSTANDING OF SCRIPTURE A GOD WHO IS SIMPLY NOT VIABLE, AND WHAT THE MIND CANNOT BELIEVE THE HEART CAN FINALLY NEVER ADORE.[22]

Let me read between the lines. Spong has decided what God is really like. He rejects any evidence he encounters in the Bible that contradicts Spong's "knowledge" about God's nature as unreliable. As we read Spong's writings, we surmise that his God has two over-riding characteristics: He is first and foremost all-loving and all-merciful. That is the trump card that overrules all other aspects of God's nature.

By contrast, the Bible describes God as a complex Being with many attributes:

- He is holy.
- He is eternal.
- He knows everything.
- He is the Creator of everything that exists.
- He is all-powerful.
- He is the force that keeps the entire universe in place.
- He is sovereign over all creation.
- He is present everywhere.
- He is all-loving.
- He is all-merciful.
- He is a God of infinite and ultimate justice.
- He is the source of all knowledge and wisdom.
- He is "jealous" for the affections of his people.
- His ways are higher than our ways and too great for us to understand.

Spong picks a single characteristic—God's love—and defines the entirety of God's being by this single trait. He elevates this one aspect of God to the apex of all his attributes. The bishop ignores the complexity of God that the Bible portrays and thereby reduces God to a simplistic and sentimental concept, rather than the eternal and holy Being who outstrips our capacity to understand him.

Spong certainly raises some important questions. There *are* many genuine theological dilemmas. For example, it is extremely difficult to understand how a loving God can let an innocent child die from brain cancer—especially if it's your child—or why many seemingly good people endure tremendous hardships, while other seemingly evil people seem to have it so easy. These are very troubling questions, and I can't pretend to answer them in a fully satisfying way.

Spong's charges against God remind me of Job's complaints against God. You will remember that Job's afflictions included the loss of his children, his wealth, and eventually his personal health. Job, proclaiming his innocence, spends a couple of chapters complaining about how God is treating him.

God allows Job to ventilate for a while, but he never really answers any of Job's questions or complaints. Instead, he turns the table by asking Job a question: "Where were you when I created the world?"

THE LORD SAID TO JOB:

"WILL THE ONE WHO CONTENDS WITH THE ALMIGHTY CORRECT HIM?

LET HIM WHO ACCUSES GOD ANSWER HIM!" (40:1–2)

Fortunately, Job is wise and humble enough to recognize the error of his ways:

THEN JOB ANSWERED THE LORD:

"I AM UNWORTHY—HOW CAN I REPLY TO YOU?

I PUT MY HAND OVER MY MOUTH." (40:3–4)

TALK TO THE ANIMALS

Philip Yancey has become one of my favorite writers. He is a thoughtful and intelligent person who is unafraid to tackle the difficult issues of the Christian life. I especially like an analogy he presents in his book *Reaching for the Invisible God* that illustrates the immeasurable distance between God and his creatures. Scientists have concluded that whales are among the most intelligent of all nonhuman creatures,[23] and researchers know that they use a variety of clicks and squeaks to communicate with each other.

Yancey ponders what might happen if someday we eventually "cracked" the whale language code and learned to communicate with them. That would be a remarkable achievement. But, asks Yancey, what would we "talk" about with them? We would have to restrict our communication to things within their sphere, such as,

- water temperature,
- light and darkness of the water,
- ocean currents, and
- the location of food.

How could I ever explain things like

- the World Series,
- the Internet,
- space travel, and
- why my teenage son's hair keeps changing colors?

Each of these is so far beyond the reach and experience of whales that it would be impossible to communicate meaningfully.[24] I can just envision the following conversation about the World Series:

ME: THE WORLD SERIES IS A BASEBALL CHAMPIONSHIP SERIES THAT TAKES PLACE EACH OCTOBER BETWEEN THE TOP BASE-BALL TEAMS FROM THE AMERICAN LEAGUE AND THE NATIONAL LEAGUE.

WHALE: WHAT'S "BASEBALL"?

ME: IT'S A GAME WHERE PLAYERS USE A STICKLIKE THING TO HIT A ROUND BALL. IF THEY HIT IT, THEY GET TO RUN AROUND SOMETHING CALLED A DIAMOND TO SEE IF THEY CAN SCORE WHAT THEY CALL "RUNS."

WHALE: WHAT'S A "GAME"?

ME: IT'S A FUN ACTIVITY USUALLY INVOLVING TEAMS THAT PEOPLE DO TO ENJOY THEMSELVES.

WHALE: WHAT'S "FUN"?

You get the idea. There is no way I could ever communicate about the World Series to a whale. Theologians who protest the God of the Bible because they can't understand him are a bit like the whale that rejects the existence of the World Series because the animal can't comprehend it. If I had to completely understand God in order to be able to worship him, he wouldn't be much of a God.

Look again at the list of God's attributes I presented a couple of paragraphs ago. The last one states that his ways are higher than our ways and too great for us to comprehend. I sincerely wish I understood everything about God and could fully explain all his actions. But I can't. He is God and I am not.

Essentially, Bishop Spong is asking for a God he can understand. Isn't this the same thing Thomas Jefferson tried to achieve? As the essayist who wrote the introduction to *The Jefferson Bible* stated, Jefferson "carved out a Gospel for himself, one whose witness he could respect and whose message he could understand."[25] With all due respect to this brilliant statesman, he was certainly finite, and his reengineered Bible reflects his theological biases more than anything else. Is it possible that God could transcend Jefferson's ability to reason and understand? If he didn't transcend Jefferson's comprehension, he would have been just a slightly idealized version of old TJ himself.

ALL YOU NEED IS LOVE

Interestingly, many, if not most, theologians who filter out many of God's attributes because of their own prejudices choose love as their ultimate value. Why? I'm not one to speak against love, but thinkers who screen out major portions of Scripture because God doesn't appear to be loving enough for them are treading on thin ice.

First of all, they are rejecting what is purportedly God's clear disclosure of himself. From cover to cover, the Bible claims to be God's special revelation to humanity. This includes the "lovely" sayings of Jesus as well as his harsh statements about weeping and gnashing of teeth in hell. If the Bible really is God's revelation, then I am obligated to accept the whole lot. If it's not, then I'm left with the challenge of determining what is true and what isn't. We're back to Thomas Jefferson's "cut and paste" methodology.

The "chop 'em up" approach to the Bible leads to the challenge of deciding which criteria I will use to determine what to keep and what to pitch.

- Do I choose what I like? I like love. I don't like judgment, so I will reject that. But I like love, so I'll keep that.
- Do I choose what fits my mental or theological constructs?
- Do I, like Jefferson and Spong, only accept what I can understand and reject the rest?
- Do I accept the parts that don't run afoul of modern thought? Will today's "modern thought" still be embraced in ten years? Fifty years? One hundred years? If not, does this mean that truth keeps changing? Do I constantly have to redefine truth so that I am not out of fashion with the then-current popular views?

NOT QUITE READY FOR *JEOPARDY*

Have you ever stopped to ponder how little any one of us really knows? Even the most brilliant among us possesses embarrassingly limited amounts of information. How many of the "facts" of the universe have I mastered? For example,

- How many grains of sand are there?
- How many people are listed in the current New York City phone book? What are their names and phone numbers? How many of them have e-mail addresses, and what are they?
- What is the height and weight of every person who has ever lived?
- How many hairs do you have on your head?
- How many hairs are on the heads of every person alive at this moment?
- For that matter, exactly how many people are alive at this moment?
- How can I reconcile the apparently contradictory characteristics of light: sometimes behaving like waves, and sometimes like particles?

So I repeat my question: How many of the facts of the universe do I possess? 1 percent? 0.1 percent? 0.00001 percent? How many "leading zeroes" do I need?

And keep in mind that these are strictly factual questions. I haven't even listed the more philosophical questions about "larger" issues of life, such as the nature of good and evil. Is it possible that my judgments are less than perfect? If so, when, based on "my knowledge of the world," I reject parts of what God has revealed, is it possible that I am mistaken? How do I know which parts to accept and which parts to reject? Perhaps most important, what are the implications if I am wrong?

That is the first challenge of those who filter revelation solely on the criterion of God's love. I'm wagering a lot on my ability to "choose wisely." The second problem "love filterers" face is the fact that, as Ricky Ricardo would say, they still have some "'splainin'" to do.

If God is, to the exclusion of all else, all-loving and all-merciful, how do I reconcile the great moral dilemmas this position creates? If there is no ultimate reckoning of justice, how will wrongs ever be righted? Where is the justice for the victims of monsters like Adolf Hitler, Joseph Stalin, Idi Amin, and others who murdered thousands, even millions, of people? How loving would God be if he let unspeakable acts of inhumanity go unpunished? Is that loving to the victims? Which is more unjust: a God who holds horrific butchers accountable for their unspeakable crimes or a God who allows them to destroy millions of lives with no consequences?

Both Thomas Jefferson and Bishop John Shelby Spong create a tidy God who appeals to their own limited, rationalistic sense of what is right. They seem unwilling to embrace truths about God that violate their own evaluation of what is loving and instead have created an idealized image of God. This is precisely what Charlotte Allen concluded in *The Human Christ*: that those who search for the "Historical Jesus" end up finding, lo and behold, a Jesus who looks just like them.[26]

PART 1 WRAP-UP

Everyone approaches the Bible with presuppositions that color their interpretation of what they read. Their lenses either add new sources of information, often from dubious sources; or they subtract parts of the Bible based on atheistic, antisupernatural, or selective theological biases. My dad has something he calls his "jelly bean theory" to explain how different people come up with such widely differing interpretations of Jesus' life and teachings. He imagines a very large fish tank filled with jelly beans of all colors and flavors. Each person picks out only the variety(ies) he or she prefers and leaves the rest uneaten. They have chosen only those flavors they prefer and discarded the rest.

Do I have biases about the Bible? Of course. I have concluded that it is reliable and accurate and is, in fact, God's inspired, inerrant, infallible, and historically reliable revelation to humanity. This is not simpleminded acceptance, but an opinion backed by considerable research and study. Are there problems with my position? Of course. I am fully aware of the intellectual challenges inherent in this theological view, but there is strong supportive evidence for my stance.

Do skeptical critics have biases? Of course. They, too, would say their positions are based on careful research, and they are correct. Are there intellectual problems with their positions? Of course.

There are enough complicated factors that neither side can claim victory based solely on the academic arguments. The point, however, is that it is possible to be a thoughtful, well-educated, well-adjusted person and to believe that the Bible is God's inspired, inerrant, and infallible revelation to all people in all ages.

Many brilliant and learned people from every walk of life have bowed their knee before the Jesus the Bible reveals and have gladly proclaimed that he has changed their lives. They have also simultaneously committed themselves to an intellectually responsible study of God's inerrant revelation and excellence in their professions. They unashamedly declare that Jesus is their Lord.

There is Warren, a successful engineer who earned his PhD in mathematics from Duke University. There is Emma, who operates a successful consulting business that has helped many organizations operate at maximum effectiveness. There is Terry, an executive who recently retired after a brilliant career leading a respected association. There is Les, an architect who has designed some of the top medical transplant centers in the nation. There is Helene, a respected high school orchestra teacher who was recognized by her peers as string teacher of the year for her entire state. There is Ron, who labored for years as vice president of finance at a liberal arts college, keeping it afloat through many rough times. There is Jim, a star basketball player and Big Man on Campus. There are dozens of senior executives who run prestigious hospitals all across the country. Each of these people has risen to the top of his or her professional field, and each of them pays first allegiance to Jesus. Perhaps if I had met some of them when I was a

high school student, I might have abandoned my pseudointellec-
tualism earlier.

The bottom line is this: Don't let people intimidate you into
thinking that anyone who believes that the Bible is inspired,
inerrant, infallible, and historically reliable is "largely poor, ignorant, and easy to command." As you interact with people who
challenge your faith, look for evidence of the filters they may be
employing.

In a recent conversation with a friend, I sensed he was drifting
toward a skeptical view of the Bible. I detected a mixture of the Filter
of Antisupernaturalism and the Filter of Selective Christian Theology
with just a dash of the Filter of Outlandish Speculation thrown in.
In cases like this, it's helpful to ask questions like these:

- What are you basing your conclusions on?
- What is the source of your authority?
- How reliable is that source?
- Is it possible that your source has biases or preconceptions?
- Have you tested the assumptions that lie behind this
  source?

You may also want to briefly describe the concept of filters as presented in this book and gently ask your friend if he or she might be
influenced by one or more of these filters.

Some skeptics, though intelligent, have developed their views
based largely on their own biases or those of their mentors. A careful look at their systems of thought can help us weed out their false
conclusions and be more confident in our explanation of the
Christian faith to people who may have set out looking for gold but
settled for brass.

Part 2

The Filter of Faith

P R I N C I P L E S   1 – 4 :
A P P R O A C H I N G   T H E
M A T E R I A L   W I T H   T H E
R I G H T   P E R S P E C T I V E

Eight words that strike terror in the heart of any male child who is out running errands with his mother are "I have to stop at the fabric store." Just the sound of those words evokes images of seemingly endless hours, wandering the button display aisle. When I was a child, I would rather weed the entire flower bed or clean up dog "stuff" from the yard than for Mom to drag me to the "Jo-Ann Chamber of Fabric Horrors." Somewhere along the way, my mom discovered that threatening a trip to "The Fabric Store" was a way to inspire model behavior. After I went away to college, I vowed I would *never* again pass the threshold of a fabric store.

Unfortunately, I overlooked the possibility that I might someday get married. What I have discovered from my whole new round of fabric store experiences is that they haven't changed much: same endless aisles of polyester, cotton, denim, corduroy, and silk material on huge cardboard tubes; same cheery-looking displays of holiday creations incongruously showcased about six months too early (to allow the home seamstress time to create a new holiday wardrobe for her entire family); same displays of thimbles and needles.

However, my latest trip to a fabric store with my wife, Annette, provided at least a glimmer of redemption. This particular store had a display of cross-stitch patterns with various sayings. One item in particular caught my eye. It read,

GIVE A MAN A FISH, AND YOU FEED HIM FOR A DAY; TEACH HIM HOW TO FISH AND YOU GET RID OF HIM FOR THE WHOLE WEEKEND.

Of course, this is a takeoff on the more familiar saying whose last line reads, "Teach him how to fish and you feed him for a lifetime." Seeing this witty cross-stitch version made up for some of the mind-numbing experience of helping Annette select just the perfect color of thread. On second thought, no, it didn't. But it at least provided some measure of amusement.

The first part of this book was devoted to looking at five filters that distort the Christian message. I will now suggest some ways to view the Bible through the "Filter of Faith." The next four chapters present principles that will help us "fish for ourselves" as we read the Bible. If we start with the premise that the Bible is inspired, inerrant, infallible, and historically accurate and then read accounts of the same story from different gospels where the details seem to be at odds, it naturally raises questions. Similarly, when we read something in the Gospels that seems at first to clash with a principle taught elsewhere in the Bible, it makes us wonder. There are only two conclusions we can reach:

- The skeptics are right after all: The Bible is not true and accurate.
- There is a reasonable explanation for the apparent problem.

Critics delight in pointing to alleged contradictions and other problem passages as a way to "prove" the Bible is unreliable, often honing their skill into a fine art form. Theoretically, you could take each book that uses specific verses to demonstrate the Bible's lack of credibility and develop the Ultimate Master List of every problem passage identified by every skeptic and then attempt to answer each one. I wager that that list would sport hundreds and hundreds, if not thousands, of verses that supposedly "disprove" the Bible.

In the spirit of "teaching a man to fish," allow me to provide some guidelines that tame the vast majority of seemingly unruly verses. In the process, I hope to equip you to effectively address future challenges with problem passages for yourself.

Of course, the objective is not to "defend" a particular theological position but to seek truthful and accurate interpretations of Scripture. Part 2 of this book presents eighteen principles that provide a solid interpretive approach to the Bible. I call these "Pearson's Principles for Approaching Puzzling, Perplexing, and Problematic Passages." If the principles are valid and if the Bible is reliable, this approach should address critiques colored by various filters and which question the validity of the biblical text.

I have arranged these principles into four chapters:

- Chapter 7. Principles 1–4: "Approaching the Material with the Right Perspective"
- Chapter 8. Principles 5–9: "Understanding the Writer's Purpose"
- Chapter 9. Principles 10–14: "Dealing with Discrepancies in Details"
- Chapter 10. Principles 15–18: "Interpreting the Text Responsibly"

I will provide examples of challenging passages and will show how to apply the principles to clear up confusion. Problems can often be reduced to bite size when we think about them in the right way. They help create a mind-set from which to resolve troubling passages. It's surprising how many foggy passages we can clarify as we apply these principles.

Some of these principles will stretch your thinking a bit. Many alleged discrepancies can be neutralized by making sure we look at them the right way. However, as much as we might like "magic" principles that erase problems, some of them may not be so easy to resolve on your own. It may be helpful to discuss difficult passages with others. You're probably not the first person to notice or read confusing passages, and Christian friends or Bible study members may be able to offer thoughtful insights.

We will sometimes have to seek answers through good old-fashioned research. Fortunately, we can access many wonderful commentaries, books, and research tools to broaden our under-standing of the background and correct interpretation of the Bible. Let's start with Principles 1–4, which deal with a proper perspective and how to avoid being trapped by skeptics' filters.

1. PRAY FOR INSIGHT

Ask God to guide you into the truth. On the night before his cruci-fixion, Jesus, speaking of the Holy Spirit, the third person of the Trinity, taught that "when he, the Spirit of truth, comes, he will guide you into all truth" (John 16:13). When people trust Christ to forgive their sins, the Holy Spirit takes up residence in their lives. James 1:5 further instructs, "If any of you lacks wisdom, he should ask God, who gives generously to all without finding fault, and it will be given to him." This is not to say that every conclusion I reach about every Bible passage is somehow divinely inspired or infallible, but it does point to Christians' belief that God is active in our lives and wants to help us grow in our understanding of his truth.

Even someone who stands outside the Christian faith can ask God to reveal the truth to him or her. It's a fair proposition because, if there really isn't a God and the Bible really isn't his revelation to all humanity, the questioner has lost nothing. Nothing "supernatu-ral" will happen, and the reader can continue on his or her way. But if there *is* a God, a prayer like this could unlock all sorts of new understandings. I know several people who found God just by read-ing the Bible after they asked him to reveal himself to them through their reading.

2. SETTLE FOR ONE REASONABLE EXPLANATION

My wife, Annette, teaches science to public school sixth graders. I expect her name to be submitted for sainthood any time now. She recently walked her students through a fascinating exercise to write hypotheses to explain the evidence they observe. Figure 1 depicts two sets of dinosaur tracks geologists discovered in Connecticut. One set of large tracks comes from the upper left down toward the center of the diagram. A smaller set of tracks comes from the upper right and also descends to the center. When the footprints meet, there is a tangle of tracks. Then the larger set moves away from the footprint knot and moves toward the lower left.

Figure 1

The students' task was to develop theories that would reasonably explain the circumstances that led to the creation of these tracks. Below are some of the students' suggestions:

- The dino-fight hypothesis, where the larger one killed the smaller one. Of course, this is the one the boys were pushing.
- The flying dinosaur hypothesis suggests that the second set of prints disappears because it was made by a flying animal that walked to the center and then flew away.
- The mother-daughter hypothesis speculates that the smaller

tracks belong to a baby dinosaur that met up with her mother (who naturally left larger prints) and was subsequently carried off by mom.

- The water hole hypothesis suggests that the animals gravitated to a water hole, perhaps at separate times. Under this hypothesis, the animals may not have even met.[1]

There may be other explanations as well. Which one is true? Of course we can't know. If we had definitive proof of one explanation, there would be no need for hypotheses. The point is that any of these theories could reasonably explain what the scientists observed.

When skeptics claim a certain set of verses "proves" the Bible is wrong, perhaps they could learn from Annette's sixth graders. For any claim that a given passage proves the Bible is unreliable, the presentation of even one feasible solution should be enough to remove it from the Ultimate Master List of passages that undercut the Bible. The onus is on the skeptic to prove that a given problem cannot be solved. If I can develop one reasonable explanation, the skeptic must retreat. If I can present two or more possible explanations, that's all the better, but one is really sufficient. When it comes to troubling verses, we may never know for sure what the "perfect" explanation is. However, the goal is not perfection, just reasonableness. I don't have to know everything about every verse.

Think of it this way. Were you part of the crowd of people who heard Jesus deliver the Sermon on the Mount (Matt. 5—7) or watched him raise Lazarus back to life (John 11) or witnessed his supernatural ascension into heaven after the resurrection (Luke 24)? Perhaps you weren't available that day. Neither was I. Neither were any of the skeptics. So when someone challenges the veracity of parts of Jesus' ministry, he or she is merely speculating and viewing the stories through one filter or another. Since, in the twenty-first century, there are no living eyewitnesses to these events, no one can definitively say that certain details are incorrect unless he or she can find evidence either from the Bible itself or from other *reliable* writings outside the Bible that clearly refute the biblical accounts. As we saw in the chapter about filters that add, there are plenty of dubious sources that energize the Filter of Outlandish Speculation. Many of these sources are commercially driven to sell books. The more eccentric the theory, the better the sales.

Several years ago, two friends and I went on a three-day backpacking trip to the beautiful Mount Washington area of New Hampshire. On day two of that trip, we decided to hike from our overnight shelter to the top of Mount Washington. None of us had ever made the trip before, so we couldn't say for sure how long it would take. To estimate our travel time, we had to consider many variables: distance, terrain, pace, and distractions along the way. Each of us guessed a different number of hours. I thought it would take 3.75 hours, Paul said 4.25, and Brad guessed 4.5. Of course, once we made the trip in four hours and five minutes, we knew exactly how long it took. If we had known the answer in advance, there would have been no need to guess. Even though Paul was closest, each of our estimates was reasonable. Eleven hours would not have been a reasonable estimate.

In the same way, when it comes to understanding difficult Bible passages, we can't *always* be 100 percent sure how they fit together. These verses are on the Ultimate Master List of problem passages precisely because they contain elements that make their interpretation challenging. There may be multiple ways to solve the riddle they present, but since we can't prove what really happened, the best we can do is guess. If we had a video recording of the actual event as it took place in time and space, there would be no confusion over what really transpired. Since we don't have that, though, some debate will continue.

But Principle 2 teaches that I have done my job if I can discover just one feasible solution. As long as my answer is reasonable (i.e., somewhere in the 3.5-to-5-hour range, to use the hiking analogy), skeptics should be satisfied. A critic says a certain passage "proves" the Bible is wrong. If I present a feasible solution, the critic loses.

(For a deeper perspective on how to face problem passages with confidence, go to www.cookministries.com/GreatQuestion and read appendix entry 7.1.)

3. THINK OUTSIDE THE BOX

As I walked into the Las Vegas hotel conference room, I was hopeful that this session might be one of the highlights of my trip. There were about seven or eight other people already there, one of whom was a carefully coiffed, blonde-haired woman who appeared to be in her late forties. By her body language and friendly greeting of each newcomer, I correctly guessed that she was the instructor.

This conference was for group purchasing managers of hospitals, mostly from the western United States. I flew in from Michigan as the guest of the sponsoring company, since my organization was considering working with the hosts. This session in particular fascinated me. It was called "Thinking Beyond the Limits" and promised to help us push through the typical barriers we place on our thinking.

There were two easels with flip-chart pads at the front of the room. After the official greeting, the instructor picked up a purple Magic Marker, drew a large circle about twenty inches in diameter, and then placed a dot about the size of a pea in the very center of the circle. Then she held the marker out to the audience and challenged us to recreate the drawing on the other flip-chart with the stipulation that, as we drew the diagram, we were *not* to lift the marker from the paper.

Hmmm! That *is* a challenge. It can't be done. Think about that for a moment. Do you have any ideas?

After puzzling over this for a few moments, I had a flash of inspiration and volunteered to demonstrate my solution. As the instructor handed me the purple marker, I could smell the artificial grape aroma of the ink. I walked to the easel and put the marker toward the lower right-hand corner of the paper (the 5:00 position) and did my best to draw a twenty-inch circle. When I got back to the starting position, I held the marker in place, lifted the lower right-hand corner of the paper and brought it to the point where it touched the marker. I then moved the marker onto the corner of the paper, onto what is really the *back* of the paper. Next I slid the corner of the paper along with the marker to the center of the page and gently eased the corner of the paper out from under the marker and proceeded to draw a small dot in the middle of the circle. Mission accomplished. I had met the criterion of recreating the image without lifting the marker from the paper.

Immediately after this, someone else stepped forward to offer another solution. This young woman drew a twenty-inch circle and then moved the marker so that its *side* was touching the paper but the point with the ink was about half an inch from the paper's surface. After she slid the marker to the center of the page, she once again returned the marker to its typical position to draw the dot. There you have it, a second solution.

If I were to repeat the exercise using a ballpoint pen instead of a marker, there would be yet a third solution: Draw the circle, retract the ink cartridge but keep the pen itself in contact with the paper, slide the pen to the center, extend the cartridge again, and complete the dot. Solution number three.

What I like so much about this example is that the speaker presented the group with a problem that appears impossible to solve. Yet within a few minutes, the audience provided two solutions to this "impossible" challenge, each with a slight variation.

What a great picture of some of the challenges some people throw at the Bible. Pick up any book about Jesus where the author has filtered his or her material through one of the five filters I described in part 1, and you will undoubtedly find various alleged contradictions and "unsolvable" problems.

THE CASE OF THE FICKLE CROWD

As I mentioned in chapter 5, NBC aired on February 20, 2004—just prior to the release of the Mel Gibson movie *The Passion of the Christ*—a special edition of *Dateline* called "The Last Days of Jesus." One of the skeptics charged that the actions of the crowd in Jerusalem as Jesus entered the city on Palm Sunday were irreconcilable with its subsequent behavior during his trial. On Palm Sunday the crowds threw palm fronds in front of Jesus as he rode astride a donkey into the city, and they blessed him as Son of David (Matt. 21:9) and the King of Israel (John 12:13). Just a few days later, however, the mob outside Pilate's court demanded his crucifixion (Matt. 27:22–23). "What happened?" the skeptics ask. How could there have been such a dramatic reversal in just a few days? On Sunday, the crowd hailed Jesus as their King; then on Thursday they called for his death. How can these two events be reconciled?

Is this inconsistency a contradiction, or is there a way to harmonize these two stories? There is. First of all, let's remember that the events recorded about Jesus' last days took place in Jerusalem during the Passover season. Scholars tell us that the population of Jerusalem, which was normally in the twenty thousand to fifty thousand range,[2] may have surged to nearly three million during Passover.[3] The atmosphere in Jerusalem was probably something like that in Times Square on New Year's Eve.

Furthermore, both Matthew and John report that the triumphal entry took place *outside* of Jerusalem:

THE NEXT DAY THE GREAT CROWD THAT HAD COME FOR THE FEAST HEARD THAT JESUS *WAS ON HIS WAY TO JERUSALEM*. THEY TOOK PALM BRANCHES AND WENT OUT TO MEET HIM, SHOUTING,

"HOSANNA!"

"BLESSED IS HE WHO COMES IN THE NAME OF THE LORD!"

"BLESSED IS THE KING OF ISRAEL!" (JOHN 12:12–13)

The crowd on Palm Sunday probably consisted of quite different people from the crowd outside Pontius Pilate's palace. The processional on Palm Sunday was a spontaneous celebration by "common" people outside Jerusalem who recognized something remarkable about Jesus. By contrast, the crowd at Jesus' trial was "worked up" by the religious leaders to demand his crucifixion. Matthew's account specifically says, "The chief priests and the elders persuaded the crowd to ask ... to have Jesus executed" (27:20). It is possible that, in their attempt to rid themselves of Jesus, the religious leaders went so far as to "create" a crowd that was sympathetic to their position. After all, they had up to three million people to choose from, and it would not have been difficult to "stack the deck" with people who would help them accomplish their objective. I don't know how large the courtyard in Pilate's palace was, but it probably wouldn't hold more than a few hundred people. How hard would it have been for the chief priests and elders to generate a crowd of that size from the millions in the city?

Although the critics highlight the dramatic change in the crowd between Sunday and Thursday, it presents no real problem. It is reasonable to assume that there were two different sets of people involved: a spontaneous and sympathetic crowd on Sunday and a handpicked antagonistic group on Thursday. Is this explanation reasonable? Yes. Does it make sense? Yes. Could it have happened? Yes. Does it explain the "dinosaur tracks"? I think so. Do we need to come up with five more alternative explanations? Not necessarily. Settle for one (Principle 2). Next!

THE PUZZLE OF PILATE

Another complaint leveled by skeptics in the NBC special was that Pilate's actions at Jesus' trial seem uncharacteristic of the brutal, cruel leader who ruthlessly slaughtered many of his subjects.[4] Instead, skeptics charge that the Pilate of the Gospels appears weak and vacillating. They complain that, even though he tries to release

Jesus, he inexplicably bows to the will of the bloodthirsty mob. Certainly, they contend, this can't be an accurate portrayal of Pilate.

There are at least three perspectives that help us explain this difficulty. First of all, let's look at Jesus' trial from Pilate's point of view. He had been in office for several years and had already dealt with a string of insurrections. His was not a peaceable tenure, partially due to his own actions, so he was quite used to dealing with agitators.

Bear in mind that, to Pilate, it was all in a day's work. Although this case may have had a somewhat higher visibility than others, there was nothing particularly remarkable about a Jewish peasant who developed a following and was charged with sedition. Had Pilate known at that time that twenty centuries later his every word would become a major source of debate about his own character, he might have been a little more conscious of his oral interactions. That's the first point. Pilate was not aware during his interviews with Jesus that he was posing for his "yearbook picture" that would affect his reputation for all of history.

The second point is that we see Pilate for a period of well under one hour. According to Luke's account, Jesus appeared before him briefly on two occasions, with a visit to King Herod in between. What we have is, at most, a one-hour slice of Pilate's life, which in some ways may be inconsistent with other information we have about him. He does seem to vacillate more than we might expect.

All it means, however, is that Pilate, just like you and I, may have acted in a manner inconsistent with his normal demeanor. Perhaps Pilate was sick or hadn't gotten a good night's sleep and was a little off kilter the day he met Jesus. Matthew reports that Pilate's wife sent him a message while he was on the judge's seat, saying, "Don't have anything to do with that innocent man, for I have suffered a great deal today in a dream because of him" (27:19). Her unsettled state may have rubbed off on him to make him uncharacteristically subdued.

The third point is based on a fuller understanding of Pilate's career. Scholar Edwin Yamauchi suggests that historical records show that Pilate may have been politically vulnerable in AD 33, the time that Jesus was probably crucified, and because of that he may have been reluctant to run afoul of his Jewish subjects, which might have caused him further political problems with Rome. Consequently, he may have been unusually willing to submit to pressure from the Jewish leaders.[5]

David O'Brien reports that it was customary for Roman legions to leave their standards, which bore the imperial Roman eagle, outside Jerusalem when they entered the city since the Jewish people were offended by the "graven image" or idol, which the Jewish religion strictly forbade. For whatever reason, Pilate had failed to follow this custom, inciting the people to riot. Pilate later attempted to impose a temple tax in order to build an aqueduct for the city, but the citizens considered this a sacrilege and once again rioted.[6] In a third show of bad judgment, Pilate later hung Roman shields in Herod's palace. The ensuing uproar forced the emperor himself to intervene.[7] By the time the Jewish leaders dragged Jesus before him, Pilate might have been unusually willing to acquiesce to their demands to avoid another violent incident.

I have provided three possible explanations of Pilate's behavior:

- He was unaware of the historical significance of this particular case and so wasn't necessarily thinking of his reputation in history.
- He may have been having a "bad hair" day.
- He may have been in a period of political vulnerability that led to an unusually acquiescent mode.

Are these explanations reasonable? Yes. Do they answer the charge that the Bible must be wrong because Pilate's character seems a little off? Indeed, they do. Can I delete this story from the Ultimate Master List? Yes.

Is it critical in this case to identify the most likely answer? No.

We, along with many Bible critics, take ourselves so seriously that we feel we *must* find absolutely the best answer. Don't get me wrong. I'm all for research and doing the hard work necessary to accurately interpret and apply the Scriptures, but when all is said and done, my personal opinion about which explanation for Pilate's unusual behavior is at best inconsequential.

In January and February 2004, I was teaching the material that eventually found its way into this book to a class at my church and had not yet made it to the principles. At the end of one class session, a young woman approached me and stated that she really wanted to believe the Bible but that there were just too many things she couldn't explain. For example, she asked, "How do you explain the fact that the Bible records that the very earliest people lived for several hundred years? And where do the dinosaurs fit in?"

My answer to her was very simple: "I don't know." These particular issues are not ones I have ever seriously examined. But I am comfortable with them for two reasons. The first is that every issue I have investigated has resulted in an answer I can live with intellectually. I just haven't gotten around to those two challenges. The other reason is that I am sure that there are very knowledgeable and credible Christians who have studied these questions, and I can trust their comfort level until I get around to investigating them for myself.

I then presented to her the Challenge of the Las Vegas Circle (sounds like a cheesy magic trick, doesn't it?), to which I referred earlier. I asked her how she would solve the puzzle. She thought for a moment and then said, "It's impossible. It can't be done." I then revealed the three different ways to solve the challenge. I said, "Five minutes ago, you stood here and told me that it was impossible to re-create this diagram without lifting the pen from the page, and I have shown you three different ways to do it. Is it possible that there are reasonable explanations to the 'long life' and 'dinosaur' problems that neither you nor I have thought of yet?" She agreed that that could be the case.

It is reasonable to live for a time with the tension of certain unanswered questions and to exercise a bit of creative thought in problem solving. It's surprising how what might appear to be impossibilities find explanations if we let the right side of our brains kick in. And if the question is important enough to me, I can research it to learn what I can about the background of the incident and how others have addressed the issue.

4. REFRAME THE CHALLENGE

Maybe the critics are barking up the wrong tree. Maybe the question itself is unfair like the classic, "Have you stopped beating your wife?" There *are* devious questions designed to make us look bad, no matter how we answer them.

This principle is the logical outgrowth of thinking outside the box (Principle 3). It can lead to solutions that at first elude us. Reframing the challenge can reveal that we, or the critics, are not even asking the right questions.

One of the great joys in life is to carve out an hour or an hour and a half to read the Sunday newspaper. Even during my two brutal years in graduate school where I had almost no disposable time, I often succeeded in sneaking in some leisure time to peruse the paper: comics, sports page, travel section, and all. One of the features I usually read from *Parade* magazine is "Ask Marilyn," where readers submit questions to the highly intelligent Marilyn vos Savant. Although I don't always agree with her answers, I enjoy following her thought patterns.

Usually at the end of the year, Marilyn compiles a list of what she kindly calls "The Year's Most Dumbfounding Questions." The 2003 list included two questions that I found particularly interesting:

- "Why were most of the Civil War battles fought in national parks?"

- "Why is the alphabet in the order it is? Is it because of that song?"[8]

The dear people who submitted these "dumbfounding" questions are in great need of applying Principle 4. They should reframe their questions to bring them more in line with standard, linear thinking.

An Arizona State University English professor named Randel Helms wrote in the late 1980s a book called *Gospel Fictions.*[9] You can imagine, based on the title, what his presuppositions are.

As a professor of literature, he subscribes to the commonly held theory that "the human imagination embroiders the careers of notable figures of the past with common mythical and fictional embellishments."[10] His thesis is that the Gospels "are largely fictional accounts about an historical figure, Jesus of Nazareth, intended to create a life-enhancing understanding of his nature."[11] He continues,

IT IS NOT MY PURPOSE HERE TO ARTICULATE A QUARREL WITH CHRISTIAN FAITH, OR TO CALL THE EVANGELISTS LIARS, OR TO ASSERT THAT THE GOSPELS HAVE *NO* HISTORICAL CONTENT; I WRITE AS A LITERARY CRITIC, NOT AS A DEBUNKER. THE GOSPELS ARE, IT MUST BE SAID WITH GRATITUDE, WORKS OF ART, THE SUPREME FICTIONS IN OUR CULTURE, NARRATIVES PRODUCED BY ENORMOUSLY INFLUENTIAL LITERARY ARTISTS WHO PUT THEIR ART IN THE SERVICE OF A THEOLOGICAL VISION.[12]

His patronizing acknowledgment of the Bible's artistic value despite its lack of historical reliability reminds me of an observation another professor of literature, C. S. Lewis, once made:

A SACRED BOOK REJECTED IS LIKE A DETHRONED KING. TOWARDS EITHER OF THEM THERE ARISES IN WELL-DISPOSED MINDS A CHIVALROUS COMPUNCTION. ONE WOULD LIKE TO

CONCEDE EVERYTHING EXCEPT THE THING REALLY AT ISSUE.
HAVING SUPPORTED THE DEPOSITION, ONE WOULD WISH TO
MAKE IT CLEAR THAT ONE HAD NO PERSONAL MALICE. JUST
BECAUSE YOU CANNOT COUNTENANCE A RESTORATION, YOU
ARE ANXIOUS TO SPEAK KINDLY OF THE OLD GENTLEMAN IN
HIS PERSONAL CAPACITY—TO PRAISE HIS FUND OF ANECDOTE
OR HIS COLLECTION OF BUTTERFLIES.[13]

Helms, it appears, would relegate the Bible to the "butterfly collection" category.

A TALE OF TWO WIDOWS

As a literary scholar, Helms correctly observes that there are some parallels between stories in the Old Testament and stories in the New Testament. In fact, he claims that the stories of miraculous deeds performed by the Old Testament prophets Elijah and Elisha, as recorded in the books of 1 and 2 Kings, provide the basis for a number of Jesus' miracles.[14] For example, Luke's account of Jesus' raising the widow of Nain's son in Luke 7, according to Helms, is based on the 1 Kings 17 story of Elijah's raising the widow of Sarepta's (or Zarephath's) son.

Because of space limitations, I won't reproduce both stories, but these are the similarities that Helms notes:

- Both stories start with the phrase "And it came to pass."
- Both accounts concern the dead son of a widow.
- In both, the prophet "went" to the town where he met the woman at the "gate of the city." Helms also claims that archaeological studies show Nain never had a wall, but that in order to make the widow of Nain story parallel to Elijah's, Luke invents one.
- In both stories, the prophet speaks and touches the dead son, who rises and speaks.
- In both stories, the miracle certifies the prophet: "Now I know

that you are a man of God and that the word of the LORD from your mouth is the truth" (1 Kings 17:24) and "'A great prophet has appeared among us,' they said" (Luke 7:16).

- Both stories conclude with precisely the same words: "And he gave him to his mother."[15]

Helms believes that "either Luke or his source consciously modeled the story set in Nain after the miracle at Sarepta."[16]

Does it make sense? First, a few comments about Helms' observations:

- The phrase "And it came to pass" is common throughout the Bible. In fact, it appears *thousands* of times in the Old Testament alone.[17] Luke himself uses the phrase forty-nine times in his gospel and fifteen times more in the book of Acts. If this phrase appeared only in the two stories about raising a widow's dead son, Helms might have a stronger case.

- Both Elijah and Jesus "went" to a lot of places. I don't find it remarkable that both accounts use this extremely common verb.

- Helms claims that archaeological study "has shown that the village of Nain in Galilee never had a wall; Nain's fictional gate is there for literary reasons—Sarepta's gate transferred."[18] Archaeologists used to question the existence of the Pool of Bethesda, the Pool of Siloam, Jacob's Well, and the probable location of the Jaffa Gate as recorded in the gospel of John. Recent discoveries have vindicated John's accounts.[19] Could it be that archaeologists just haven't yet found the wall?

- Next, Helms says that the prophet speaks and touches the dead son. But Jesus regularly spoke to and touched the people he was healing. There is nothing particularly noteworthy about that. Again, his case would be stronger if this were the *only* time Jesus touched the person while healing him.

- Then the dead sons rise. Well, these *are* stories of raising dead people. What else are they supposed to do?

Now consider some of the differences between the two accounts:

- In 1 Kings, Elijah receives from God specific instructions to go to Sarepta for the purpose of meeting the widow who will be his source of sustenance. In Luke's story, Jesus just shows up in Nain.

- Elijah had an ongoing relationship with the widow. In fact, she fed him for some period of time by taking flour and oil from vessels that miraculously never ran out. It was only after Elijah had lived with the widow for quite a while that her son got sick and died. In Luke's story, the son was already dead before Jesus showed up. He apparently had no previous contact with the son or the widow before their initial contact and none afterward.

- The widow implies that Elijah might be in some way responsible for her son's death: "She said to Elijah, 'What do you have against me, man of God? Did you come to remind me of my sin and kill my son?'" (1 Kings 17:18). There is no similar charge against Jesus.

- It's true that the prophet spoke in both cases, but in the Old Testament account, Elijah's words were directed toward God in prayer:

> THEN HE CRIED OUT TO THE LORD, "O LORD MY GOD, HAVE YOU BROUGHT TRAGEDY ALSO UPON THIS WIDOW I AM STAYING WITH, BY CAUSING HER SON TO DIE?" THEN HE STRETCHED HIMSELF OUT ON THE BOY THREE TIMES AND CRIED TO THE LORD, "O LORD MY GOD, LET THIS BOY'S LIFE RETURN TO HIM!" (1 KINGS 17:20–21)

> IN THE NEW TESTAMENT STORY, INSTEAD OF PRAYING TO GOD, JESUS SPOKE TO THE BOY AS HE SIMPLY TOLD HIM, "YOUNG MAN, I SAY TO YOU, GET UP!" (LUKE 7:14).

- Yes, touch was involved in both cases, but Elijah "stretched himself out on the boy three times" (1 Kings 17:21), while Jesus merely touched the *coffin* and not even the boy (Luke 7:14). So Helms' contention that both prophets "touch the dead son"[20] is not even accurate. Just like I "knew" that the word *sleep* was on the conference speaker's list, apparently Helms "knew" that Jesus touched the dead son.

Did Luke compose his story based on the 1 Kings account of Elijah's raising the widow's son? If you have either a fertile imagination or a wonderfully powerful filter that is predisposed to seeing stories as literary fabrications based on earlier narratives, I suppose you can conclude that. Most of the similarities between the two accounts, though, are tangential at best. There are at least as many differences between the stories as there are similarities.

STAND THE PROBLEM ON ITS HEAD

Helms has fabricated an outlandish theory based on speculation. Like other filterers, he appears to have a theory about the parallels in Bible stories; then he looks for the evidence to support his theory. Too often we allow critics to set the table and let them go unchallenged in their skeptical inventions. Although his argument sounds credible and he bears the title of "professor," all it takes to debunk his theory is a careful reading of the two stories. Rather than letting Helms get away unchallenged with his dubious theory, we can easily point out its shortcomings and (politely) tell him he has to do better than that.

Helms argues that, since there are certain similarities between the story of Elijah raising a widow's son and Jesus raising a widow's son, Luke consciously patterned his widow of Nain's story after the widow of Sarepta's story. There are also similarities between the various New Testament accounts of Jesus healing different individuals. He often touched them; he often spoke to them; their healing was usually instantaneous; he sometimes instructed them not to tell anyone; they often went away rejoicing. Do these similarities indicate that he really only healed one person during his entire three-year ministry and that the gospel writers remodeled and recycled the story over and over again, putting it into different historical frames? There is no reason to conclude that. It makes more sense to assume that Jesus healed different people on various occasions and that sometimes the details were similar.

Helms correctly observes some similarities between the miracles of 1 and 2 Kings and the Gospels. But to Helms, the similarities point to intentional fabrications on the part of the New Testament writers.

We can reframe the issue by recalling an important principle of literary interpretation: foreshadowing, which is the practice of an author to give hints in advance of things to come. As an English professor, Helms should be familiar with foreshadowing. In the case of the two similar events, the author—the transcendent God— foreshadowed the second story with the events of the first.

I would turn Helms' argument around and consider the similarities more of a pattern than a copy. Just as many of Jesus' teachings had precedents in the Old Testament, so did many of his actions. In fact, he himself went out of his way to point to similarities between Old Testament stories and aspects of his ministry:

- In indicating the time of his return, he referenced the people of Noah's day.

> AS IT WAS IN THE DAYS OF NOAH, SO IT WILL BE AT THE COMING OF THE SON OF MAN. FOR IN THE DAYS BEFORE THE FLOOD, PEOPLE WERE EATING AND DRINKING, MARRYING AND GIVING IN MARRIAGE, UP TO THE DAY NOAH ENTERED THE ARK; AND THEY KNEW NOTHING ABOUT WHAT WOULD HAPPEN UNTIL THE FLOOD CAME AND TOOK THEM ALL AWAY. THAT IS HOW IT WILL BE AT THE COMING OF THE SON OF MAN. (MATT. 24:37–39)

- When the Pharisees and teachers of the law demanded a miraculous sign from Jesus, he told them,

A WICKED AND ADULTEROUS GENERATION ASKS FOR A MIRAC-ULOUS SIGN! BUT NONE WILL BE GIVEN IT EXCEPT THE SIGN OF THE PROPHET JONAH. FOR AS JONAH WAS THREE DAYS AND THREE NIGHTS IN THE BELLY OF A HUGE FISH, SO THE SON OF MAN WILL BE THREE DAYS AND THREE NIGHTS IN THE HEART OF THE EARTH. (MATT. 12:39–40)

- When the Pharisees criticized him for picking grain on the Sabbath, which they considered to be unlawful, Jesus retorted,

HAVE YOU NEVER READ WHAT DAVID DID WHEN HE AND HIS COMPANIONS WERE HUNGRY AND IN NEED? IN THE DAYS OF ABIATHAR THE HIGH PRIEST, HE ENTERED THE HOUSE OF GOD AND ATE THE CONSECRATED BREAD, WHICH IS LAWFUL ONLY FOR PRIESTS TO EAT. AND HE ALSO GAVE SOME TO HIS COM-PANIONS. (MARK 2:25–26)

Of course there are similarities between Old Testament events and New Testament ones. Why wouldn't there be? Bible advocates believe that the Scriptures report the unfolding story of God's work in human history. In fact they notice a certain "style" that God seems to employ in the patterns of how he deals with people. Why wouldn't God do things in a consistent way from one time period to another? Wouldn't we *expect* a certain degree of consistency if God is, indeed, behind various historical incidents? Is he only "allowed" to perform a certain action one time? Is it a technical foul for God to do something that is reminiscent of something he had already done? Apparently Helms thinks so.

A SECOND LOOK AT THE CROWD

Let's return to the charge, as discussed under Principle 3, that the dramatic shift in the Jerusalem crowd between the Sunday and

Thursday leading up to Jesus' crucifixion undermines the credibility of the Gospels. I provided a very reasonable solution; namely, that there were probably two different crowds involved. For me, this meets the threshold of "one reasonable explanation" suggested by Principle 2.

Let's revisit the basis of the challenge. The critics essentially say that it is impossible for a crowd to reverse itself so quickly. How could they go from being an adoring throng on Sunday into a bloodthirsty mob four days later? Is this really true that such a shift is impossible? Many a public figure has seen his or her image turn overnight based on some dramatic revelation or scandal.

One such person is Richard Jewell, a former sheriff's deputy, who spotted a suspicious-looking knapsack in Centennial Olympic Park during the 1996 Atlanta Olympics and alerted authorities. His actions helped get several people away from the bomb before it exploded, probably saving their lives. Jewell was paraded before national television audiences as a hero until law enforcement officials realized that he fit the profile sometimes typical of bombers: a loner with a law enforcement background that would have provided the know-how to construct a bomb. Within days, Jewell went from being an international hero to becoming the target of unrelenting scrutiny. He was finally exonerated after what he called "88 days in hell."[21]

We know from Matthew 27:20 that the religious leaders in Jerusalem actively whipped up opposition to Jesus among the crowd, urging them to demand Pilate's release of Barabbas the criminal instead of Jesus and undoubtedly spreading false information about him. Even if it were the same crowd on the two different days (which I doubt), I don't think the skeptics have proved their case that this incident disproves the Bible. A passing knowledge of how fleeting popularity can be is enough to undermine their theory.

Sometimes all it takes is to stand back a few feet and to challenge the premise behind the accusation.

RECAP

Here is a review of the four principles that deal with perspective:

1. *Pray for insight.* Ask God to guide your study and help you understand the truth.

2. *Settle for one reasonable explanation.* All it takes is one reasonable explanation to remove a passage from the Ultimate Master List of verses that allegedly disproves the Bible.

3. *Think outside the box.* Perhaps you can think of a credible explanation for what at first might appear to be an impossibility.

   - The Challenge of the Las Vegas Circle
   - The Case of the Fickle Crowd
   - The Puzzle of Pilate

4. *Reframe the challenge.* Maybe the challenge has been framed to stack the deck against the Bible, especially if it is presented by a skeptical critic. Think about different ways to view the issue.

   - Similarities between Elijah's raising of the widow of Sarepta's son and Jesus' raising of the widow of Nain's son
   - A second look at the Case of the Fickle Crowd

PRINCIPLES 5 – 9:
UNDERSTANDING THE
WRITER'S PURPOSE

Because of their generally mindless nature, comic books were off-limits in the Pearson home when I was growing up, except for a series called Classics Illustrated that presents comic book versions of such literary masterpieces as *Treasure Island* and *The House of the Seven Gables*.

Partly because of this unusual ban, I actually looked forward to going to the doctor's office. And since Dr. Vanore was also an old family friend whose office was actually in his beautifully preserved Victorian home, a simple office visit would turn into an all-afternoon event, visiting with his family and enjoying homemade cookies. Another fringe benefit was the fact that he had a terrific stash of comic books in his waiting room. I guess my parents considered doctors' offices as a kind of "duty-free zone" for Batman and his friends.

My absolute favorites were the Superman comics, probably because that guy could do *anything*. For some reason, I remember one particular story that involved something called Silver Kryptonite. Standard Kryptonite, you will remember, was a green rock that originated on Superman's home planet. It was the one substance in the universe that could not only temporarily weaken

Superman but even kill him if he was exposed to it for long enough.

Everyone knows about "Green" Kryptonite, but only those of us devoted to the comic books of the 1960s knew that there were actually other kinds (that is until the recent *Smallville* television series revived the popularity of the Kryptonite "variety pack"). The 1960s' mutations of Kryptonite each had a different effect on Superman: Red Kryptonite didn't harm him, but it would affect him for forty-eight hours in odd ways, like making him stupid or giving him an extra finger on each hand; Blue Kryptonite affected only Bizarro Superman (a warped clone of the real hero) in the same way that Green Kryptonite affected the real Superman; and Gold Kryptonite would permanently remove Superman's powers. I guess the publishers never did much with the gold version because that would effectively end the comic book series.

This particular story, however, introduced a strange new variety called Silver Kryptonite. Throughout the comic book, Clark Kent—who was Superman incognito—happens to see his friend Jimmy Olsen quietly collecting silver objects from Superman's various friends so Jimmy could make something "Silver Kryptonite." Clark/Superman is shocked. No matter how you hack it, Kryptonite is bad, and here are his friends willingly donating to create something sinister that Superman has never even heard of. As the story progresses, both Superman and I get increasingly alarmed as his friends seem to happily plot Superman's demise. The circumstances are suspicious.

Eventually, Jimmy lures Superman into a little room and pulls back a curtain, revealing a large silver rock. Superman is shocked. How could this be? He is being trapped by one of his best friends. What would this unknown rock do to the Man of Steel? It wasn't looking good.

While Superman stands stunned, waiting for the impact of Silver Kryptonite to kick in, Jimmy steps over to the glittering rock, snaps a latch on the side, and reveals that it is actually nothing more than a hollow display case holding little silver busts of his friends (Lois Lane, Perry White, etc.) on a shelf inside the rock. It turns out that Silver Kryptonite is actually a special tribute to Superman created by his friends to commemorate the twenty-fifth anniversary (hence the silver) of his arrival on Planet Earth.

Up to this point, all the details of Superman's friends' actions pointed in a sinister direction. With only partial information, Superman came to the erroneous conclusion that his friends were plotting his destruction. However, once their real purpose was understood, the whole story looks very different.

Similarly, certain aspects of the Gospels might appear to undercut their historical reliability. But once we understand the writers' intentions, recognize their filters, and view the stories accordingly, many difficulties greatly diminish. A number of the challenges to the Gospels' accuracy come from a misunderstanding of the authors' purposes or a misinterpretation of what Jesus was trying to communicate in his teaching. So let's look at five principles that address the writers' intentions, which will clear up many of the alleged contradictions.

5. CONSIDER THE WRITER'S UNIQUE PURPOSE

Each writer recorded the story the way he did in order to fulfill a particular objective he had that other writers did not have. One key to the harmonization of apparently contradictory gospel passages is to remember that each writer had a style that affected the selection and presentation of his material. Matthew is not John. Luke is not Mark. Each author had his particular background, personality, level of education, and target audience. Plus, Matthew and John were probably the only gospel writers who had face-to-face relationships with Jesus. As a result, each writer brought to his writing a unique background and set of objectives.

GENEALOGICAL CONFUSION

If there were a contest for the alleged contradiction that receives the most attention, the blue ribbon would probably go to Jesus' two genealogies as presented by Matthew and Luke. Skeptics love these passages.

A comparison reveals that there are some pretty significant differences. For one, Matthew begins his genealogy with Abraham (the father of the Jewish people) and moves forward to Jesus, while Luke starts with Jesus and runs backward, past Abraham and on to Adam. The other major difference is that, although the two genealogies from Abraham to David are almost identical, there are significant variations from David onward. Skeptics relish the idea of pointing to these differences as proof positive that the Gospels are riddled with errors. What's a Bible advocate to do?

Well, there is a relatively simple explanation, and it has to do with the writer's purpose (Principle 5). It seems probable that Matthew—who wrote for a primarily Jewish audience—traced the royal line through Joseph, Jesus' legal father. Luke, who wrote for a largely Greek audience, likely presents the natural bloodline of Jesus through his mother, Mary. This is consistent with each writer's orientation and purpose. Matthew emphasizes Jesus' ties to the Old Testament and how he is the culmination of God's promise to Abraham. Consequently, it is important for him to present Jesus as rightful heir to David's throne, which is claimed through his legal father, Joseph.

Luke, on the other hand, writes primarily to a non-Jewish Greek audience that is far less interested in the Jewish monarchy, so he spotlights Jesus' true bloodline through Mary. Of the four gospels, Luke's is the one that places the most stress on the universal application of Jesus' message to all people. Remember, he is the one who records the angel's message to the shepherds at Jesus' birth: "I bring you good news of great joy that will be *for all the people*" (2:10), underscoring the gospel's relevance to all people, not just the Jews. As a result, he traces Jesus all the way back to the very first man.

Since each genealogy is for a different parent, and since each parent has a different set of ancestors, they differ.[1] R. A. Torrey notes that each genealogist's emphasis parallels that of his respective gospel birth narrative. Most of the action in Matthew focuses on Joseph (Jesus' legal father), while Mary is barely mentioned. By contrast, Luke makes Mary the focal point of the story, while Joseph hovers around the periphery.[2] Remember, it is Luke who includes the extended picture of Jesus' birth as seen through Mary's eyes. It also includes her cousin Elizabeth's miraculous conception of John the Baptist, the angelic announcement to Mary, and Mary's prophetic song that preceded Jesus' birth—all of this in Luke 1—2.

Luke starts his genealogical list with the statement that Jesus "was the son, so it was thought, of Joseph" (3:23). This statement downplays Joseph's role and reinforces Jesus' virgin birth through Mary. As *The NIV Study Bible* somewhat wryly observes, "Although tracing a genealogy through the mother's side was unusual, so was the virgin birth."[3]

TEMPTED TO SEE A DISCREPANCY

Another apparent contradiction between Matthew and Luke concerns the order of Jesus' temptations at the beginning of his ministry. Although Matthew and Luke both list the same three temptations, they report them in different orders. Matthew's version describes the challenge to turn stones into bread, the temptation to jump off the highest point of the temple, and the offer to gain all the kingdoms in the world in exchange for worshipping Satan. Luke reverses the order of the last two. Why the discrepancy?

Walter Kaiser suggests that the difference between the respective authors' purposes explains the variation. Matthew's objective is to show parallels between Jesus' temptations and the experience of

Israel as they wandered through the desert. After God miraculously and dramatically rescued Israel from Egyptian slavery (remember Charlton Heston and the Red Sea?), Israel's lack of faith caused God to condemn them to forty years of wandering through the desert. Kaiser believes that Matthew attempts to draw a contrast between Israel's testing in the desert (they flunked) and Jesus' testing in the desert (he passed). To provide contrast with Israel's failure to worship only God, Matthew brings his version of Jesus' testing to a climax with the temptation to worship Satan. Unlike Israel, Jesus passes with flying colors.[4]

Luke's objectives were different from Matthew's. Rather than stress Old Testament fulfillment, Luke depicts the kingdom of God as an invasion of the kingdom of Satan as illustrated by Jesus' "mission statement": "to preach good news to the poor ... to proclaim freedom for the prisoners and recovery of sight for the blind, to release the oppressed" (4:18). Jesus here declares his intention to weaken Satan's death grip on many people. In Luke, Jesus is the Son of God who starts out at the edge of Satan's kingdom and moves steadily toward the center where "the final drama of salvation history will be played out."[5]

Kaiser also notes a "directionality" in Luke's gospel, which ultimately leads Jesus to Jerusalem. Luke devotes an entire section (9:51—18:34) to tracing Jesus' journey from Galilee to Jerusalem with occasional comments about where Jesus was in relation to Jerusalem. Of course, he ends up in the city itself, where he is eventually killed and resurrected. When it comes to recording the temptation accounts, Luke's order parallels this geographical zeroing in on the Holy City, culminating in the temptation to leap from the highest point of the temple.[6] So an understanding of the authors' respective purposes helps explain how they arrange their material.

The important point is this: Keep the author's purpose in mind. It explains a lot.

6. REMEMBER THAT BIBLICAL WRITERS DIDN'T SHARE OUR OBSESSION WITH TIME

The gospel writers did not write in order to satisfy our twenty-first-century obsession with the creation of a precise minute-by-minute chronology. To criticize them for not having done so is unfair. Some material is intentionally out of sequence or lacks sufficient detail to pinpoint exact times and orders of events. To obsess over perceived differences in the timelines of each gospel writer has become a favorite indoor sport of many skeptics who unjustly impose a modern mind-set onto ancient writings.

Principle 5 teaches that each writer composed his book to be consistent with his purposes. It's safe to say that none of them had as his primary objective the construction of an impeccably precise chronological account. Instead, the gospel writers often arranged their material thematically. For example, a quick overview of Matthew's gospel reveals that the backbone of the book is a series of Jesus' sermons interspersed with narrative that describes his actions. As Paul Copan observes,

> [SKEPTICS] OFTEN GIVE THE IMPRESSION THAT THE GOSPEL MATERIAL MUST BE PURELY CHRONOLOGICAL, OR ELSE IT IS NOT HISTORICAL.... WE MUST ALLOW THE BIBLICAL WRITERS FREEDOM TO INCLUDE, EXCLUDE, AND EDIT PARTICULAR MATERIAL ACCORDING TO A PARTICULAR THEME THEY WANT TO EMPHASIZE.[7]

Let's back up a moment and consider the reasonableness of what the skeptics demand. Does their requirement that the Gospels adhere to a strict historical chronology unfairly impose a twenty-first-century criterion onto documents written two millennia ago? We live in an age of instant communication and twenty-four-hour-a-day news coverage, which results in immediate and continuous documentation. We don't want a poem. We don't want an allegory. We want the *facts*, and we want them in precise chronological order. At any moment I can turn on CNN, MSNBC, or Fox News to learn the latest from the national or international scene. I subscribe to an Internet news notification service that blasts out e-mail bulletins of breaking news, so I often know of a momentous event that takes place on the other side of the globe within thirty minutes of its occurrence.

The Iraq War of 2003 introduced a new term to the American news lexicon: *embedded journalists*. These are reporters who join American military units; travel with them; and provide live, instant updates from the actual battle sites. This is a far cry from the speed with which battleground news was disseminated even two hundred years ago, much less two thousand years in the past. Let me illustrate.

One of the curiosities of military history is the fact that the Battle of New Orleans at the end of the War of 1812 actually extended beyond the official end of the war. The Treaty of Ghent, which formally ended the war, was signed on December 24, 1814, in Belgium, and yet the Battle of New Orleans raged on until January 8, 1815.[8] The opponents in that battle were not even aware that the war had been over for more than two weeks before the fighting ended.

Even more recently—less than 150 years ago—the Pony Express was established to speed communications to the West Coast of the United States. In 1860, St. Joseph, Missouri, was the westernmost point to which railroad and telegraph lines reached. Mail normally took twenty-four days by stagecoach to get from Missouri to San Francisco. The coming of the Pony Express in April 1860 reduced this to an unheard-of ten days between St. Joseph and San Francisco. The fastest trip on record was the lightning-fast seven-day-and-seventeen-hour trip that carried President Lincoln's inaugural address from St. Joseph to Sacramento.[9]

Little did those pioneer mailmen realize that, within twenty-five years, people who lived hundreds of miles apart would be able to have real-time, voice-to-voice conversations by holding a device to their ears and speaking into a box or that, within 140 years, someone in Atlanta could send a written message with no paper, ink, or stamp to a friend in Madrid and that it would reach him in a matter of seconds. If you had told them, they would think that you were on your way to a straitjacket fitting. Our sense of time, including our expectations of instant and precise communications, has surely changed.

TIME IS ON OUR SIDE

Along with our obsession with instant communication, we are also fixated on time. I recently acquired a new watch, bringing my total up to an embarrassing six. Well, it's actually eight if you count the watch I bought in Switzerland in college and which no longer works but still looks cool, and the now-broken watch Annette gave me as a wedding present that has high sentimental value but none as a timepiece.

Our culture is so obsessed with time that we are seldom more than a glance away from a timepiece. An outgrowth of our fascination with time is the cultural fixation with documentation of the exact timing of events. Whenever there is a particularly dramatic incident, such as the February 1, 2003, explosion of the *Columbia* space shuttle, newspapers and magazines typically provide minute-by-minute details of the events as they unfolded:

- 8:53 a.m.—Sensor failures on left wing
- 9:00 a.m.—Shuttle disintegrates over Texas
- 9:16 a.m.—Scheduled touchdown in Cape Canaveral, Florida

I understand that after President Ronald Reagan was shot as he left the Washington Hilton in 1981, a new policy was enacted to always videotape the president as he is entering or leaving buildings, "just in case" something dramatic were to happen. That way we would always have a permanent record of the events to study and to measure the events down to the millisecond.

Not every culture is as time and precision crazed as is the United States. Back in the mid-'70s, several Campus Crusade for Christ music groups went on a three-week concert tour of the Greater Manila area in the Philippines. As part of our orientation once we got there, one of the Filipino staff members asked all the Americans to raise our left hands into the air. "What do you notice?" he asked.

We all kind of looked around and said in a rather matter-of-fact way, "Well, we see a lot of Americans with their left hands raised."

"What else do you notice?" he asked.

We all sat silently, our hands still in the air. Our host pointed out that every one of us was wearing a wristwatch. "Here in the Philippines," he stated, "we are far less time oriented than you Americans are." It turns out, in fact, that some of the locals play a game by going up to Americans to ask them what time it is, just so they can see them look at their watches. Sure enough, he was right. His countrymen *are* far less conscious of time. A Filipino concert scheduled for 7:00 p.m. means that people will often start to *arrive* at 7:30.

Typically, the cultures that are less time oriented are far more relationship oriented. If this is true for contemporary non-Western cultures, how much more was it true for the ancient Middle Eastern culture out of which the Bible sprang? A few of the ancients used sundials to approximate the time of day, but most people judged time by the sun and the moon and the seasons. Today, we can set our watches by an atomic clock located in Boulder, Colorado. We wouldn't want to be two seconds off, now would we? While Bible authors sometimes used days to estimate the distance between places, we now use hundredths of seconds to measure Olympic victory margins.

Some ancient civilizations didn't even maintain uniform "hours" throughout the year. Instead, they merely divided the interval between sunrise and sunset into twelve equal parts. As the percentage of the day when it was light varied, so did the length of each hour.[10] In the modern age where many people wear sports watches that record time down to the hundredth of a second, it seems incredible that hours in Jesus' time would expand or shrink according to the time of year.

Is it any surprise that the gospel writers' emphasis on precise chronology does not always satisfy our nanosecond mind-set? The Pony Express riders of 1860 would be astounded at our manic attitude toward instant communication and time. They felt they were doing the world a huge service by cutting mail delivery time down from twenty-four days to ten. Nowadays, we get frustrated if an e-mail attachment takes more than fifteen seconds to download. The Pony Express operated less than 150 years ago. We have to multiply that time span by thirteen to reach back to the days of Matthew, Mark, Luke, and John. If the gap in communications and orientation toward chronology between the Pony Express riders and twenty-first-century Americans would be incomprehensible to them, how much more so the gap between the gospel writers and today's Bible critic?

THE GREAT FIG TREE MYSTERY

Let's examine a famous challenge to the Gospels' authenticity based upon the sequence of events. It is the episode where Jesus curses a fig tree, which subsequently withers. Matthew places this incident after Jesus' expulsion of the money changers from the temple. Mark, on the other hand, breaks the account into two parts, with the cursing of the tree prior to the temple cleansing and with the actual withering of the tree taking place afterward.

Which sequence reflects what actually happened? Was it before or after the cleansing of the temple? Does this difference mean that Matthew was right and Mark was wrong, or vice versa? Furthermore, Matthew seems to report that Jesus threw the money changers out of the temple on Sunday of Holy Week, while Mark states that it was Monday. How do we explain this and the hundreds of other chronological variations among the four accounts of Jesus' life?

This story is recorded in both Matthew 21:18–22 and Mark 11:12–14 and 20–25. Here is a summary of the two versions:

Matthew's gospel:

- As Jesus and the disciples approached Bethphage on the Mount of Olives, Jesus sent two disciples ahead to bring him a particular donkey and her colt (see vv. 1–7).
- A large crowd gathered; spread their cloaks and palm branches on the road; and went ahead of him, proclaiming him to be the Son of David (see vv. 8–9).
- "When Jesus entered Jerusalem, the whole city was stirred and asked, 'Who is this?' The crowds answered, 'This is Jesus, the prophet from Nazareth in Galilee'" (vv. 10–11).
- Jesus entered the temple area and drove out the merchants (see vv. 12–13).
- Jesus and the disciples left Jerusalem for Bethany, where they spent the night (see v. 17).
- Early the next morning, he saw a fig tree by the road and cursed it because it had nothing but leaves on it (see v. 18). "'May you never bear fruit again!' Immediately the tree withered" (v. 19).
- The disciples were amazed that the tree withered so quickly (see v. 20).

Mark's gospel:

- As Jesus and the disciples approached Jerusalem, Jesus sent two disciples ahead to get the colt (see vv. 1–7).
- The crowds spread their cloaks and branches on the road and proclaimed blessings on Jesus (see vv. 8–10).
- "Jesus entered Jerusalem and went to the temple. He looked

around at everything, but since it was already late, he went out to Bethany with the Twelve" (v. 11).

- The next day as they were leaving Bethany, Jesus saw the fig tree, discovered it had no fruit, and cursed it (see vv. 12–14).
- "On reaching Jerusalem, Jesus entered the temple area and began driving out those who were buying and selling there" (v. 15).
- The chief priests and the teachers of the law began to look for a way to kill him (see v. 18).
- "When evening came, they went out of the city" (v. 19).
- "In the morning, as they went along, they saw the fig tree withered from the roots" (v. 20).

To summarize, Matthew's order is

- the triumphal entry (Sunday),
- the cleansing of the temple (not stated but implied as Sunday),
- cursing and withering of fig tree ("early in the morning"— although no particular day is specified, the implication may be that it was the next day, that is, Monday).

Mark's chronology appears to be different:

- the triumphal entry (Sunday),
- a *visit* to the temple (Sunday),
- cursing of the barren fig tree on the way back to Jerusalem (Monday morning),
- ejection of the money changers (Monday),
- observation by the disciples of the withered tree (Tuesday).

What actually happened, and when?

Gleason Archer points out that both Matthew and Mark agree that Jesus visited the temple on Sunday. Although the reader might conclude from Matthew's account that Jesus cleared the temple on Sunday, Mark indicates that after his visit to the temple, Jesus left

Jerusalem "since it was already late" (see 11:11). He probably cursed the fig tree on his way back to Jerusalem the next morning, after which he cleansed the temple. On Tuesday morning, the disciples noticed that the tree had withered.

Archer also reaffirms Matthew's tendency to arrange his material topically instead of strictly chronologically. "Once a theme has been broached, Matthew prefers to carry it through to its completion, as a general rule."[11] Mark probably recorded the "correct" chronology, and Matthew, true to his form, arranges his stories thematically. Immediately after he introduces the concept of Jesus' visiting the temple, he goes on to record the subsequent ejection of the money changers. Similarly, he treats both "halves" of the fig tree story in a single account. This treatment seems well within Matthew's thematic methodology. His expanded account then reflects the actual historical sequence and provides additional details.

(For a discussion of how Principle 6 helps us understand chronology problems concerning Jesus' crucifixion, go to www.cookministries.com/GreatQuestion and read appendix entry 8.1.)

Walter Kaiser summarizes it well: "Exact chronology is a relatively modern fixation; ancient writers were very happy to compromise chronology if by so doing readers got a better grasp on the inner meaning and real significance of the facts."[12] So it should be no surprise that the Gospels don't conform to the scientifically rigid demands of precise twenty-first-century chronological analysis. Does that mean that the writers were mistaken? No, it only means that they were consistent with their objective of communicating the significance of their narratives.

7. DON'T LISTEN TO "NOTHING"

Be careful about entertaining arguments from silence. Silence, in and of itself, proves nothing. An "argument from silence" is weak. Just as the television show *Seinfeld* was allegedly about "nothing," so are some of the charges skeptics hurl at the text. Based on what they *don't* see, they impute an error, not recognizing that the author had his reasons for including or excluding certain information. Although we don't always know why, a particular fact or detail may be missing because the author intentionally excluded it.

Let me give you an example of how critics with negative mental grids turn silence into a problem. Antisupernatural filterer C. Milo Connick questions several elements of Jesus' triumphal entry into Jerusalem on the Sunday before his crucifixion, including whether or not it showed that Jesus saw himself as the Messiah.[13] The New Testament writers relate that Jesus entered the city riding a colt, which Bible advocates see as a fulfillment of the Old Testament prophecy about the coming of the Messiah as recorded in Zechariah 9:9:

> REJOICE GREATLY, O DAUGHTER OF ZION!
> SHOUT, DAUGHTER OF JERUSALEM!
> SEE, YOUR KING COMES TO YOU,
> RIGHTEOUS AND HAVING SALVATION,
> GENTLE AND RIDING ON A DONKEY,
> ON A COLT, THE FOAL OF A DONKEY.

This appears to be yet another example of Jesus' declaration that he was the Jewish Messiah. Connick agrees that Jesus probably did ride into Jerusalem on a donkey. But he concludes that it was the early church, which was aware of the messianic overtones of Zechariah 9:9, that injected the messianic elements into the story.

Connick rationalizes his doubts about Jesus' self-identity as the Messiah by saying, "If the manner of the entry was obviously Messianic—why was not this fact presented at the trial as proof of Jesus' treasonable ambitions?"[14] He asserts that the silence of the Gospels on this aspect of Jesus' claim to be the Messiah during his trials demonstrates that it didn't exist.

Is there any validity to this charge? Let's look at what we know about Jesus' trials to see if Connick has a point or not. Here's part of what Matthew says about the trial before the Jewish council:

> THE CHIEF PRIESTS AND THE WHOLE SANHEDRIN WERE LOOK-
> ING FOR FALSE EVIDENCE AGAINST JESUS SO THAT THEY
> COULD PUT HIM TO DEATH. BUT THEY DID NOT FIND ANY,
> THOUGH MANY FALSE WITNESSES CAME FORWARD.
>
> FINALLY TWO CAME FORWARD AND DECLARED, "THIS FEL-
> LOW SAID, 'I AM ABLE TO DESTROY THE TEMPLE OF GOD AND
> REBUILD IT IN THREE DAYS.'" (26:59–61)

Mark adds a few interesting details:

> MANY TESTIFIED FALSELY AGAINST HIM, BUT THEIR STATE-
> MENTS DID NOT AGREE.
>
> THEN SOME STOOD UP AND GAVE THIS FALSE TESTIMONY
> AGAINST HIM: "WE HEARD HIM SAY, 'I WILL DESTROY THIS
> MAN-MADE TEMPLE AND IN THREE DAYS WILL BUILD ANOTHER,
> NOT MADE BY MAN.'" YET EVEN THEN THEIR TESTIMONY DID
> NOT AGREE. (14:56–59)

Notice that Matthew refers to "many" who gave false witness. Mark adds that their statements did not agree. How many of the witnesses' specific charges against Jesus are actually recorded in the gospel accounts? Exactly one: the allegation that he said he would destroy the temple and rebuild it in three days. What other specific charges were leveled at him? Did any of the false witnesses refer to Jesus' implicit messianic claim demonstrated by his riding into Jerusalem on a colt? We don't know. The text is silent on that matter. Why didn't the writers include the specifics of the other false witnesses' allegations? All we have is the testimony about destroying and rebuilding the temple. Apparently it was not within their purposes to include any of the other charges.

Is it possible that one of the other false witnesses brought up the colt incident? Certainly. We just don't know for sure.

Luke records the trial before Pilate where the Jewish leaders specifically charged that he "claims to be Christ, a king" (23:2). Luke doesn't elaborate on what exactly Jesus did to lead them to the conclusion that he claimed to be the Christ (Messiah). But it is possible that they referenced the triumphal entry donkey incident. Remember that we can read aloud the accounts of Jesus' trials in a mere three or four minutes. Yet the trials certainly lasted much longer. Who knows what else was said? Is it reasonable to assume that one of the many false witnesses may have tied in the "riding on a colt" story? Yes.

How can Connick be so confident that nothing about the colt was mentioned? He really can't be sure. To expose this argument as one from silence and to combine it with Principle 2 (that one reasonable explanation is enough to defang a claim of error) neutralizes Connick's allegation and is sufficient to remove this passage from the Ultimate Master List of problem passages.

READING THE AUTHOR'S MIND

Let's look at another instance where a skeptic argues from silence. In my coverage of Principle 4 about reframing the issue, I discussed Randel Helms' treatment of the two stories regarding the raising of the two widows' sons. You will remember that Helms posits that Luke fabricated his story from his knowledge of the vaguely similar Old Testament story of Elijah raising another widow's son. Luke alone, of all the gospel writers, records the Nain incident.

Helms betrays his skeptical filter by commenting that "only Luke of the four evangelists *knew* the story of the widow of Nain" (italics added).[15] Oh, really? How does Helms know that Luke is the only one of the four familiar with this story? Did he interview the other writers before their deaths to verify this fact, or did he discover a document that declares they were ignorant of this event? Or could it be that, for reasons of their own, the other writers chose not to include this particular incident? I have yet to mention baseball legend Babe

Ruth in this book. Does that mean I don't know that he existed? Helms seems to claim the ability to reach across the centuries and read ancient minds when he concludes the other gospel writers didn't even know of the widow of Nain.

(For a further example of arguments from silence, go to www.cookministries.com/GreatQuestion and read appendix entry 8.2.)

Keep in mind that none of the Gospels is particularly long, and God guided each writer as he selected the material that was consistent with his objectives. In fact, the very last verse in the gospel of John declares that "Jesus did many other things as well. If every one of them were written down, I suppose that even the whole world would not have room for the books that would be written" (21:25). Remember that Jesus' ministry lasted about three years, and we can read all four gospels in just a few hours. A lot more happened than what we know about, and each writer was intentionally selective.

What we have in the gospel records is only a fraction of what could have been written. Each writer selected his material from the universe of Jesus' lifetime according to his own purposes. It requires an unreasonable negative bias to turn this selectivity into a lack of knowledge or a contradiction. As David O'Brien says, "When a writer chooses not to record an event, or a detail involved in an event, he hasn't made a mistake; he's made a decision."[16] My friend Les Saunders once quipped that if we take the skeptics' arguments to the logical extreme, we would conclude that Jesus never played games as a child, kissed his mother, or ate more than about a dozen meals in his entire life.

8. RECOGNIZE THAT TIMELESS TREASURES AND LIMITED LESSONS ARE NOT THE SAME THING

There is a difference between the record of a principle that transcends the time in which it was written and the record of a historical event or teaching intended for limited application. Readers some-times misinterpret or misapply a particular passage and end up with a view of the Bible that borders on the "magical." When we fail to recognize the author's or speaker's intention, we set ourselves up for misunderstandings. Let me explain.

The book of Proverbs contains many wonderful insights into human nature that generally hold true. Some people view that book in particular as full of promises to "claim," such as,

THE LORD DOES NOT LET THE RIGHTEOUS GO HUNGRY. (10:3)

TRAIN A CHILD IN THE WAY HE SHOULD GO,
    AND WHEN HE IS OLD HE WILL NOT TURN FROM IT. (22:6)

COMMIT TO THE LORD WHATEVER YOU DO,
    AND YOUR PLANS WILL SUCCEED. (16:3)

THE FEAR OF THE LORD ADDS LENGTH TO LIFE. (10:27)

These truths reflect the way God usually deals with us and also present general observations about human behavior. But sometimes Christians consider these verses to be ironclad promises that God cannot violate. Observation tells us, though, that there are many cir-cumstances where these "promises" seem to go unfulfilled. What about the righteous believers in sub-Saharan Africa who are victims of devastating famine and starve to death? What about the faithful Christian parents whose child rebels and runs amok during his or her teenage years or early adulthood? What about the Christian who prays about and carefully executes a business plan, only to see her venture crumble into bankruptcy? What about the faithful family whose daughter dies of cancer at twelve years of age? Do the bad out-comes mean that these people did something wrong or that God broke his word? It looks that way if you view these verses as invio-lable promises from God.

Author Jack Kuhatschek observes that many people misinterpret the nature of proverbs. Some "promises," he says, are really more principles that generally hold true. "Before applying a biblical promise, we should ask whether it really *is* a promise."[17]

It's interesting that I have never heard anyone "claim" such promises as

A POOR MAN'S FIELD MAY PRODUCE ABUNDANT FOOD,
   BUT INJUSTICE SWEEPS IT AWAY. (PROV. 13:23)

A PERVERSE MAN STIRS UP DISSENSION,
   AND A GOSSIP SEPARATES CLOSE FRIENDS. (PROV. 16:28)

AS A DOG RETURNS TO ITS VOMIT,
   SO A FOOL REPEATS HIS FOLLY. (PROV. 26:11)

Few people ask God to "deliver" on the promises to sweep away someone's food, stir up dissension, separate close friends, or encourage foolish people to mimic dogs' gastrointestinal habits. These particular proverbs are clearly not promises at all but, instead, observations about life. Don't get me wrong. We certainly can and should pray for the blessings the positive proverbs communicate. But there is a difference between reverently asking God to accomplish certain things in our lives and "demanding" that he do so because he is obligated by a phrase that he intended simply as wise counsel. A "magical" view of the Bible treats biblical phraseology as having intrinsic power that we can invoke without regard for the author's original intent.

This less-than-discerning approach to the Bible can sometimes lead us to believe that a certain passage is problematic when it needn't be. A great way to cut through the fog is to ask why the passage was recorded as it was.

FOR JEWS ONLY?

I once pointed out to an adult Sunday school class that Jesus forbids us to minister to anyone who is not Jewish. Stunned, they asked, "What did you say?" I assured them that the Bible clearly teaches that we should never minister to non-Jewish people.

"Look at Matthew 10:1–8," I said. "In verse 1, Jesus calls the twelve disciples together and gives them authority to drive out evil spirits and heal every disease and sickness." Verses 5–8 read as follows:

> THESE TWELVE JESUS SENT OUT WITH THE FOLLOWING INSTRUCTIONS: "DO NOT GO AMONG THE GENTILES OR ENTER ANY TOWN OF THE SAMARITANS. GO RATHER TO THE LOST SHEEP OF ISRAEL. AS YOU GO, PREACH THIS MESSAGE: 'THE KINGDOM OF HEAVEN IS NEAR.' HEAL THE SICK, RAISE THE DEAD, CLEANSE THOSE WHO HAVE LEPROSY, DRIVE OUT DEMONS. FREELY YOU HAVE RECEIVED, FREELY GIVE."

"There," I said. "Clearly, he wants us to avoid anyone who is not Jewish. That means that every time a Christian performs any type of ministry to a Gentile (that is, anyone who is not Jewish), we are violating a specific commandment delivered by Jesus himself."

What's wrong with this picture? All my observations are exactly correct, but I have applied them incorrectly because I violated Principle 8 and failed to take into account the purpose and context of Jesus' instructions. I mistakenly applied the text to all of his followers in all generations. Just because the Bible is eternally true and just because it records a given event or teaching doesn't mean that every teaching is equally applicable to all people in all ages.

There is such a thing as timeless teaching, such as when Jesus described himself as the Bread of Life. His is a kind of food intended for all people at all times. Then there are limited application lessons: specific teachings whose use is confined to a particular time and/or domain. This type of food comes in small cans with expiration dates and is only intended to serve a limited number of people. We must read the content label carefully to determine if the can is past date.

Jesus delivered his instructions in Matthew 10 rather early in his ministry, while his reputation was still growing. Among his purposes was to multiply his presence through his disciples and to give them a sense of how God could help others through them. A lot of people would also be helped in the process.

My suggested application is wrong on two accounts: Jesus meant these instructions to apply only to the original hearers, and he intended them only for a specific period of time. How do I know? Let's go to the very end of the same gospel, to Matthew 28:16–20 to witness Jesus' last words right before he miraculously goes up to heaven:

> THEN THE ELEVEN DISCIPLES WENT TO GALILEE, TO THE MOUNTAIN WHERE JESUS HAD TOLD THEM TO GO. WHEN THEY SAW HIM, THEY WORSHIPED HIM; BUT SOME DOUBTED. THEN JESUS CAME TO THEM AND SAID, "ALL AUTHORITY IN HEAVEN AND ON EARTH HAS BEEN GIVEN TO ME. THEREFORE GO AND MAKE DISCIPLES OF ALL NATIONS, BAPTIZING THEM IN THE NAME OF THE FATHER AND OF THE SON AND OF THE HOLY SPIRIT, AND TEACHING THEM TO OBEY EVERYTHING I HAVE COMMANDED YOU. AND SURELY I AM WITH YOU ALWAYS, TO THE VERY END OF THE AGE."

Notice that Jesus delivered these instructions to the very same disciples (minus Judas, of course). It supersedes the instructions of Matthew 10 and tells them to go to *everyone, everywhere*. Furthermore, this new instruction applies to all his followers, including Jesus' disciples down through the ages. We know this because he tells the eleven to teach *everything* that he had commanded them, which includes instructions about sharing the message with everyone.

A skeptic who took a literalistic interpretation of these verses from Matthew 10 and Matthew 28 could charge Jesus with contradicting himself. That would be a gross misreading of the obvious intent. It's possible for a specific teaching of Jesus to apply to a particular historical circumstance and not to all people in all times.

"GETTING RIGHT WITH GOD"

One of the central issues of the Bible is what it takes to become acceptable to God. A casual reading of various parts of the Gospels could lead to some confusion. Mark 10:17–27 recounts the story of someone we usually call "the rich young ruler." The young man one day runs up to Jesus, kneels before him, and asks what he must do to inherit eternal life. Jesus tells him that he must keep the commandments: don't murder, commit adultery, lie, etc. Notice the young man's response:

> "TEACHER," HE DECLARED, "ALL THESE I HAVE KEPT SINCE I WAS A BOY."
>
> JESUS LOOKED AT HIM AND LOVED HIM. "ONE THING YOU LACK," HE SAID. "GO, SELL EVERYTHING YOU HAVE AND GIVE TO THE POOR, AND YOU WILL HAVE TREASURE IN HEAVEN. THEN COME, FOLLOW ME."
>
> AT THIS THE MAN'S FACE FELL. HE WENT AWAY SAD, BECAUSE HE HAD GREAT WEALTH. JESUS LOOKED AROUND AND SAID TO HIS DISCIPLES, "HOW HARD IT IS FOR THE RICH TO ENTER THE KINGDOM OF GOD!" (VV. 20–23)

Gospel writer John records another incident where a crowd follows Jesus right after he miraculously feeds five thousand men. Jesus accuses them of following him primarily because they see him as the ultimate meal ticket. Then he admonishes:

> "DO NOT WORK FOR FOOD THAT SPOILS, BUT FOR FOOD THAT ENDURES TO ETERNAL LIFE, WHICH THE SON OF MAN WILL GIVE YOU. ON HIM GOD THE FATHER HAS PLACED HIS SEAL OF APPROVAL."
>
> THEN THEY ASKED HIM, "WHAT MUST WE DO TO DO THE WORKS GOD REQUIRES?"
>
> JESUS ANSWERED, "THE WORK OF GOD IS THIS: TO BELIEVE IN THE ONE HE HAS SENT." (6:27–29)

Wait a minute. Didn't Jesus tell the rich young man that in order to receive eternal life he had to perform a very specific action (sell all he had and follow Jesus)? But now he says that the work God requires is to believe in the one he sent (Jesus). Isn't this a contradiction? If you push Jesus' teaching in Mark to the extreme, you could conclude that anyone who owns anything cannot be acceptable to God. And yet Jesus doesn't even mention possessions in the John story. How do we reconcile these apparently conflicting teachings?

It's actually fairly simple. Jesus' response to the individual young man in Mark is based on his diagnosis of this particular person's misunderstanding of what it takes to be acceptable to God. As seminary professor William L. Lane observes,

> THE FORM OF THE QUESTION ("WHAT MUST I DO TO INHERIT ETERNAL LIFE?") IMPLIES A PIETY OF ACHIEVEMENT WHICH STANDS IN CONTRAST TO JESUS' TEACHING THAT A MAN MUST *RECEIVE* THE KINGDOM (OR LIFE) AS A GIFT FROM GOD IN HIS OWN HELPLESSNESS. [18]

Jesus detects this man's misplaced confidence in his own achievements to please God. As Professor Lane states,

> THE SPECIFIC FORM OF THE SACRIFICE JESUS DEMANDED OF THIS MAN IS NOT TO BE REGARDED AS A GENERAL PRESCRIPTION TO BE APPLIED TO ALL MEN.... THE COMMAND TO SELL HIS PROPERTY AND DISTRIBUTE THE PROCEEDS TO THE POOR WAS APPROPRIATE TO THIS PARTICULAR SITUATION. THE SUBSEQUENT REDUCTION TO POVERTY AND HELPLESSNESS WOULD DRAMATIZE THE FACT THAT MAN IS HELPLESS IN HIS QUEST FOR ETERNAL LIFE, WHICH MUST BE BESTOWED AS THE GIFT OF GOD. [19]

The crowd's question in John's gospel betrays a similar misunderstanding of what God requires for eternal life. "What must we *do* to do the works God requires?" they ask (6:28). Jesus quickly redirects them away from works and toward belief.

The end point in both cases is the same. Both the rich young man and the crowd should have come away with the recognition that they were incapable of doing enough to make themselves acceptable to God. As Jesus said, the only work required is to believe in him. In the case of the young man, the bottom line for him was not just selling his goods, which is the part of the instruction we usually trip over. It was as much the rest of the command: "Follow me." Jesus just happened to see that, in this particular case, before the man could follow Jesus, he first had to stop following the money.

Jesus' instructions about who to target in ministry and his statement about requirements for salvation are two examples of gospel stories that, on the surface, appear to contradict each other but which, after an examination of Jesus' purpose, are not problematic after all. He intended some of what he taught to apply to all Christians in all generations and other parts to apply only to the primary hearers. It's important to distinguish between the two.

9. THE FACT THAT IT'S THERE DOESN'T GUARANTEE IT'S RIGHT

The Bible often reports people's words, even if they are wrong. In such cases, the writers' purpose is to report what was said without necessarily endorsing it. To misunderstand the writers' reason for inclusion of a particular event can lead to muddled interpretations or to the conclusion that the Bible contradicts itself.

The clearest example in the Gospels may be the question of whether or not John the Baptist was the prophet Elijah. In Matthew 17, Jesus has a conversation with Peter, James, and John about the coming of God's kingdom. Why, they ask, do the teachers of the law say that Elijah must come before the kingdom is ushered in?

JESUS REPLIED, "TO BE SURE, ELIJAH COMES AND WILL RESTORE ALL THINGS. BUT I TELL YOU, ELIJAH HAS ALREADY

COME, AND THEY DID NOT RECOGNIZE HIM, BUT HAVE DONE
TO HIM EVERYTHING THEY WISHED. IN THE SAME WAY THE
SON OF MAN IS GOING TO SUFFER AT THEIR HANDS." THEN
THE DISCIPLES UNDERSTOOD THAT HE WAS TALKING TO THEM
ABOUT JOHN THE BAPTIST. (VV. 11–13)

Contrast this with the interchange between John the Baptist and
religious leaders recorded in the gospel of John:

NOW THIS WAS JOHN'S TESTIMONY WHEN THE JEWS OF
JERUSALEM SENT PRIESTS AND LEVITES TO ASK HIM WHO HE
WAS. HE DID NOT FAIL TO CONFESS, BUT CONFESSED FREELY,
"I AM NOT THE CHRIST."

THEY ASKED HIM, "THEN WHO ARE YOU? ARE YOU
ELIJAH?"

HE SAID, "I AM NOT."

"ARE YOU THE PROPHET?"

HE ANSWERED, "NO."

FINALLY THEY SAID, "WHO ARE YOU? GIVE US AN ANSWER
TO TAKE BACK TO THOSE WHO SENT US. WHAT DO YOU SAY
ABOUT YOURSELF?"

JOHN REPLIED IN THE WORDS OF ISAIAH THE PROPHET, "I
AM THE VOICE OF ONE CALLING IN THE DESERT, 'MAKE
STRAIGHT THE WAY FOR THE LORD.'" (1:19–23)

Was he Elijah, or wasn't he? Jesus seemed to think so, but John
didn't. Given the choice, I'd put my money on Jesus. This may be a
case where John the Baptist's answer was affected by the fact that he
was not omniscient and was, frankly, wrong. Jesus said John was
Elijah; John said he wasn't.

At one point, Jesus said of John, "Among those born of women
there has not risen anyone greater than John the Baptist" (Matt.
11:11). Yet he was not infallible. Remember, it was John who had
enough doubts about who Jesus was that he sent messengers to

him after John's arrest to ask, "Are you the one who was to come, or should we expect someone else?" (Matt. 11:3).

This was the same John who publicly declared of Jesus, "Look, the Lamb of God, who takes away the sin of the world!" (John 1:29). Yet his experience in the wretched Roman prison apparently was enough to undermine his confidence and cloud his vision a bit.

Think of the evidence that John had about Jesus' identity:

- John's own miraculous birth (as recorded in Luke 1:5-25) involved an angel appearing to his father and announcing his birth even though his mother was barren and "they were both well along in years" (Luke 1:7). John undoubtedly heard this story many, many times as he was growing up.
- The fact that, as cousins, Jesus and John certainly interacted with each other countless times through their early years. This would have given John plenty of opportunities to observe Jesus' character and sinless life.
- God the Father's testimony in both word and physical manifestation at Jesus' baptism:

  > AS SOON AS JESUS WAS BAPTIZED, HE WENT UP OUT OF THE WATER. AT THAT MOMENT HEAVEN WAS OPENED, AND HE SAW THE SPIRIT OF GOD DESCENDING LIKE A DOVE AND LIGHTING ON HIM. AND A VOICE FROM HEAVEN SAID, "THIS IS MY SON, WHOM I LOVE; WITH HIM I AM WELL PLEASED." (MATT. 3:16-17)

  Luke adds that the Spirit descended "in bodily form" (see 3:22), visible to all.
- The fact that John had heard stories about Jesus' miraculous deeds.

After all this unbelievable evidence, John still wasn't sure that Jesus was really the Messiah! That's incredible. But it reinforces the fact that, despite his stature in Jesus' eyes, John was still human and, therefore, capable of error. So when John denies being Elijah, he could be wrong. And if John was rattled enough to seek confirmation from Jesus that he really was the Messiah, is it possible that John could have been mistaken about his own identity? I think so.

We have a somewhat tongue-in-cheek saying in our family that something can be "encouraging in a perverse way." What makes it encouraging is the realization that we are not alone in our struggles. What makes it perverse is that our "encouragement" comes from someone else's misfortune, failures, or difficulties. John's struggle in prison meets the criterion of being "encouraging in a perverse way." The fact that someone as great as he was had his doubts comforts me in my own feeble faith.

Principle 9 teaches that just because it's there, it doesn't guarantee it's right. I doubt that many would advocate that we, like John did from jail, question whether Jesus is really the Promised One.

Dr. Robert Stein proposes an alternative resolution of Jesus' and John's apparent disagreement over John's identity that doesn't require John to be wrong. His explanation hinges on the concept of what it means to "be" Elijah. Stein suggests that we recognize that John correctly denied being the prophet Elijah physically returned from heaven in bodily form, even though Jesus recognized John's Elijah-like role in preparing the way for the Messiah.[20] F. F. Bruce adds that even the angel Gabriel's prediction to John the Baptist's father that John would go before the Lord "in the spirit and power of Elijah" (see Luke 1:17) falls short of stating that John would actually be Elijah physically reincarnated. Instead, John would be the one to fulfill the Old Testament prophecy about Elijah paving the way for the Messiah. Regarding John the Baptist's denial in the gospel of John, Bruce comments, "In any case, John was wise to leave it to others to make such claims on his behalf."[21]

Which explanation is better? Was John wrong, or did he and Jesus just differ in their definitions of what it meant to "be" Elijah? If John was wrong, it's a good example of a highly righteous man demonstrating his fallibility. In any case, both explanations are reasonable, so the requirement of Principle 2 (settle for one reasonable explanation) is fulfilled regardless of which way you go. Delete this one from the Ultimate Master List. (For other examples in the Bible where lead characters messed up in their thinking, go to www.cook ministries.com/GreatQuestion and read appendix entry 8.3.)

R ECAP

The following is a summary of the five principles, along with examples from this chapter, about recognition of the author's purpose:

5. *Consider the writer's unique purpose.* Each author presents his material the way he does in order to support his themes.
    - Differences between Matthew's and Luke's genealogies of Jesus
    - The order of Jesus' temptations
6. *Remember that biblical writers didn't share our obsession with time.* They lived in a very different world, and we shouldn't criticize them because their Gospels don't conform to twenty-first-century expectations of how chronologies should be presented.
    - The cursing of the fig tree
    - The time of crucifixion (see online appendix 8.1)
7. *Don't listen to "nothing."* Arguments from silence are very weak.
    - Jesus' alleged failure to assert his messianic role during his trial
    - Whether Luke was the only gospel writer who knew about the widow of Nain story
    - Whether Jesus carried his cross or Simon of Cyrene did (see online appendix 8.2)

8. *Recognize that timeless treasures and limited lessons are not the same thing.* Sometimes we mistakenly interpret a teaching or event as being universally applicable when it may not be.

- If we should we minister only to Jewish people
- The requirements for salvation

9. *The fact that it's there doesn't guarantee it's right.* Even God's heroes can sometimes be wrong about things they said or did.

- Whether or not John the Baptist was really Elijah

For other examples of mess-ups by characters in the Bible, see online appendix 8.3.

PRINCIPLES 10 – 14:
DEALING WITH
DISCREPANCIES IN
DETAILS

Three of the best summers of my life took place between my freshman and senior years of college. I spent them as a camp counselor at Dorothy B. Flint Nassau County 4-H Camp in beautiful eastern Long Island. The setting was incredible and the people were tops. Two or three times each summer the counselors would go all out and develop a full-day themed event that preempted the normal routine of swimming, athletics, woodland activities, and science classes. All-day events are *really* tough to pull off. To develop enough activities to keep 125 grade school boys engaged for eight or ten hours is enough to cause gastrointestinal problems for even the most seasoned of counselors.

Somehow one summer, a junior counselor named Bernie Schwartz—a high school student—managed to convince the rest of us to let him spearhead an all-day program. I can't remember why we allowed such an obvious lapse in judgment. Bernie was a bright but scatterbrained kid whose behavior occasionally rose to the level of the campers'. Since Bernie was fascinated with outer space and the prospect of life on other planets, we found ourselves anticipating an "Alien Invasion Day."

The other counselors grew increasingly alarmed as "A. I. Day" approached and Bernie seemed blissfully detached from anything remotely resembling planning. In fact, two nights before A. I. Day, the only things Bernie had managed to complete were four or five exquisitely drawn 8 1/2 x 11–inch posters (he was also an artist) to hang up in the dining hall "to get the kids psyched about the day." No activities planned. No counselors enlisted to run various segments of the day. No delegation of any functions. Zippo.

Although the posters added a glitzy dimension to the day, they were merely tinsel-like additions that would be meaningless without the foundation of decent programming. We all knew Bernie was in trouble; the campers, like ravenous piranhas, would strip the flesh from his bones by 9:15 a.m. To the credit of the staff, we recognized his peril and stepped in at the last minute to organize a day of activities that ultimately came off rather well.

Bernie's problem was that, despite his level of intelligence, he focused on a few details and missed the larger picture. For Bernie, the details overshadowed the basics. Details like the neat posters for A. I. Day are important, but they are not the whole story.

When it comes to reading the Gospels, details are similarly important. In fact, one of the reasons I love the Gospels so much is that parallel versions of the same story provide fascinating, complementary details that offer 3-D insights into Jesus' life and ministry.

Bible skeptics also focus on details. However, their motivation is often to search for inconsistencies and problems. Like Bernie, they can so fixate on relatively minor issues, blowing alleged mistakes all out of proportion, that they miss the big picture of Jesus' deity and what his ministry was all about. This chapter provides five principles designed to help navigate problematic details.

By the way, Bernie Schwartz went on to earn a PhD in meteorology, and I understand that he has developed a national reputation as an expert in his field, even to the point of being featured on CNN and the History Channel. Go figure.

The next five principles teach us how to avoid letting apparent problems with details filter out the big picture.

10. Remember That Details Are Just Details, Not the Whole Story

Small differences in details don't necessarily constitute a contradiction.

Article 13 of *The Chicago Statement on Biblical Inerrancy* states in part:

> WE ... DENY THAT INERRANCY IS NEGATED BY BIBLICAL PHE-
> NOMENA SUCH AS A LACK OF MODERN TECHNICAL PRECISION,
> IRREGULARITIES OF GRAMMAR OR SPELLING, OBSERVATIONAL
> DESCRIPTIONS OF NATURE, THE REPORTING OF FALSEHOODS,
> THE USE OF HYPERBOLE AND ROUND NUMBERS, THE TOPICAL
> ARRANGEMENT OF MATERIAL, VARIANT SELECTIONS OF MATE-
> RIAL IN PARALLEL ACCOUNTS, OR THE USE OF FREE
> CITATIONS.[1]

These issues represent inconsequential variations that can coexist with the concept of inerrancy. I would add to this list some other minor variations in details, such as where events took place, who said what, apparently conflicting numbers, and the like.

Precisely Right but Fundamentally Wrong

Our church men's group meets every other Saturday morning at 7:00 a.m. A few weeks ago, one of guys started the session with a prayer that went something like this: "Lord, thank you for all the men who come out to our group every week." Did you catch that? I said we meet every *other* week, and this guy thanked God for the guys who come *every* week. Guess what? No one jumped up and shouted, "Hold it! That's wrong. No one comes *every* week. You made a mistake."

The typical Bible critic would leap all over this discrepancy and cast doubt on the accuracy of the prayer, perhaps going so far as questioning whether the one who prayed actually attends the men's group since he obviously doesn't even know how often it meets. Technically, the skeptics would be correct in noting the inaccuracy of the prayer. No men come every week because we don't meet every week, but many come every time we *do* meet, so the sentiment is exactly right, and the "error" is strictly one of technicality.

Critics who view the New Testament through eyes of unbelief tend to pounce on every opportunity to make it look bad. Ian Wilson, whom I would classify as a "semi-skeptic," takes to task some of his more cynical brethren who seem to go beyond an even-handed and fair-minded approach that allows for small variations in details. Wilson observes that, over the last couple of centuries, New Testament criticism has gone beyond reasonableness, "and in some quarters there is a fashion for each new critic to try to outdo his predecessors in casting doubt on the gospels' authenticity."[2] I have to wonder if critics are forgetting that, as a fundamental rule of interpretation, the reader's job is to step into the writer's mind-set. If they were more motivated to do that, they might detect fewer flaws.

Today, every important public event is recorded in excruciating detail, immediately beamed around the world, and posted on the Internet. Not so in Jesus' day. As David O'Brien observes, it is not likely that, for example, a recording secretary sat in the corner of the room as Jesus instituted the Last Supper. Even if there had been one, he or she would have been more intent on recording exact meaning than exact wording. O'Brien comments:

> THAT SOUNDS ODD TO US BECAUSE WE ARE PROGRAMMED TO THINK THAT THE ONLY WAY TO KNOW MEANING IS THROUGH DIRECT QUOTATIONS. BUT MEANING CAN BE EXPRESSED IN A VARIETY OF WAYS. AN ALMOST INFINITE NUMBER OF SENTENCE STRUCTURES, SYNONYMS, AND VARIANT WORDINGS CAN BE USED TO SAY THE SAME THING.[3]

He wonders how we would remember Lincoln's famous

Gettysburg Address if we didn't have a written copy. The famous opening line, "Fourscore and seven years ago our fathers brought forth of this continent ..." could be rendered, "Eighty-seven years ago the first American patriots introduced to North America ..." or "America's founders, eighty-seven years ago, initiated ..." Although some versions are more poetic than others, they all communicate the same information and are equally "accurate" in their presentation of Lincoln's meaning.[4] This principle holds true when we consider variations in Jesus' conversations and sermons in the New Testament.

SERMON ON THE MOUNT OR SERMON ON THE PLAIN?

Let's look at some discrepancies in details from the Gospels and how those of us with less skeptical perspectives might explain them. Matthew relates the famous Sermon on the Mount in chapters 5 through 7 of his gospel. Luke records a similar message in his chapter 6. Because of the overlap between the sermons, some believe that Matthew and Luke report on the same event, while others suggest they are different messages altogether.

If these are, indeed, two different accounts of the same sermon, the apparent discrepancies force Bible advocates to address a two-part question: *When* did Jesus deliver this message, and *where* was he when he gave it? Concerning when, Matthew includes his account immediately after his report of Jesus' teaching, preaching, and healing ministry in Galilee (see 4:23–25). Luke, on the other hand, reports his sermon immediately after the selection of the twelve disciples. Matthew, however, describes the selection of the twelve disciples three chapters *after* the Sermon on the Mount, so the two writers have inverted chronological orders.

Concerning Jesus' location, Matthew introduces his story by stating, "Now when he saw the crowds, he went up on a mountainside and sat down. His disciples came to him, and he began to teach them" (5:1). Luke, on the other hand, states that Jesus went down from the mountain with his disciples "and stood on a level place"

(6:17). So Matthew places Jesus "up on a mountainside," while Luke describes "a level place," leading some to refer to Matthew's version as the "Sermon on the Mount" and Luke's as the "Sermon on the Plain." The variation in locale does appear to be a troubling detail. "See!" cry the skeptics. "Matthew and Luke obviously contradict each other. Was Jesus on a mountain or on a level place?"

Furthermore, some point out that Matthew reports that Jesus "sat down" while Luke states that he "stood on a level place." Was he sitting or standing? Let's deal with this one straightaway. It was customary for teachers in Jesus' day to sit as they delivered their messages. It's entirely possible that Jesus stood among some of his followers and eventually sat down to begin his talk after more people joined the original group. If this is what indeed happened, Matthew is correct in stating that Jesus sat, and Luke is correct in mentioning he stood. Not a big deal.

We already dealt with the question of varying chronologies in Principle 6 and have seen that the writers often arrange their material thematically. Therefore, the discrepancy in chronology probably reflects the authors' respective topical presentations, so there is no fundamental "error" in chronology.

From what type of terrain did Jesus deliver this sermon? Was it a mountain or a level place? Let's think about this. Principle 3 (think outside the box) provides help. Luke's version immediately follows his account of the selection of the Twelve, which he describes as follows: "One of those days Jesus went out to a mountainside to pray, and spent the night praying to God. When morning came, he called his disciples to him and chose twelve of them, whom he also designated apostles" (6:12–13). Matthew reports that Jesus went *up* on a mountainside (5:1), and Luke reports that he "went *down*" with his disciples (6:17). Well, if he went "down," he must have started from "up." It could be that he went up on a mountainside (as Matthew reports) and then came partway down to a level area in the mountains to address the crowd.

Anyone who has ever gone hiking in the mountains knows that mountain ranges have many stretches of level meadows. I have extensively hiked the Rocky Mountains in Colorado, and within those mountains are many lush meadows and flatland areas. If I am standing in one of those meadows, am I up in the mountains? Yes. Am I in a level place? Yes. Does this solve the problem? Yes.

Some scholars have even identified a level piece of ground on a ridge that runs parallel with the Sea of Galilee between Tell-Hum and Et-Tabgha as a location that meets the criteria of both mountainside and level place.[5] Could this be where Jesus delivered the Sermon on the Mount? We don't know for sure, but it certainly could be. If so, it adequately deals with the alleged discrepancy and satisfies Principle 2. It is a reasonable explanation.

Another possible solution is that perhaps Matthew and Luke report on different sermons that had similar elements. Principle 12 presents the possibility that what may appear to be two accounts of the same story may actually be reports of two different events. Both the one-sermon theory and the two-sermon theory are reasonable. If that is the case, we have a second possible explanation for why details of the timing and location vary.

Although we can't say for sure which explanation actually accounts for what happened, Principle 2 doesn't force us to decide. All it requires is that we develop one reasonable explanation, and we have two—more than enough to remove this from the Ultimate Master List of problem passages.

A QUICK LOOK AT FASTING

Let's consider another potential discrepancy, the question of who asked Jesus why he didn't fast. Fairly early on in Jesus' ministry, Matthew threw a dinner party for Jesus and included many "sinners" and tax collectors on his guest list. The Pharisees considered it entirely inappropriate for Jesus to mix with such a crowd. Anyone who was truly "holy" would never mingle with such vermin. They couldn't understand why Jesus and his disciples didn't follow the typical and highly admired practice of skipping meals for God. As is often the case, we have three different versions of a question to Jesus in the Synoptic Gospels:

THEN JOHN'S DISCIPLES CAME AND ASKED HIM, "HOW IS IT THAT WE AND THE PHARISEES FAST, BUT YOUR DISCIPLES DO NOT FAST?" (MATT. 9:14)

NOW JOHN'S DISCIPLES AND THE PHARISEES WERE FASTING. SOME PEOPLE CAME AND ASKED JESUS, "HOW IS IT THAT JOHN'S DISCIPLES AND THE DISCIPLES OF THE PHARISEES ARE FASTING, BUT YOURS ARE NOT?" (MARK 2:18)

BUT THE PHARISEES AND THE TEACHERS OF THE LAW WHO BELONGED TO THEIR SECT COMPLAINED TO HIS DISCIPLES, "WHY DO YOU EAT AND DRINK WITH TAX COLLECTORS AND 'SINNERS'?" ... THEY SAID TO HIM, "JOHN'S DISCIPLES OFTEN FAST AND PRAY, AND SO DO THE DISCIPLES OF THE PHARISEES, BUT YOURS GO ON EATING AND DRINKING." (LUKE 5:30, 33)

Who posed the question about fasting? Matthew reports that it was John the Baptist's disciples. Mark states that it was "some people." Luke indicates that it was the Pharisees and teachers of the law. Who exactly was it? Is this a contradiction?

This is an example of a single-sentence question that may be a summary of a much longer conversation. The question of fasting was obviously important within the contemporary religious climate. Imagine a healthy dinnertime debate. Questions, opinions, and challenges are flying faster than shoppers racing to Thanksgiving Day early bird sales. Perhaps various people have the same question, and it ends up being posed several times by different people. Any report of the mealtime discussion could reasonably summarize a key question and correctly attribute it to any of several different individuals or groups. Matthew's version of the banquet and the conversations is clearly a summary that we can read aloud in less than two minutes. Of course the banquet would have lasted for several hours, so there were undoubtedly many other conversations. It is likely that there was preliminary conversation that led up to this final question.

The Pharisees posed their question to challenge Jesus' status as a religious authority. When John the Baptist's disciples asked the same question, though, it was with more friendly intentions. Perhaps they were truly puzzled by Jesus' lack of fasting. There may also have been other bystanders, neither Pharisees nor John's followers, who joined in. "Yes, Jesus. We have the same question. Why is it that you don't fast?" The banquet proceedings may even have stopped as everyone waited to hear Jesus' response.

The difference in detail among the three accounts of who asked the question is not important. The point is that several groups were at the dinner, and they presented to Jesus questions about fasting. According to Principle 2, all I need is a single feasible explanation of what happened, and we have one. It explains how the fasting question could have come from John's disciples (according to Matthew), from "some people" (in Mark's version), and from the Pharisees and teachers of the law (as reported by Luke). (For a discussion of other alleged discrepancies concerning how many blind men Jesus healed on one occasion and where they were healed, and regarding how Judas died, go to www.cookministries.com/GreatQuestion and read appendix entry 9.1.)

11. STUDY THE DETAILS FOR CLUES

Critics who employ various skeptical filters are sometimes so committed to their positions that they miss details that contradict their pet theories. We've already seen three instances where skeptics, in attempts to advance their theories, have misread or overlooked details of the biblical text.

- In the chapter on the Filter of Atheism (chapter 4), I pointed out that Bertrand Russell misquoted Matthew 16:28, making Jesus appear to say that some people who heard him speak on a particular day would not die until the Son of Man came into his kingdom. What Jesus really said was that some of his hearers wouldn't die until they *saw* the Son of Man *coming* in his kingdom. This might seem to be a minor difference, but the implications are huge. Russell's rendering allows him to declare that the Jesus of the Gospels was flat-out wrong since he didn't physically ascend any kind of throne during the lifetime of his listeners. Flip back to chapter 4 to review the argument. Suffice it to say that a careful study of the details exposes Russell's error.

- In the Case of the Fickle Crowd the people who hailed Jesus as Son of David on Palm Sunday seemed to turn against him dramatically just four days later. Careful observation reveals that the triumphal entry took place as Jesus approached Jerusalem, while the angry mob scene took place inside the city. Given that millions of people typically gather in Jerusalem during the Passover, it is reasonable to suggest that two different crowds were involved.

- We also saw under Principle 4 how Professor Randel Helms attempts to undercut the Bible's trustworthiness with his theory that Luke's story of Jesus raising the widow of Nain's son from the dead was consciously patterned after a vaguely similar Old Testament story that involved the prophet Elijah. A quick flyover of the story reveals some similarities between the stories. But once again, a closer study of the details undermines Helms' theory.

(For a discussion of how one scholar suggests that at least one of

Jesus' alleged miracles was nothing more than a literalization of one
of Jesus' parables, go to www.cookministries.com/GreatQuestion
and read appendix entry 9.2.)

12. KEEP IN MIND THAT SIMILAR DOES NOT MEAN THE SAME

Jesus' ministry lasted three years. Some of the supposed discrepancies may be the result of different events that share similar elements.
The most-reported miracle in the Gospels is the feeding of thousands
of people. The feeding of the five thousand is the only miracle (other
than Jesus' resurrection) reported by all four evangelists. Beyond the
feeding of the five thousand, Matthew and Mark also report a separate event of the feeding of four thousand. This means that there are
six different accounts of Jesus' miraculous feeding of thousands of
people. The records of both stories specify that the numbers reflect
men only, meaning that the women and children present could easily have brought the total to twelve to fifteen thousand.

Some skeptics suggest that the feedings of the five thousand and
the four thousand are variations of a single incident. Critic C. Milo
Connick suggests that Jesus' disciples react in Mark's gospel to the
second miracle involving the four thousand as if they were totally
unaware of the previous feeding. "Where in this remote place can
anyone get enough bread to feed them?" they asked (Mark 8:4).
According to Connick, their apparent lack of knowledge of the previous incident supports the theory that there was really only one free
lunch, not two. If Jesus had already fed five thousand men, why
didn't the disciples seem to remember?[6]

What about this allegation? Was this really a single event that
somehow morphed over the years and became two independent stories? There are three ways this could have happened. First, if the
Gospels were written years and years after the events, no one who
recalled the circumstances of the single miracle would have been

alive to blow the whistle on the faulty reporting. The greater the gap between the event and the writing, the more plausible this theory becomes. This helps explain why skeptics like to date the Gospels as late as possible.

There is considerable evidence to support the belief shared by hundreds of New Testament scholars that the Gospels were composed within a few decades of Jesus' death. If the Gospels were, indeed, written while eyewitnesses were still alive and the split was fabricated, it's likely that at least some of the many thousands of participants would have exposed the inaccuracy.

The New Testament itself appeals to this "eyewitness logic" concerning Jesus' bodily resurrection. In 1 Corinthians 15, Paul refers to "more than five hundred" eyewitnesses who saw the resurrected Christ "most of whom are still living" (v. 6). Paul says that if someone doubted his account, he or she could easily track down one of the five hundred to see if he was telling the truth. Many Bible scholars—among them, the editors of The NIV Study Bible[7]— believe Mark and 1 Corinthians may have been written at roughly the same time. If this dating is accurate, many of the twelve to fifteen thousand participants at the feeding incident would also have been alive to set the record straight. I am unaware of even the faintest hint from biblical history that any members of the crowds Jesus fed later disputed that there were two separate feedings.

The second way this "one became two" theory could make sense would be if the critics assume that neither Matthew nor Mark realized that they were telling the same story twice. But that doesn't make sense. When Mark recorded the feeding of the four thousand in chapter 8 he certainly remembered that he had just recounted a similar story two chapters earlier! He and Matthew obviously believed them to be separate events; otherwise, they would not have written them both. The skeptics seem to imply condescendingly that the first-century writers weren't bright enough to recognize that they were repeating themselves.

A third explanation would be that the writers intentionally "multiplied the miracle" to exaggerate Jesus' powers. But that theory questions the integrity of the writers, something that Bible advocates reject. If the second feeding was fictitious but presented as historical fact, what other alleged "facts" were also fabrications? Of course, this is the slant taken by many adherents of the Quest for the Historical Jesus and is the product of antisupernaturalist filters.

All this speculation is unnecessary. The significant differences in details between the two stories support the writers' integrity in treating these as separate incidents.

	Feeding of the five thousand (Mark 6 and Matthew 14)	Feeding of the four thousand (Mark 8 and Matthew 15)
Where the feeding took place	The shore of the Sea of Galilee (i.e., Jewish territory)[8]	The Decapolis region, a largely Gentile area east of the Jordan River[9]
How long the crowd was with Jesus	Less than a day (Matt. 14:13–15)	Three days (Matt. 15:32)
Who brought up the topic of the crowd's hunger	The disciples (Mark 6:35–36)	Jesus (Mark 8:2–3)
The initial amount of food	Five loaves and two fish (Matt. 14:17)	Seven loaves and "a few" small fish (Matt. 15:34)
How much food was left over	Twelve baskets (Mark 6:43)	Seven baskets (Mark 8:8)

Despite certain skeptics' claims that these stories evolved from a single incident, there is no compelling reason to treat these as contradictory accounts of a single event. The only similarities between the two versions—the five thousand and the four thousand—are that Jesus miraculously fed thousands of people from a few loaves and fish and that there were leftovers. Many other details differ considerably between the stories.

Another problem with treating these as corruptions of a single story is the fact that Jesus himself later references two separate feedings in a conversation with his disciples:

> "DON'T YOU REMEMBER? WHEN I BROKE THE FIVE LOAVES FOR THE FIVE THOUSAND, HOW MANY BASKETFULS OF PIECES DID YOU PICK UP?"
>
> "TWELVE," THEY REPLIED.
>
> "AND WHEN I BROKE THE SEVEN LOAVES FOR THE FOUR THOUSAND, HOW MANY BASKETFULS OF PIECES DID YOU PICK UP?"
>
> THEY ANSWERED, "SEVEN." (MARK 8:18–20)

In order for the skeptics' theory to hold up, these verses would have to be the result of either creative editing or a fabricated tradition.[10]

What about Connick's charge that the disciples act as if they didn't know anything about first miracle recorded in Mark 6 when they get to chapter 8? Does this observation prove that they were unaware of the previous incident because it never happened? There are many instances in the Gospels where characters seem to have forgotten even the simplest facts and lessons. Consider Peter. He spent nearly three years walking with Jesus every day; saw him perform countless miracles; walked on the water with Jesus (Matt. 14:22–33); declared him to be the Christ, the Son of the living God (Matt. 16:16); witnessed Jesus' transfiguration (Matt. 17:1–8); and swore that he would be willing to go to his own death to support Jesus (Matt. 26:33). Yet, after Jesus' arrest, he denied three times even knowing him (Matt. 26:69–75). How can that be? Wasn't Peter taking notes?

Recall as well that, even though Jesus preached numerous times about humility, James and John approached Jesus right before the triumphal entry into Jerusalem to request special seats of honor in Jesus' kingdom (Mark 10:37). How could they so totally miss Jesus' message?

And what about us? How many times do we learn the hard way a lesson about gossip, conflict, and repentance, only to forget the lesson so soon?

The fact that the disciples didn't realize, "Maybe he could multiply the bread again," isn't altogether surprising and probably reflects more of a spiritual lapse than poor short-term memory. Despite their ongoing interaction with Jesus, they still lacked the faith to recognize his ability to do the miraculous.

This explanation for the disciples' alleged lack of familiarity with the previous feeding meets the threshold of Principle 2 that says one reasonable explanation is enough. But there is another possible solution as well. Commentator William Lane suggests that when the disciples approach Jesus about the lack of fast food for the second crowd, it is only after Jesus himself brought up the fact that many in the crowd had been with him for three days and had no food. The disciples respond, "But where in this remote place can anyone get enough bread to feed them?" (Mark 8:4). According to Lane, their question amounts to a request for Jesus to clarify how he would meet their needs. "It would have been presumptuous for the disciples to have assumed that Jesus would, as a matter of course, multiply a few loaves as he had done on an earlier occasion."[11] In other words, they knew he could do it but, out of respect, waited for him to bring it up. This is a perfectly reasonable explanation. Let's cross this item off the Ultimate Master List of verses that disproves the Bible.

(For an additional example of a popular skeptic's theory, concerning when Jesus threw the money changers out of the temple, go to www.cookministries.com/GreatQuestion and read appendix entry 9.3.)

WHAT ABOUT THE PARABLES?

Just as similar stories can actually record different events, so can similar-sounding parables actually record different teachings. Jesus may have presented similar but separate parables and other sayings multiple times and in different settings. Skeptics, of course, assume the worst and treat them as contradictions.

(For a discussion of one skeptic's theory that two clearly different parables evolved from a single story, go to www.cookministries.com/GreatQuestion and read appendix entry 9.4.)

AM I REPEATING MYSELF?

Under Principle 10, I raised the possibility that the Sermon on the Mount (in Matt. 5—7) and the so-called Sermon on the Plain (in Luke 6) might be two versions of a sermon Jesus delivered on different days. People on the speaking circuit often give pretty much the same talk to different crowds, despite minor "tweaks" tailored for a particular audience. The fact that Jesus may have preached fairly similar messages on subsequent days is neither shocking nor blasphemous. If he did recycle some of his material, why would it surprise us that wording and details vary a bit from one delivery to the next? If I give essentially the same talk several times, it evolves and improves, based on audience reaction and feedback. I might toss in a line that ends up getting a laugh, so it shows up again the next time. Another attempt at humor falls flat, so out it goes.

During my senior year of college, I student-taught five different sections of eleventh-grade English. Although I covered the same material with each group, transcripts of the five classes would reveal differences. I always felt the second class got the best deal. The first time through the material, I stumbled through my explanations of gerunds and participles. Based on either student questions or the nonverbal feedback of blank stares, by the time I went through the material a second time, my explanations were crisper. On the third pass, the challenge was pretty much over, and by fifth period, I was so sick of the material that I usually wished I could have played a video of second period and gone out for some coffee. I taught the same material. Each presentation was similar. But they were not identical.

Since Jesus spent three years ministering to people, we can

assume that he probably performed similar miracles and made similar points to different people in different settings. Actually, I'd be surprised if he did not.

13. Recognize That Discrepancies Can Be Good

As strange as it may seem, the fact that some details in various stories don't quite "add up" actually strengthens the argument for the reliability of the Bible.

Most biblical scholars believe that there was some sharing of documents among the synoptic writers. At a minimum, Matthew and Luke were probably familiar with Mark's gospel and may even have borrowed from it as they wrote their own accounts. When it comes to the gospel of John, it appears that he was familiar with all three Synoptics since he omits several prominent stories, such as Jesus' birth, the temptations in the desert, and the institution of the Last Supper. He apparently did so because he assumed his readers were already familiar with these events reported in the Synoptics. Since we can assume some cross-familiarity among the Gospels, what do we do with details that seem to conflict? Didn't the authors know that twenty-first-century skeptics would notice these problems?

Reliability does not require exact agreement. Lifelong member of Marietta First Presbyterian Church and former United States Court of Appeals judge Samuel Sibley used to say that if two witnesses showed up in his courtroom with exactly the same story, he would suspect collusion. Agreement that is perfect is suspicious.

A Gold Mine for Critics

Next to the observed difficulties with the two versions of Jesus' genealogy, skeptics may have devoted more ink to the accounts of Jesus' resurrection than to any other problem of inconsistency in the

Gospels. Countless writers have observed the differences in the number of Jesus' appearances reported by each writer: how many women went to the empty tomb, how many angels appeared, and who got to the tomb when. Their conclusion? The accounts are impossible to reconcile.

It is beyond the scope of this book to provide a detailed harmonization of the gospel resurrection accounts, but many such efforts exist.[12] Each provides credible timelines and harmonized reconstructions that provide enough explanation to meet the criterion of one reasonable solution (Principle 2).

For example, Kaiser suggests that it is possible to resolve the conflicts if we think in terms of different "scenes" that took place in and around Jesus' tomb. First, Mary Magdalene and some other women visit to find the stone guarding the tomb has been removed, and they see angelic visitors. They run to tell the disciples and meet Jesus on the way. Next, Peter and John investigate the empty tomb. Then the guards report to the chief priests, who bribe them. Then two disciples see Jesus on the Emmaus road.[13] These are the broad strokes. Kaiser and company not only harmonize various details, but also point out that we must read the accounts in light of the individual writers' perspectives and theological objectives.

MATTHEW WANTS TO UNDERLINE THE MIRACULOUS AND ALSO EXPLAIN A RUMOR THAT THE BODY OF JESUS WAS STOLEN. LUKE STRESSES THE FULFILLMENT OF THE WORDS OF JESUS AND YET THE DISBELIEF OF THE APOSTLES. JOHN, BY FOCUSING ON A SINGLE CHARACTER AND HER INTIMATE DISCUSSION WITH JESUS, POINTS OUT THAT IN THE RESURRECTION AND ASCENSION OF JESUS THE PROMISES OF JOHN 13—16 ARE FULFILLED. JESUS CANNOT BE HELD, FOR IT IS BETTER FOR HIM TO GO TO THE ONE WHO IS NOT ONLY HIS FATHER BUT IS NOW ALSO OUR FATHER.[14]

Kaiser and the others actually utilize my Principle 5—consider the writer's unique purpose—to show how the writers' objectives influence their selection of material.

Another point to consider is that Jesus' resurrection is central to the Christian faith. As the apostle Paul later wrote, "If Christ has not been raised, our preaching is useless and so is your faith. More than that, we are then found to be false witnesses about God, for we have testified about God that he raised Christ from the dead" (1 Cor. 15:14–15). The disciples surely recognized the controversial nature of the claim that Jesus returned from the dead. They had to have known that the resurrection accounts would undergo intense scrutiny.

Although we don't know for sure whether Matthew, Mark, Luke, or John had their comrades' texts in front of them as they wrote, it's likely that they were each familiar with the others' writings. For example, we know from Luke's introduction to his gospel that he carefully researched Jesus' life: "I myself have carefully investigated everything from the beginning" (1:3). If his gospel was one of the later ones to be written, which most scholars agree is the case, he certainly would have known about other resurrection accounts. The fact that such a meticulous historian recorded his story the way he did indicates that, rather than his recording discrepancies, he saw his account as consistent with the others. Differences between his accounts and the earlier ones were intentional on Luke's part and aligned with his purposes.

John's gospel supports the same point. He didn't attempt to harmonize his account with the others, which indicates his integrity as a writer. He honestly presented the details as he saw them, even if he suspected that doing so might help create a cottage industry for professional skeptics a couple of thousand years later. Despite John's probable familiarity with the Synoptics, and Matthew's and Luke's presumed acquaintance with Mark, there is little effort among the various authors to minimize differences among their accounts. Even though the first-century Middle Eastern mind-set certainly doesn't match the modern obsession with chronology and precision in details, it is unlikely that the gospel writers would have overlooked outright contradictions. Their obvious lack of collusion supports the trustworthiness of their stories.

TROUBLE WITH THE TRIALS

Another area that receives a high level of criticism is the record of Jesus' trial before the Jewish council. The example of the resurrection is a case where there appear to be discrepancies among the Gospels themselves. This one looks at what appear to be contradictions between the Gospels and external information about Jewish legal practice. C. Milo Connick identifies as many as fourteen violations of Jewish judicial procedure in Jesus' trial before Caiaphas. These include the facts that

- it was conducted at night;

- it took place during a religious festival;

- because of the rushed nature of the trial, it probably took place without a full quorum;

- there were no defense witnesses;

- the condemnation and execution occurred on the same day; and

- the penalty of death didn't fit the "crime" of blasphemy.[15]

Connick also reports that some scholars consider the entire Jewish trial to be a fabrication.[16] They base this charge on the irregularities above as well as the observations listed below. How does the Bible advocate overcome such objections? Consider the following problems along with their solutions in italics:

- No mention of Jesus' Jewish trial was made during his trial before Pilate. *But this is an argument from silence—a violation of Principle 7.*

- The false witnesses from the Jewish trial "were conspicuous by their absence." *Once again, an argument from silence.*

- Instead of going to Pilate with a charge of blasphemy, the religious leaders accuse Jesus of sedition. *This is a particularly weak charge and is an example of Principle 4, critics who inappropriately frame the challenge to prove their points. John's version of the trial before Pilate includes the admission by the Jewish leaders that they have no right to execute anyone (18:31). But Pilate, as enforcer of Roman rule, did. Because Pilate couldn't care less about Jewish religious controversies, the religious officials had to come up with something that would motivate him—Jesus' claim to be a king. Hence the charge of sedition.*

- The penalty was Roman execution by crucifixion instead of the Jewish practice of stoning. *Of course the Romans crucified him. It was their trial, and that's how they executed people.*

- There was no mention in John's account of the trial by the Jewish court, only the examination by Annas and Caiaphas, the priests. *This is yet another example of arguing from silence.*[17]

Let's get back to the question of irregularities in the Jewish trial. If Luke (as a Gentile who would not have been entirely familiar with Jewish customs) was the only synoptic writer to record the irregularities, there might be a bit more merit in the charge that he, in his ignorance, invented details that violated the religious rules. However, Matthew (as a Jew writing for Jews) and Mark (as a Jew writing primarily to Romans) also include many of these alleged problems. Certainly, Matthew knew better than to make up elements that his Jewish readers would instantly recognize as illegal, and Mark as a Jew himself would not have invented details that contradicted his faith background. Perhaps these "errors" were recorded because that's exactly what happened. Has the world never witnessed a trial conducted illegally? I think that is a better explanation than to suggest that two experts in Jewish customs would perpetuate wrong information, especially since one of them was writing to his fellow countrymen.

14. BLAME MY AGENT

A number of so-called problems evaporate when we recognize the principle of agency, where one person acts on behalf of another. The Synoptics include several stories where this principle is in play.

Perhaps the best example of this is the story of the healing of the Roman centurion's servant, which both Matthew and Luke record. Here are the two versions with the passage from Matthew first:

WHEN JESUS HAD ENTERED CAPERNAUM, A CENTURION CAME TO HIM, ASKING FOR HELP. "LORD," HE SAID, "MY SERVANT LIES AT HOME PARALYZED AND IN TERRIBLE SUFFERING."

JESUS SAID TO HIM, "I WILL GO AND HEAL HIM."

THE CENTURION REPLIED, "LORD, I DO NOT DESERVE TO HAVE YOU COME UNDER MY ROOF. BUT JUST SAY THE WORD, AND MY SERVANT WILL BE HEALED. FOR I MYSELF AM A MAN UNDER AUTHORITY, WITH SOLDIERS UNDER ME. I TELL THIS ONE, 'GO,' AND HE GOES; AND THAT ONE, 'COME,' AND HE COMES. I SAY TO MY SERVANT, 'DO THIS,' AND HE DOES IT."

WHEN JESUS HEARD THIS, HE WAS ASTONISHED AND SAID TO THOSE FOLLOWING HIM, "I TELL YOU THE TRUTH, I HAVE NOT FOUND ANYONE IN ISRAEL WITH SUCH GREAT FAITH. I SAY TO YOU THAT MANY WILL COME FROM THE EAST AND THE WEST, AND WILL TAKE THEIR PLACES AT THE FEAST WITH ABRAHAM, ISAAC AND JACOB IN THE KINGDOM OF HEAVEN. BUT THE SUBJECTS OF THE KINGDOM WILL BE THROWN OUTSIDE, INTO THE DARKNESS, WHERE THERE WILL BE WEEPING AND GNASHING OF TEETH."

THEN JESUS SAID TO THE CENTURION, "GO! IT WILL BE
DONE JUST AS YOU BELIEVED IT WOULD." AND HIS SERVANT
WAS HEALED AT THAT VERY HOUR. (8:5–13)

WHEN JESUS HAD FINISHED SAYING ALL THIS IN THE HEARING
OF THE PEOPLE, HE ENTERED CAPERNAUM. THERE A CENTU-
RION'S SERVANT, WHOM HIS MASTER VALUED HIGHLY, WAS
SICK AND ABOUT TO DIE. THE CENTURION HEARD OF JESUS
AND SENT SOME ELDERS OF THE JEWS TO HIM, ASKING HIM TO
COME AND HEAL HIS SERVANT. WHEN THEY CAME TO JESUS,
THEY PLEADED EARNESTLY WITH HIM, "THIS MAN DESERVES TO
HAVE YOU DO THIS, BECAUSE HE LOVES OUR NATION AND HAS
BUILT OUR SYNAGOGUE." SO JESUS WENT WITH THEM.

HE WAS NOT FAR FROM THE HOUSE WHEN THE CENTURION
SENT FRIENDS TO SAY TO HIM: "LORD, DON'T TROUBLE YOUR-
SELF, FOR I DO NOT DESERVE TO HAVE YOU COME UNDER MY
ROOF. THAT IS WHY I DID NOT EVEN CONSIDER MYSELF WOR-
THY TO COME TO YOU. BUT SAY THE WORD, AND MY SERVANT
WILL BE HEALED. FOR I MYSELF AM A MAN UNDER AUTHORITY,
WITH SOLDIERS UNDER ME. I TELL THIS ONE, 'GO,' AND HE
GOES; AND THAT ONE, 'COME,' AND HE COMES. I SAY TO MY
SERVANT, 'DO THIS,' AND HE DOES IT."

WHEN JESUS HEARD THIS, HE WAS AMAZED AT HIM, AND
TURNING TO THE CROWD FOLLOWING HIM, HE SAID, "I TELL
YOU, I HAVE NOT FOUND SUCH GREAT FAITH EVEN IN ISRAEL."
THEN THE MEN WHO HAD BEEN SENT RETURNED TO THE
HOUSE AND FOUND THE SERVANT WELL. (LUKE 7:1–10)

According to Matthew, the centurion himself came and made the
request, but Luke indicates that it was Jewish elders and the centurion's friends who actually came and did the speaking. This is easy
to explain once we recognize that the Jewish leaders and the friends
spoke on behalf of the centurion. Kaiser points out that in the

Middle Eastern culture of the day, to send an intermediary to request a favor was quite common.[18] The intermediary would serve three purposes: to avoid putting the person who is being petitioned on the spot, to minimize the embarrassment to the petitioner if the request was not granted, and to serve as someone likely to engender a positive result.

But Matthew states that the centurion made the request. Doesn't this mean that Matthew was wrong? Not at all. Almost all countries send diplomats to other countries to "speak" for their leaders. When the United States ambassador to Italy delivers a message from the president, it is as if the president himself were speaking, even though the words are coming from the ambassador's mouth.

The centurion well understood the concepts of authority and agency. He had men under him who were required to carry out his wishes and who could speak in his name. In this sense, they were an extension of the centurion and were, in fact, acting as his representatives. He knew that Jesus could do the same. When the centurion sent the Jewish leaders and his friends to Jesus, it was as if he himself were there.

This concept of agency helps explain other alleged discrepancies as well. Right before the triumphal entry into Jerusalem, James and John approached Jesus to request choice seats at Jesus' right and left hands when he came into his kingdom (Mark 10:35–37). The parallel account in Matthew (20:20–21), though, reports that it was actually James' and John's mother who made the request. Mark's version skips over the "ambassador" role their mother played. This resolves the problem of the discrepancy.

THE BLESSING IS IN THE DETAILS

This chapter has focused on reconciling differing details in parallel accounts. Rather than being wary of details as sources of potential problems, we should recognize that they actually add richness and insights. They reinforce the fact that each author honestly tells the story of Jesus from his own perspective and in accordance with his own objectives. As my good friend Rick Satterthwaite suggests, we should recast the well-worn adage that the devil is in the details to see that it is really the blessing that is in the details. Sometimes we gain wonderful insights as we wrestle through the challenge of "cracking" puzzling details.

For example, in the stories of the feeding of the five thousand and the feeding of the four thousand, we notice that the first story took place in Israel and resulted in twelve baskets of leftovers, while the second was in largely Gentile territory and yielded seven baskets. Jesus conducted this miracle of multiplication for two different audiences. The first group was almost exclusively Jewish, and the second would have been a mixed crowd of both Jewish and non-Jewish people. He may have repeated this miracle to show that God's blessings would be available to both the nation of Israel and also the "mixed" population of the church (of both Jewish and Gentile backgrounds).

Leon Morris observes that the feeding of the five thousand resulted in twelve baskets left over, one for each of the twelve disciples,[19] which is probably a reminder of God's ability to provide for them. Twelve, of course, is also the number of Israel's tribes, perhaps suggesting Jesus' ultimate adequacy for and fulfillment of God's promises to Israel over the generations. Some also see significance in the seven baskets left over from the second miracle. In the Bible, seven is often associated with perfection or completeness,[20] and the fact that there were seven baskets remaining might suggest that God's blessing is intended for all humanity, not just the Jews.

So rather than filter details through skeptical lenses to find cause to dismiss the Gospels, we should look to details in order to supplement our understanding of Jesus' life and ministry.

RECAP

In this chapter, we discussed five principles that help navigate problems with details:

10. *Remember that details are just details, not the whole story.* Small differences in detail don't necessarily constitute a contradiction.

- Whether the Sermon on the Mount and the Sermon on the Plain were the same message
- Who asked Jesus about fasting
- How many blind men Jesus healed and whether they were healed while Jesus was entering or leaving Jericho (see online appendix 9.1)
- How Judas died (see online appendix 9.1)

11. *Study the details for clues.* Skeptics sometimes overlook details that don't support their theories.

- Bertrand Russell's contention that Jesus believed he would literally "come into his kingdom" during the lifetime of his hearers
- The Case of the Fickle Crowd in Jerusalem
- Randel Helms' contention that Luke patterned his story of the raising the widow of Nain's son after a similar Old Testament story
- Bishop John Shelby Spong's theory that the writer of John's gospel turned Jesus' parable of the rich man and Lazarus into a literal resurrection (see online appendix 9.2)

12. *Keep in mind that similar does not mean the same.* Jesus' ministry lasted about three years, and sometimes what appears to be the same story or parable recorded differently by different writers may actually be records of two different events.

- How many miraculous feedings there were
- When Jesus expelled the money changers from the temple (see online appendix 9.3)

- Whether Luke's parable of the great feast and Matthew's parable of the marriage feast were different versions of the same story (see online appendix 9.4)

13. *Recognize that discrepancies can be good.* The fact that all details do not completely line up shows the writers didn't consciously collude to make their stories correlate perfectly.
    - Jesus' resurrection accounts
    - Jesus' Jewish trial

14. *Blame my agent.* Many stories record conversations as delivered by one character when in reality there may have been an intermediary who was authorized to speak for him.
    - Who really asked Jesus to heal the Roman centurion's servant
    - Who asked for James and John to get special seats in the kingdom

PRINCIPLES 15–18: INTERPRETING THE TEXT RESPONSIBLY

To return to the "teaching someone how to fish" metaphor, how is the fishing so far? In addition to making an attempt to clear up some well-known problem passages, I have sought to provide solid principles you can use to "feed yourself." You may already have read parts of the Gospels that at first perplexed you, but which became clearer as you utilized these principles. I hope so. The application of them to new situations is an art. The more you practice it, the better you will get.

So far we have looked at principles that deal with our perspective, with the writers' and speakers' purposes, and with handling details that, at first blush, don't seem to add up. This final chapter presents principles that will help in interpretation of the Bible. There is a whole field of study called *hermeneutics*, which forms a core element of seminary education. Both popular- and seminary-level hermeneutics texts describe various principles of interpretation for any kind of literature. Among the concepts under consideration are the type of literature (narratives, poetry, prophecy, proverbs), context (historical, cultural, logical), principles of grammar (verb forms, noun forms, tenses, prepositions, clauses), figures of speech (analogies, similes, metaphors, irony, euphemism), and other aspects of language.

In this last set of principles, I will address a few specialized problem areas that sometimes contribute to confusion over biblical interpretation and will point out how literary, linguistic, and cultural confusion can create distorted filters.

15. RECOGNIZE THE DIFFERENCE BETWEEN A PARADOX AND A CONTRADICTION

Although the Bible teaches many paradoxical principles, it does not contradict itself. Do you remember Philip Yancey's whales and how we would have very little to "talk" about with them? If the gap between people and whales is so great, imagine how much more significant is the one between God and us. Consequently, when Jesus tries to communicate truth about God and his dealings with us, we will never fully comprehend it all. Paradoxes, by definition, are situations with *apparently* contradictory elements but which ultimately fit together without contradiction. The Bible is full of many such paradoxes. Consider the following:

- God is all-loving and all-just at the same time.
- Jesus was simultaneously fully God and fully man.
- God is one, yet he is three persons: Father, Son, and Holy Spirit.
- People have the ability to choose or reject God, yet God predestines those he will save.

Each pair contains apparently contradictory elements, yet both parts are true. We are unable to reconcile completely the conflicting elements. But I'm not sure I would want to worship a God I could fully understand. Would he be worthy of my worship if my finite mind could grasp everything about him? As we saw in the chapter on the Filter of Selective Christian Theology, Thomas Jefferson searched for a gospel "whose witness he could respect and whose message he could understand."[1]

There are many things in life that we can't explain. One of the few useful tidbits I recall from my college physical chemistry class is the fact that scientists have developed two different descriptions of the nature of light. One is that light is composed of waves. The other is that light is made up of packets of energy that behave like particles. Light exhibits characteristics that are consistent with both theories. The only problem is that these two views seem mutually exclusive. How can light be made up of both waves and packets of energy? Yet it apparently is.

Does the fact that I can't explain this conflict mean that I refuse to use the headlights on my car until someone reconciles this scientific anomaly? I don't think so. Skeptics often camp on paradoxes in the Bible, turning them into contradictions and showcasing them as examples of how the Christian faith isn't trustworthy. They then walk away from a strongly Bible-focused faith.

Let's look at some paradoxical aspects of Jesus' life and teaching. Most of these "paradox pairs" are from the gospel of Matthew. The existence of apparent contradictions in the same gospel could lead some to adopt a relatively low view of Matthew's intelligence. After all, couldn't he at least detect the logical inconsistencies in events he so naively reports?

TEACHING PARADOXES

Some of Jesus' statements are inherently paradoxical, such as,

WHOEVER FINDS HIS LIFE WILL LOSE IT, AND WHOEVER LOSES HIS LIFE FOR MY SAKE WILL FIND IT. (MATT. 10:39)

I TELL YOU, IT IS EASIER FOR A CAMEL TO GO THROUGH THE EYE OF A NEEDLE THAN FOR A RICH MAN TO ENTER THE KINGDOM OF GOD.... WITH MAN THIS IS IMPOSSIBLE, BUT WITH GOD ALL THINGS ARE POSSIBLE. (MATT. 19:24, 26)

MANY WHO ARE FIRST WILL BE LAST, AND MANY WHO ARE LAST WILL BE FIRST. (MATT. 19:30)

How can these pronouncements make sense? Fortunately, most readers recognize them for what they are—statements that teach truths that, at first, seem self-contradictory, but that call attention to a higher truth by the use of contrast.

Some of Jesus' statements, spoken in different contexts, seem to create inconsistencies. In the Sermon on the Mount, for example, Jesus teaches, "If someone strikes you on the right cheek, turn to him the other also" (Matt. 5:39), yet his instructions to his twelve disciples as he sends them out on their ministry trip include the surprising statement "Do not suppose that I have come to bring peace to the earth. I did not come to bring peace, but a sword" (Matt. 10:34). How can Jesus, the Prince of Peace who just five chapters earlier teaches disciples to turn the other cheek, later declare that he came to bring a sword? Is there a way that both teachings make sense together?

It helps to read further in the Matthew 10 passage to see how Jesus elaborated on his sword statement. He states that he came to turn

- a man against his father,
- a daughter against her mother,
- a daughter-in-law against her mother-in-law—
- a man's enemies will be the members of his own household. (vv. 35–36)

He says that loyalty to Jesus and his message must transcend even family allegiance. The sword is actually a metaphor for the division within families that a radical commitment to Jesus sometimes fosters. This in no way contradicts the admonition to turn the other cheek.

"Do What I Say, Not What I Do"

Critics sometimes accuse Jesus of hypocrisy when they compare his words and his deeds. As I explained in the selective Christian theology chapter, Bishop John Shelby Spong takes Jesus to task for a number of behaviors he considers inconsistent with the teachings attributed to

him. Let's briefly consider once again the statements from Spong I
included in that chapter. He was troubled by passages that, in his
mind, portray Jesus of Nazareth as narrow-minded, vindictive, and
even hypocritical. In these passages, Jesus seemed to contradict his
own teachings about how to treat your enemies (he called them
vipers) and family members (he appeared to disown them).[2]

There are only three possibilities concerning Spong's complaint:

- Jesus never said some of the things or did some of the things
  attributed to him, meaning we can't trust the gospel records.
- Jesus really said and did them, and the contrast between the
  two renders Jesus morally impotent.
- Jesus really said and did them and there are ways to reconcile
  the apparent hypocrisy of his deeds compared to his words.

I choose to throw my hat into the ring with countless believers
through the centuries who have been able to handle the paradoxical
aspects of Jesus' life and teaching. It takes especially powerful negative filters to fail to see the internal consistency between Jesus' words
and his actions, even if we can't adequately explain all their nuances.

In the chapter on the Filter of Selective Christian Theology, I
observed that Spong has decided that love is God's primary attribute.
Clearly, as 1 John 4:8 says, "God is love." But he has many other
characteristics, such as omnipotence, holiness, justice, even "jeal-
ousy" for our affections. If you pick one attribute out and
subordinate all others to it, you end up with a distorted picture of
God. To keep God's complex nature in mind will help us avoid
Spong's somewhat simplistic trap.

THEOLOGICAL CONTRADICTION?

Jesus' theology (stated or implied) sometimes prompts skeptics
to see contradictions. Further examination, however, reveals that
these teaching are paradoxical, not contradictory. For example, Jesus
warns at the end of the Sermon on the Mount:

NOT EVERYONE WHO SAYS TO ME, "LORD, LORD," WILL ENTER
THE KINGDOM OF HEAVEN, BUT ONLY HE WHO DOES THE WILL
OF MY FATHER WHO IS IN HEAVEN. MANY WILL SAY TO ME ON
THAT DAY, "LORD, LORD, DID WE NOT PROPHESY IN YOUR
NAME, AND IN YOUR NAME DRIVE OUT DEMONS AND PERFORM
MANY MIRACLES?" THEN I WILL TELL THEM PLAINLY, "I NEVER
KNEW YOU. AWAY FROM ME, YOU EVILDOERS!" (MATT.
7:21–23)

This set of instructions makes it sound like we enter heaven based on whether or not we have a relationship with Jesus. What we do doesn't even come up.

Yet in the very same gospel (Matthew), in the parable of the sheep and the goats (25:31–46), which describes the judgment at the end of time, the "goats" are condemned because they failed to feed the hungry, give drink to the thirsty, take in strangers, or clothe the naked. It sure sounds like salvation based on what we do or don't do.

So which is it? Do we get to heaven because we know Jesus, or do we get there based on what we do? Again, we are faced with the same three choices as with the Spong illustration mentioned above:

- Jesus didn't really say both these things. Implication: Matthew, intentionally or unintentionally, included fallacious material.
- He said them, but they are self-contradictory. Implication: Neither Jesus nor Matthew was clever enough to detect the self-contradictory nature of these teachings.
- He said them, and they actually fit together in some way.

The relationship between faith and works that evangelical Christians understand is that salvation is based entirely on Jesus' sacrificial death to pay for our sins. There are no works that anyone can do to earn this standing because it is a free gift. *After* a person receives the pardon that Jesus offers, the most natural way to demonstrate his or her gratitude to God is with a life that reflects well on God by obeying his instructions and ministering to other people. This distinction is by no means trivial. There is a world of difference between someone who performs good deeds to earn God's favor and someone who does those deeds out of gratitude.

This tension between faith and works runs throughout the Bible. Perhaps it is best illustrated by the fact that the very same verse from the book of Genesis (15:6) is used by two different New Testament writers to arrive at seemingly opposite conclusions. That verse says, "Abram believed the LORD, and he credited it to him as righteousness." The apostle Paul quotes this verse in Romans 4:3, specifically noting that Abraham was not justified by his works or by his deeds (Rom. 4:2).

Yet the apostle James includes the same Genesis verse as part of his argument that faith must be verified by good deeds:

> YOU FOOLISH MAN, DO YOU WANT EVIDENCE THAT FAITH WITHOUT DEEDS IS USELESS? WAS NOT OUR ANCESTOR ABRAHAM CONSIDERED RIGHTEOUS FOR WHAT HE DID WHEN HE OFFERED HIS SON ISAAC ON THE ALTAR? YOU SEE THAT HIS FAITH AND HIS ACTIONS WERE WORKING TOGETHER, AND HIS FAITH WAS MADE COMPLETE BY WHAT HE DID. AND THE SCRIPTURE WAS FULFILLED THAT SAYS, "ABRAHAM BELIEVED GOD, AND IT WAS CREDITED TO HIM AS RIGHTEOUSNESS," AND HE WAS CALLED GOD'S FRIEND. YOU SEE THAT A PERSON IS JUSTIFIED BY WHAT HE DOES AND NOT BY FAITH ALONE. (2:20-24)

These examples are relatively easy to reconcile. Paul and James address the question of salvation from different perspectives because they write to different audiences. Paul wants to make sure that his Jewish hearers are not reverting to their Old Testament concept that salvation is achieved by keeping God's law (which, by the way, is impossible to do). Instead, Jesus' ultimate sacrifice to pay for our sins opens the door to a restored position with God. James, on the other hand, addresses a group of Christians who have lowered their definition of faith to the point that some believed it was possible to have a version of faith that made no difference in their lives. This dead faith was worthless to save them even though they called it "faith."

There is no contradiction. Both Paul and James would say that both aspects are necessary. They merely address different sides of the salvation coin. Paul focuses on the theological basis of our salvation—faith in Jesus' death to pay for our sins—and James emphasizes the gratitude that true faith generates and which it expresses in obedience to Jesus Christ.

In the same way, Jesus teaches in Matthew 7 that our deeds are not what bring us into a relationship with God. He teaches in Matthew 25, however, that they are a natural outgrowth of salvation. Those who possess a high view of the Scriptures see how these apparent contradictions in Jesus' teaching actually complement each other. When we encounter seemingly conflicting concepts, our goal should be to look beyond the apparent problem to understand the heart of the message. We must at the same time remember that we are dealing with a God who is infinitely greater than we are, and we can't always reduce his actions to tidy sound bites that we can neatly explain.

16. LOOK FOR LINGUISTIC OR TRANSLATION MIX-UPS

The New Testament was written nearly two thousand years ago in a form of Greek that is no longer spoken. Think how much the English language has changed even in the last four centuries.

A few years ago I saw a magazine ad for framed and mounted pages from an early edition King James Bible that maintained the 1611 language. We ordered two pages, one for home and one for my office. Despite the fact that these pages are written in English, they're amazingly difficult to read. The English language has morphed a lot since the early 1600s. The most noticeable difference is the fact that many of the letters *s* are written to resemble our contemporary letter *f*. So, for example, the title of the book we refer to as 1 Peter reads,

THE FIRFT EPIFTLE GENERALL OF PETER

The little commentary at the beginning of chapter 1 reads in part,

HE BLEFFETH GOD FOR HIS MANIFOLD FPIRITUAL GRACES; FHEWING THAT THE FALUATION IN CHRIFT IS NO NEWES, BUT A THING PROPHEFIED OF OLD.

Obviously, my Microsoft Word spell-checker didn't like this sentence. By the way, in case you couldn't tell, the word "faluation" above is our word "salvation."

We are reading from the same language, and we are only separated by four centuries, yet comprehension of the sentences requires significant work. How much more of a challenge is it to multiply that time span by five *plus* translate from Greek, a language that doesn't even use the Western alphabet, into English?

TO TOUCH OR NOT TO TOUCH

Linguistic confusion is also the culprit in Jesus' apparently contradictory instructions about touching him that he gave to Mary and Doubting Thomas. More than one reader of John's gospel has observed that Jesus seems to contradict himself within ten verses. Early on resurrection Sunday morning, Mary Magdalene went to Jesus' tomb to mourn. When she first saw Jesus, she mistook him for the gardener; but when she realized it was Jesus, she very naturally tried to embrace him out of sheer joy. As translated in the King James Bible, Jesus' response was, "Touch me not; for I am not yet ascended to my Father" (John 20:17). Yet a few verses later, he issues the following invitation to Doubting Thomas (again in the King

James Version): "Reach hither thy finger, and behold my hands; and reach hither thy hand, and thrust it into my side: and be not faithless, but believing" (John 20:27). Why does he tell Mary not to touch him, but invites Thomas to do just that?

As usual, our choices are either that these sayings attributed to Jesus are not accurate, John wasn't bright enough to recognize this apparent contradiction that takes place within the span of a few paragraphs, or there is a reasonable way to reconcile these verses.

In this case, the problem is a poor translation. As beautiful as the King James Version is, it's not always the most accurate, and it certainly is not the most contemporary. The New American Standard Bible, which provides a rather literal, word-for-word rendering, translates Jesus' response to Mary like this: "Stop clinging to Me, for I have not yet ascended to the Father." F. F. Bruce admits that the exact meaning of this verse is a bit unclear, but certainly Jesus is not saying that she shouldn't touch him at all. "The most natural interpretation is that Mary, in her delight at finding her Lord alive, clutches him lest she should lose him again."[3]

Leon Morris suggests that Jesus might also be telling her that there is no need to latch on to him since he'll still be around for a while and she will have other chances to see him.[4] Jesus' instruction to Mary is to stop clinging to him, while his invitation to Thomas is to verify his physical resurrection by touching his wounds. These are very different concepts and not at all contradictory. (For an additional example of the language gap discussing whether Jesus said the "poor" or the "poor in spirit" are blessed, go to www.cookministries.com/GreatQuestion and read appendix entry 10.1.)

INSCRIPTION CONFUSION

Some have alleged that the inscription on Jesus' cross indicates contradictions in the various accounts. The Romans often posted an offender's crime as a warning to other would-be troublemakers. All four gospels record the wording on Jesus' placard, and each is somewhat different:

- Matthew 27:37—"This is Jesus, the King of the Jews"
- Mark 15:26—"The King of the Jews"
- Luke 23:38—"This is the King of the Jews"
- John 19:19—"Jesus of Nazareth, the King of the Jews"

This appears to be an outright contradiction until you read an important detail in John 19:20: the fact that the sign was written in Aramaic, Latin, and Greek.

In recent years, as Spanish has become more pervasive in the United States, we have witnessed an increase in the number of bilingual signs. I find it mildly interesting that even though the English and Spanish versions of the messages usually communicate the same sentiment, the exact wording of the Spanish message, when translated word for word into English, doesn't always exactly match. For example, I recently saw a list of safety precautions posted in three languages (English, Spanish, and Chinese) on New York's Staten Island Ferry. The sign read in part,

- In case of emergency, listen for announcements and instructions from the crew [English—but you knew that].
- En caso de emergencia, escuche los anuncios y siga las instrucciones de la tripulación [Spanish].

A word-for-word translation of the Spanish line is

- In case of emergency, listen to the announcements and *follow* the instructions of the crew [emphasis added].

Notice how the word *follow* crept into the Spanish instructions. Obviously, the sense of the two sets of instructions is the same, but for whatever reason, whoever created the sign chose a slightly different wording for the Spanish. I'm not even going to attempt the Chinese translation.

This phenomenon could very well explain the differences in the inscriptions written in three languages on the cross. Gleason Archer suggests the following resolution:

- Matthew may reflect the Aramaic version, since according to Papias, Matthew's gospel was originally composed in Aramaic.
- Mark and Luke both include the Latin (Mark drops the first two words, "this is").
- John includes the Greek version, which would be consistent with the fact that much of his ministry focused on the Greek-speaking world.[5]

So even though the inscriptions said essentially the same thing, the language instructor for the Roman soldiers may not have given an A grade to the soldier who wrote and translated the sign. (For additional examples of linguistic confusion dealing with what type of structure Jesus was born in and how many animals he rode during his triumphal entry into Jerusalem, go to www.cookministries.com/GreatQuestion and read appendix entries 10.2 and 10.3.)

17. Look for Cultural Confusion

There are few things that broaden our worldviews more than a firsthand exposure to cultures different from our own. Whenever I travel abroad, I am fascinated to see how other cultures handle everyday aspects of life.

One example is the difference in driving protocols. People in the British-influenced world drive on the left-hand side of the road, while drivers in most of the rest of the world use the right side. What was the thinking behind these "cultural decisions"?

I once visited South Africa, where people drive on the left-hand side, and I had the life-threatening experience of crossing a road in downtown Johannesburg. I looked, as I always do, to the left, only to narrowly escape a driver coming from the right. After several similar incidents, I reached the uncomfortable realization that I couldn't even trust my instincts for something as simple as crossing the road. Every time I approached a street, I had to pause and consciously think about which way to look. Experiences like this make interaction with another culture thrilling, if occasionally dangerous.

When you think about it, there are two ways to "experience" a different culture. One is to hop a plane and land somewhere else. The other is to travel back through time, so to speak, by studying a past culture.

What would it have been like to drive from New York to Los Angeles by car in 1930? With no interstate highways, Hampton Inns, or Burger Kings, what would the trip have been like? How long would it have taken? Since tires used to wear out after only a few thousand miles, would I have been able to make the trip on one set? How hard would it have been to find a clean restroom? Come to think of it, how hard is it to find one today?

Believe it or not, I find thoughts of life in past decades fascinating. To step back into another time would provide an experience similar to boarding a plane and landing in a foreign country.

I also find it intriguing that we can witness the progression of history within our own lifetimes. One night as we sat around the dinner table, Annette, who teaches sixth-grade science, related an amusing illustration of this from her class. She often incorporates a "joke" answer on a few of her multiple choice tests to lighten the mood a bit and to give the kids a small break by reducing the number of "legitimate" answer selections, thus increasing the kids' odds of getting the question right.

On the most recent test, she included a question that read, "Scientists have determined that a major factor contributing to lake pollution is the fact that." Among the "real" possibilities, Annette included the following selection: "Workers empty their Thermoses into rivers that feed into the lakes." She was surprised that the kids failed to see the humor in this option until she realized that, in the age of ubiquitous vending machines and Starbucks drive-throughs, many of the sixth graders had never even seen a Thermos and didn't know what they were.

Sometimes we barely recognize the cultural evolution until we pause to think how much change we have personally witnessed. For example, in my own lifetime, I have seen the following items all but disappear from American life:

- Slide rules—done in by calculators
- Phones with rotary dials—replaced by touch-tone phones
- First 78 rpm records, then 45 rpm singles (the ones with the big holes), and then finally 33 1/3 rpm LP vinyl records—each upstaged by emerging music technologies culminating (at least for now) in compact discs and MP3 players
- Car windows with hand cranks—replaced by power windows
- Carbon paper—made obsolete by photocopy machines and personal computers, which allow printing on demand
- Eight-character personal computer file names—which became unnecessary once the Windows operating system took over
- Dot matrix printers—whose original advantage as the economical choice was lost as ink-jet and laser printers kept dropping in price
- Full-service gas stations—which, in most states, lost out to self-service stations as a way to lower gas prices during the Arab oil embargo of the 1970s
- Wooden tennis rackets—upstaged by a host of alternative materials

If you draw a blank on what some of these items are, ask your older siblings or parents. They can tell you what they were.

THE CHALLENGE TO READERS OF THE GOSPELS

If people living in America today are not familiar with what used to be a standard part of our culture just a few years ago, how much more is this true when we reach back to Bible times? If we can lose touch with recent cultural trends, how much more difficult is it to reach across vastly different cultural mind-sets and over dozens of generations to understand some of the stories and sayings in the New Testament? Cross-cultural phenomena often contribute to the impression that things Jesus said contradict other parts of the Bible. For example, in Matthew, Jesus informs his would-be disciples of the cost of following him:

> WHEN JESUS SAW THE CROWD AROUND HIM, HE GAVE ORDERS TO CROSS TO THE OTHER SIDE OF THE LAKE. THEN A TEACHER OF THE LAW CAME TO HIM AND SAID, "TEACHER, I WILL FOLLOW YOU WHEREVER YOU GO."
>
> JESUS REPLIED, "FOXES HAVE HOLES AND BIRDS OF THE AIR HAVE NESTS, BUT THE SON OF MAN HAS NO PLACE TO LAY HIS HEAD."
>
> ANOTHER DISCIPLE SAID TO HIM, "LORD, FIRST LET ME GO AND BURY MY FATHER."
>
> BUT JESUS TOLD HIM, "FOLLOW ME, AND LET THE DEAD BURY THEIR OWN DEAD." (8:18–22)

Doesn't this sound harsh? Jesus seems to tell the man that he can't even go to his own father's funeral. How is that consistent with the fifth commandment to honor one's father and mother?

Two different insights into the cultural background of this episode may help to explain Jesus' apparent insensitivity to normal family relationships. First, when the prospective disciple asked to be excused until his father was buried, the older man may have still been alive. If this was the case, the son was asking for an excused absence for an indeterminate period of time to take care of his elderly father. This was akin to saying that someday, when his circumstances changed, he would get serious about being a disciple.[6] Jesus' response echoes what he says in Luke 14:26: "If anyone comes to me and does not hate his father and mother, his wife and children, his brothers and sisters—yes, even his own life—he cannot be my disciple." The meanings are similar in both passages: Even our most fundamental human obligations are to take a backseat to our radical commitment to Jesus.

The second possible explanation has to do with a cultural tendency in Jesus' day to request burying a father as an excuse to avoid an obligation. This is like today's joke about the employee who must have seven grandmothers because he keeps asking for time off to go to her funeral. In her little book *Strange Scriptures That Perplex the Western Mind,* Barbara M. Bowen observes,

THE PALESTINIAN UNDERSTANDS THIS AS BEING NOTHING IN THE WORLD BUT AN EXCUSE, AND AN EXCEEDINGLY COMMON ONE IN THAT COUNTRY. NO DOUBT THE FATHER WAS PERFECTLY WELL AND STRONG, BUT THE SON DID NOT WANT TO FOLLOW CHRIST....

IF YOU ASK SOME NATIVES EVEN TODAY TO DO ANYTHING THEY DO NOT WANT TO DO, THEY WILL NOT ANSWER THAT THEY DO NOT FEEL WELL, OR HAVEN'T THE TIME, BUT THEY WILL INSTANTLY SAY TO YOU, "NO, I CANNOT, MY FATHER IS DEAD."[7]

Either insight makes Jesus' response seem less uncaring or contradictory to his teaching about honoring our parents. (For an additional example of cultural misunderstandings caused by differing social customs regarding greetings, go to www.cookministries.com/ GreatQuestion and read appendix entry 10.4.)

A LESSON IN CONSTRUCTION TECHNIQUES

Cultural confusion also comes into play in one of the healing stories where a crowd was so huge that a paralyzed man's friends couldn't work their way into the house where Jesus was teaching. They resorted to climbing onto the roof, digging a hole in the roof, and lowering the man right in front of Jesus to be healed. And Jesus did heal him.

Unfortunately, Mark and Luke seem to contradict each other regarding what type of roof the men dug through. Here are the relevant verses from the two gospels:

> SOME MEN CAME, BRINGING TO HIM A PARALYTIC, CARRIED BY FOUR OF THEM. SINCE THEY COULD NOT GET HIM TO JESUS BECAUSE OF THE CROWD, THEY MADE AN OPENING IN THE ROOF ABOVE JESUS AND, AFTER DIGGING THROUGH IT, LOWERED THE MAT THE PARALYZED MAN WAS LYING ON. (MARK 2:3–4)

> SOME MEN CAME CARRYING A PARALYTIC ON A MAT AND TRIED TO TAKE HIM INTO THE HOUSE TO LAY HIM BEFORE JESUS. WHEN THEY COULD NOT FIND A WAY TO DO THIS BECAUSE OF THE CROWD, THEY WENT UP ON THE ROOF AND LOWERED HIM ON HIS MAT THROUGH THE TILES INTO THE MIDDLE OF THE CROWD, RIGHT IN FRONT OF JESUS. (LUKE 5:18–19)

Since houses in ancient Israel did not have tile roofs, skeptics charge Luke with a technical foul. They point out that Jewish roofs employed beams about three feet apart, across which they arranged short sticks covered with thickly matted thorn bushes. They plastered that layer with a coat of mortar and topped it off with earth.[8]

Luke, however, talks about tiles. How could the men lower their friend through the tiles if there were none? Robert Stein suggests that Luke, who wrote for a predominantly Greek audience that would have had little familiarity with Jewish housing codes, translates the situation into terms his readers could understand. Since Greek houses usually had tile roofs, Luke translates the concept of digging through a roof into a cultural equivalent that would be familiar to his readers.[9] So this really is a translation issue, not from one language to another, but from one culture to another.

FROM ROOFS TO FOUNDATIONS

Another case in which Luke translates culture rather than words occurs in Jesus' Sermon on the Mount (Matt. 5—7) and the Sermon on the Plain (Luke 6:17–49). At the end of the sermon, Matthew records Jesus' words:

> THEREFORE EVERYONE WHO HEARS THESE WORDS OF MINE AND PUTS THEM INTO PRACTICE IS LIKE A WISE MAN WHO BUILT HIS HOUSE ON THE ROCK. (7:24)

Luke, on the other hand, records his comments like this:

> HE ... WHO COMES TO ME AND HEARS MY WORDS AND PUTS THEM INTO PRACTICE ... IS LIKE A MAN BUILDING A HOUSE, WHO DUG DOWN DEEP AND LAID THE FOUNDATION ON ROCK. (6:47–48)

Why does Matthew's version describe building on a preexisting rock while Luke's describes the process of digging a hole and laying a foundation? As with the roof tile incident, the answer, according to Paul Copan, lies in different construction techniques in the Jewish and Greek worlds. Greeks customarily dug and laid foundations, while the Jews did not. "Rather than keeping the exact words of Jesus ... Luke captures Jesus' intention ... to communicate architectural stability to his particular audience."[10]

So an understanding of cultural differences can clear up what might otherwise be considered errors. Both of these construction-related challenges should be relegated to the "deleted items" of the Ultimate Master List file.

18. GIVE THE BIBLE THE BENEFIT OF THE DOUBT

In chapter 1, I used the example of meeting my friend Phil for lunch. You may recall my willingness to give him the benefit of the doubt for his tardiness, based on my prior positive history with him. Since he had shown his reliability over the years, I was willing to give him a break if he stood me up.

This is also how we should approach the Gospels and, indeed, the entire Bible. I have, over the years, come across dozens of issues in the biblical text that at first seem to create credibility problems for the Bible. Upon further research, however, they prove to have reasonable explanations. I have learned that, just like my friend Phil, the Bible has proved itself over and over to be reliable. Now, when I come across something that may be difficult to understand, I suspend judgment until I can further investigate the problem. In the small number of cases where I cannot fully explain the apparent contradiction, because so much of the Bible has proved to be rock solid, I am able to live with the ambiguity.

I suspect that many theologians who would label themselves theologically liberal often espouse a worldview that is "open" to various cultures and traditions. Certainly, my very liberal Unitarian upbringing stressed inclusiveness and respect for various worldviews, faith traditions, and sacred writings. Yet, ironically, many of these same theologians who urge openness and respect for holy books of other religions sometimes fail to afford the same courtesy to the Bible. Can it be that their filters create a more gracious attitude toward Hindu and Muslim writings than for the Bible?

RECAP

The following are principles we considered in chapter 10:

15. *Recognize the difference between a paradox and a contradiction.*
    - Various paradoxes in Jesus' sayings
    - Alleged contradictions between Jesus' words and his actions
    - The road to salvation

16. *Look for linguistic or translation mix-ups.*
    - To touch or not to touch
    - What did the inscription on Jesus' cross really say?
    - "Poor" vs. "poor in spirit" (see online appendix 10.1)
    - Whether Jesus was born in a house or a stable (see online appendix 10.2)
    - If Jesus somehow rode on both a donkey and a colt at the same time (see online appendix 10.3)

17. *Look for cultural confusion.*
    - What Jesus meant about the dead burying their own dead
    - Whether Jesus wants us to greet other people (see online appendix 10.4)
    - If Mark and Luke contradict each other about the roof some people dug through to help their friend get healed
    - Whether Matthew and Luke contradict each other about Jesus' instructions about building on a rock

18. *Give the Bible the benefit of the doubt.* Trust the Bible in the same way that you would trust a friend who has proved his reliability over the years.

So there you have them: Pearson's Principles for Approaching Puzzling, Perplexing, and Problematic Passages. I hope they have provided some perspectives on how to handle passages that don't necessarily make sense on the surface. These principles may not solve every intellectual problem, but I can say that having applied them over the years has helped me resolve many challenges to the Gospels.

Before we close the door on this book, I want to provide an example of how *not* to approach the biblical texts. Keep reading.

FORTY-FIRST-CENTURY HUNGARIAN SCHOLARS

As I mentioned in the introduction, all four of my grandparents were either born or raised in Hungary. My Hungarian relatives had some some great names: Ilona Balazs (my mom's given name on her birth certificate), Bela Danko (an uncle's name), and Zolton Varjassy (my all-time favorite Hungarian moniker, which belonged to another uncle). My kids got a real kick out of learning that I had an uncle Zolton. They thought he must have been some kind of futuristic comic book superhero.

Although my family had mastered the culture of Greater Budapest, their sense of popular American ways was a bit lacking. When I got to high school, my grandmother kept trying to get me to the Grape Festival at Liberty Hall so I could meet a "nice Hungarian girl." The Grape Festival may not have had the hottest girls in town, but when it came to accordion music, it was unsurpassed.

FAST FORWARD

The year is AD 4000. Hungary has become one of the major intellectual centers in the world. It so happens that the future Hungarian

Institute of Technology (HIT) has a small department that specializes in the study of ancient (i.e., late twentieth century) American culture.

After weeks of careful sifting through debris found in the famous Great Lakes Sinkhole, archaeologists from Budapest have unearthed documents containing transcripts of several conversations that one of their ancestors—that would be me—had with various people concerning a summer vacation his family took in 1993. There is great hope among these experts that finally an answer can be found to a question plaguing the department: Why did this ancient culture spend so much time writing essays titled "What I Did on My Summer Vacation," and why was the grammar uniformly terrible in those essays?

THE PEARSONS' 1993 SUMMER VACATION

Before we review the transcripts, let me go over with you what we actually did in that rather unremarkable week. Please contact the author if you would like copies of the videos.

MONDAY

I went to work.

We ate a quick dinner at home.

Packed the van.

Drove from Grand Rapids to Adrian, to Annette's parents' (Ron and Helene) house.

Picked up doughnuts on the way.

TUESDAY

Slept in till about 9:00 a.m.

Ate doughnuts from yesterday.

Went to two wood mills to try to get cherry top made for small kitchen cabinet.

Attended Lenawae County Fair.

Got rained out about 5:00 p.m.

Had dinner at El Gordo Mexican restaurant in Adrian.

WEDNESDAY

Went swimming (kids only).

Went to downtown Adrian for a drill bit.

Used drill bit on kids' play structure parts that I brought with me.

Annette made fancy dinner.

THURSDAY

Went swimming (kids and all adults).

Annette and I drove to Ann Arbor, Michigan—remember, we used to live there.

Stopped at shopping mall in Ann Arbor.

Ate at one of our favorite fancy restaurants, the Moveable Feast.

FRIDAY

We all went out for breakfast at a local café.

Went back to mill to pick up tabletop. It wasn't ready.

Went swimming.

Helped father-in-law assemble his new walk-in greenhouse—the in-law good deed of the trip.

SATURDAY

Went swimming.

Went back to mill. This time, tabletop was ready.

Used father-in-law's table saw to cut boards for play structure.

Patched flashing around the in-laws' house's chimney and roof seams—tried to get head start on good deed for next trip.

Went out for ice cream after dinner.

SUNDAY

Attended church.

Went swimming.
Ate Sunday dinner.
Packed up.
Drove back to Grand Rapids.

Despite the dull and boring account, we had a great week. Now, let's look at the mysterious documents recently unearthed by the Hungarian researchers. They record my conversations with various people describing our week off.

ELEVATOR TALK

Elevator talk, like elevator music, is lighter than lite. During those uplifting seconds between the first floor and the tenth floor "dings," this is about all I would be able to say.

YUP, I WAS OUT LAST WEEK. VACATION. WE VISITED MY WIFE'S FAMILY IN ADRIAN. IT WAS GREAT! WE REALLY DIDN'T DO MUCH OF ANYTHING. SEE YA!

LETTER TO MY MOM

Mom, of course, wants details about each day.

WE LEFT FOR VACATION ON MONDAY AND POPPED THE KIDS' FAVORITE TAPE IN TO THE CASSETTE PLAYER ON THE WAY DOWN IN THE CAR. THEY WERE REALLY EXCITED ABOUT GOING TO THE LENAWAE COUNTY FAIR ON TUESDAY. UNFORTUNATELY, IT STARTED TO POUR ABOUT 5:00 P.M., SO WE RACED OVER TO A RESTAURANT AND ATE SOME MEDIOCRE MEXICAN FOOD. WE ALL WENT TO BED PRETTY EARLY THAT NIGHT.

FOR THE REST OF THE WEEK, WE WENT SWIMMING EVERY DAY. ACTUALLY, ANNETTE AND I DIDN'T SWIM ON WEDNESDAY, SINCE THE RAIN MADE THE WATER PRETTY COLD.

ON THURSDAY, ANNETTE AND I DROVE UP TO ANN ARBOR AND GOT TO EAT OUT AT THE MOVEABLE FEAST IN ANN ARBOR.

I ALSO HELPED RON ON HIS GREENHOUSE. THEY ALSO
NEEDED THE FLASHING AROUND THEIR CHIMNEY RE-TARRED.
THE KIDS GOT A KICK OUT OF WATCHING ME CRAWL ALONG
THE EDGE OF THE ROOF THIRTY FEET OFF THE GROUND AS IF
MY LIFE DEPENDED ON IT. COME TO THINK OF IT, IT DID!

WE HAD A TERRIFIC FAMILY DINNER AFTER CHURCH ON
SUNDAY AND THEN WENT HOME. IT WAS NONSTOP ACTION,
BUT WE HAD A GREAT TIME!

BREAKFAST BUDDIES

This is how I might describe the week to the guys I meet with for
breakfast every week.

WE HAD A GREAT TIME ON VACATION LAST WEEK. ACTUALLY, I
WORKED ON MONDAY, AND THEN WE LOADED UP THE VAN
AFTER DINNER AND DROVE DOWN TO ADRIAN. WE DID A LOT
OF FAMILY THINGS. WE WENT TO THE LENAWAE COUNTY FAIR
AND WENT SWIMMING EVERY DAY. OH, AND I BROUGHT STUFF
FOR THE KIDS' PLAY STRUCTURE PROJECT WITH ME SO I
COULD USE SOME OF MY FATHER-IN-LAW'S TOOLS. IT SEEMS
LIKE WE WERE RUNNING THE WHOLE TIME. I THINK I NEED A
VACATION FROM OUR VACATION!

GYM BUDDIES

If you've ever belonged to a gym or a health club and you have
developed some friendships, you recognize the dynamic of down-
playing your physical condition in some kind of false modesty
drama. This is the version those guys might hear.

I CAN'T BELIEVE HOW FAT I FEEL! WE WENT TO MY IN-LAWS'
HOUSE AND DID NOTHING BUT EAT ALL WEEK. ANNETTE AND I
DROVE UP TO ANN ARBOR AND ATE AT ONE OF OUR FAVORITE
FANCY RESTAURANTS: NOT EXACTLY LOW-FAT FARE. ONE NIGHT,
ANNETTE COOKED A GREAT GOURMET MEAL FOR THE WHOLE

FAMILY. AND THEN THERE WAS THE PIG-OUT AT EL GORDO MEXICAN RESTAURANT. THE FOOD MAY NOT HAVE BEEN VERY GOOD, BUT THEY SURE KNEW HOW TO INJECT GREASE INTO THEIR CHIPS. PLUS ANNETTE'S FOLKS TOOK US TO BREAKFAST ONE DAY. AND WE ALSO MANAGED TO SQUEEZE IN ICE CREAM AND DOUGHNUTS! I GUESS I'LL HAVE TO BE ON THE BIKE FOR THREE DAYS STRAIGHT TO MAKE UP FOR ALL THAT FOOD.

FIX-UP BUDDY

Finally, here's what I might tell to a friend who is into home repair and fix-up projects.

YEAH, LAST WEEK AT MY IN-LAWS WAS PRETTY COOL. I BROUGHT THE LUMBER FOR MY KIDS' PLAY STRUCTURE PROJECT SO I COULD USE MY FATHER-IN-LAW'S DRILL PRESS. ALSO, WE HAVE THIS CABINET THAT WE'RE REDOING, AND WE DECIDED TO SEE IF WE COULD GET A CHERRY-WOOD TOP MADE FOR IT. I KNEW THERE WERE TWO WOOD MILLS DOWN THERE, SO WE TRAIPSED AROUND TRYING TO SEE IF ONE OF THEM COULD HANDLE THIS FOR US.

ANNETTE AND I ALSO GOT TO HELP MY IN-LAWS ASSEMBLE THEIR 6-FOOT x 18-FOOT GREENHOUSE. IT'S A GREAT STRUCTURE! PLUS, THEY NEEDED SOME HELP RE-TARRING THE FLASHING AROUND THEIR CHIMNEY, SO I SPENT A HALF HOUR DANGLING ABOUT THIRTY-FIVE FEET OFF THE GROUND.

A HUNGARIAN PUZZLE

As the Hungarian scholars try to make sense of the various vacation accounts, they have quite a challenge on their hands. In order to correctly understand what the Pearson family did on our vacation those many years ago, they have to overcome two significant barriers. The first is language, which involves a shift from twenty-first-century English to forty-first-century Hungarian. Even to go from twenty-first-century English to forty-first-century English would be a challenge. Add to that going from one language to a totally unrelated one, and you'll have an idea about the difficulty of the task.

The other challenge is the cultural gap. Despite a few similarities, Hungarian culture and American culture are different. There was little resemblance between mainstream American culture and what I experienced at the Grape Festivals at Liberty Hall during my high school years. We can reasonably assume each culture has continued to evolve in its own unique way between the twenty-first and forty-first centuries. If they started out somewhat different, how far apart did they continue to drift?

So between the linguistic and the cultural gaps, the challenge to the Hungarian scholars parallels that of twenty-first-century non-Greek and non-Hebrew readers of the Bible.

CONTRADICTIONS GALORE

Let's assume that the future Hungarians approach the recently discovered manuscripts with the same mind-set of many of today's Bible critics. The following is an account of what their commentary might look like.

THESE VARIOUS ACCOUNTS ALLEGEDLY DESCRIBE A SINGLE VACATION BY THE PEARSON FAMILY ABOUT TWO THOUSAND YEARS AGO. HOWEVER, NOTING THE MANY CONTRADICTIONS IN THE ACCOUNTS, SOME SCHOLARS QUESTION THE ACCURACY OF THESE STORIES. THERE APPEAR TO BE IRRECONCILABLE CONFLICTS REGARDING THE NUMBER AND TYPE OF ACTIVITIES THE PEARSONS SUPPOSEDLY DID ON THEIR VACATION. IN THE BRIEF SUMMARY ATTRIBUTED TO A CONVERSATION IN AN ELEVATOR, PEARSON INDICATED THAT HE DIDN'T DO ANYTHING. YET THE "LETTER TO MOM" ACCOUNT MENTIONS NONSTOP ACTIVITY AND THE "GYM BUDDIES" TRADITION LISTS NOTHING BUT

EATING. DID THEY DO NOTHING? WAS IT A NONSTOP WEEK? DID THEY RESTRICT THEIR ACTIVITIES TO EATING ONLY? MOST SCHOLARS HAVE CONCLUDED THAT IT IS IMPOSSIBLE TO REC-ONCILE THESE THREE ACCOUNTS. SPECIFICALLY, THE "GYM BUDDIES" AND THE "FIX-UP BUDDY" VERSIONS BEAR ALMOST NO RESEMBLANCE TO EACH OTHER.

SOME SUGGEST THAT THERE WERE ACTUALLY TWO SEPARATE VACATIONS THAT, OVER TIME, WERE COMBINED INTO A SINGLE EVENT. SOME CRITICS HAVE SUGGESTED THAT, TAKEN TOGETHER, THESE VARIOUS ACCOUNTS PRESENT A RATHER STYLIZED AND IDYLLIC VIEW OF FAMILY LIFE DURING THIS PERIOD. THEY SHOW A FAMILY ENJOYING LEISURE ACTIVITIES TOGETHER, FELLOWSHIPPING OVER MANY GOOD MEALS, INVOLVED IN INDUSTRIOUS CONSTRUCTION PROJECTS DESIGNED TO CREATE AN ENJOYABLE ENVIRONMENT FOR THE FAMILY, AND EVEN PARTICIPATING IN DEVOTIONAL ACTIVITY. IT IS EASY TO VIEW THESE ACCOUNTS AS AN APOLOGETIC FOR WHAT WAS CALLED "TRADITIONAL FAMILY LIFE" LATE IN TWENTIETH-CENTURY AMERICAN CULTURE.

THAT THESE ACCOUNTS ACTUALLY RECORD EVENTS FROM MULTIPLE VACATIONS IS EVIDENT FROM THE FACT THAT THE DURATION OF THE VACATION TRIPS VARIES FROM VERSION TO VERSION. IN SOME (THE "ELEVATOR TALK," THE "GYM BUDDIES" ACCOUNT, AND THE "FIX-UP BUDDY" STORY) THE VACATION IS DESCRIBED AS LASTING A WEEK, WHEREAS THE "LETTER TO MOM" VERSION RECOUNTS A SHORTER TRIP. WHICH WAS IT?

ANOTHER PROBLEMATIC ASPECT OF THESE ACCOUNTS CON-CERNS THE TYPE OF VEHICLE PEARSON HAD. HE CALLED IT A "CAR" IN THE LETTER TO HIS MOTHER BUT TOLD HIS BREAKFAST BUDDIES THAT HE HAD A "VAN." ARCHAEOLOGISTS HAVE DETER-MINED THAT VANS WERE FOUR-WHEELED VEHICLES SOMEWHAT LARGER THAN CONVENTIONAL CARS AND WERE OFTEN USED TO

TRANSPORT CARGO. ESPECIALLY IN THEIR EARLIEST FORM, THEY WERE RATHER STARK AND NOT PARTICULARLY SUITED TO CONVEYING PEOPLE. MANY WERE USED BY A CLASS OF WORKERS CALLED "REPAIRMEN," WHO WOULD TRANSPORT TOOLS TO PEOPLE'S HOMES TO REPAIR SUCH THINGS AS THE WATER SUPPLY TO THEIR HOMES OR DEVICES TO ASSIST IN DAILY LIVING THAT WERE CONTROLLED BY SOMETHING CALLED "ELECTRICITY."

THIS ARCHAEOLOGICAL INSIGHT CASTS SOME DOUBT ON THE ACCURACY OF THE SO-CALLED "BREAKFAST BUDDIES" CONVERSATION. WHY WOULD PEARSON CARRY HIS FAMILY IN AN UNCOMFORTABLE COMMERCIAL VEHICLE? MANY VANS HAD SEATING FOR ONLY TWO RIDERS, SO IT IS HARD TO SEE HOW AN ENTIRE FAMILY COULD HAVE TRAVELED IN SUCH A MOTORIZED VEHICLE. THIS PROBLEMATIC OBSERVATION MAY INDICATE THAT THE "BREAKFAST BUDDIES" ACCOUNT WAS WRITTEN AS LATE AS THE 2060S, LONG AFTER VANS STOPPED BEING USED AND THE RECOLLECTION OF THEIR TYPICAL PURPOSE WAS FORGOTTEN.

ADDITIONAL DIFFERENCES IN INDIVIDUAL ACCOUNTS ARE NOTEWORTHY. NOTE THAT THE "LETTER TO MOM" STORY INDICATES THAT PEARSON WAS THIRTY FEET ABOVE THE GROUND WHILE RE-TARRING THE CHIMNEY, AND THE "FIX-UP BUDDY" VERSION DESCRIBES IT AS THIRTY-FIVE FEET. WHICH WAS IT? THIS CONTRADICTION SUPPORTS THE HYPOTHESIS THAT THESE TWO ACCOUNTS GREW UP INDEPENDENTLY AND WERE SUBSEQUENTLY MERGED. HOWEVER, WHOEVER EDITED THE DOCUMENTS APPARENTLY FAILED TO NOTICE OR WASN'T CONCERNED ABOUT THE CONFLICTING NUMBERS.

ALSO, IF ONE READS THE "GYM BUDDIES" ACCOUNT CAREFULLY, ONE DETECTS A PATTERN IN THE FOOD DESCRIPTIONS. IT APPEARS THAT EACH MEAL DESCRIBED IS SUCCESSIVELY LESS EXPENSIVE. THE ACCOUNT PROGRESSES FROM AN EXPENSIVE MEAL IN A FANCY RESTAURANT, TO A RATHER ELABORATE

HOME-COOKED MEAL (WHICH WOULD UNDOUBTEDLY HAVE
BEEN LESS COSTLY THAN A RESTAURANT-PURCHASED MEAL),
TO INCREASINGLY CHEAPER MEALS EATEN IN RESTAURANTS.
PERHAPS THIS DOWNWARD PROGRESSION POINTS TO A MONEY
MANAGEMENT PROBLEM ON THE PART OF THE FATHER. HIS
POOR MANAGEMENT OF THE VACATION BUDGET CULMINATES
(IN THE "GYM BUDDIES" VERSION) WITH THE FAMILY BEING
REDUCED TO EATING NOTHING BUT ICE CREAM AND DOUGH-
NUTS. MODERN HISTORIANS HAVE BEEN UNABLE TO
UNDERSTAND THE ROLE THAT THESE FOODS PLAYED IN THE
DIETS OF AMERICANS DURING THE LATE TWENTIETH CENTURY,
BUT THEY SEEM TO HAVE BEEN ITEMS CONSUMED PRIMARILY
FOR NUTRITIONAL SUSTENANCE. ICE CREAM CONSISTED
MOSTLY OF DAIRY PROTEIN, AND DOUGHNUTS PROVIDED CAR-
BOHYDRATES NECESSARY FOR A BALANCED DIET.

You get the idea. This description reflects the type of analysis to
which skeptics often subject the Bible, and it violates several of the
principles I presented in part 2: failure to consider the writer's purpose, demanding precise chronology, refusal to allow for small
differences in details, ignoring linguistic and cultural differences,
and unwillingness to give the text the benefit of the doubt.

Are these explanations any more ludicrous than a suggestion
Luke was so inspired by reading about the Old Testament prophet
Elijah's miracle of raising a widow's son that he fabricated a similar
event to tap into that literary stream? Come to think of it, the
Hungarians' analysis is mild compared to some of the crazy theories
that many of today's biblical scholars have proposed.

The four gospels clearly tell four versions of Christ's life from
four perspectives by four authors. We must take into account that
reality in a manner similar to the way we would harmonize the various versions of my 1993 weeklong vacation. Anyone can twist and
debunk varying accounts by filtering them.

W R A P - U P

So where have we been?

The introduction reviewed some of the "image" problems of Christianity that stem from various high-profile lapses. We discussed how skeptics view anyone who takes the Bible seriously as a bit shy on the brain-power scale. I also revealed that in high school I rejected any notion that the Bible was inspired or reliable. My stereotypes found reinforcement as I attended churches that appealed to my academic snobbery. I had virtually no sense of my own personal spiritual need. It never dawned on me that the Christian faith might offer some answers for life's biggest questions.

Part 1 examined five filters commonly used by those outside the historic Christian faith to view the Bible and Jesus. Two of them add to the Bible, and three of them subtract from the Bible.

- The Filter of New Revelation
- The Filter of Outlandish Speculation
- The Filter of Atheism
- The Filter of Antisupernaturalism
- The Filter of Selective Christian Theology

Part 2 offered Pearson's Principles for Approaching Puzzling, Perplexing, and Problematic Passages: eighteen principles that help to reconcile apparently irreconcilable contradictions in parallel versions of the same story. They are as follows:

Approaching the Material with the Right Perspective

1. *Pray for insight.* Ask God to guide your study and help you understand the truth.
2. *Settle for one reasonable explanation.* All it takes is one reasonable explanation to remove a passage from the Ultimate Master List of verses that disprove the Bible.
3. *Think outside the box.* Perhaps you can think of a credible explanation for what at first might appear to be an impossibility.
4. *Reframe the challenge.* A skeptical critic will sometimes frame an issue in a manner that stacks the deck against the Bible. Think about different ways to view the issue.

Understanding the Writer's Purpose

5. *Consider the writer's unique purpose.* Each author presents his material the way he does in order to support his themes.
6. *Remember that biblical writers didn't share our obsession with time.* They lived in a very different world. We shouldn't criticize them because their Gospels don't conform to twenty-first-century expectations regarding chronology.
7. *Don't listen to "nothing."* Arguments from silence are weak.
8. *Recognize that timeless treasures and limited lessons are not the same thing.* We sometimes misinterpret a teaching or event as universally applicable when its application was for a specific time and place.
9. *The fact that it's there doesn't guarantee it's right.* Even God's heroes can sometimes be wrong about things they said or did. The Bible reliably records statements and actions of people who were sometimes wrong.

DEALING WITH DISCREPANCIES IN DETAILS

10. *Remember that details are just details, not the whole story.* Small differences in details don't necessarily constitute a contradiction.

11. *Study the details for clues.* Skeptics sometimes overlook details that don't support their theories.

12. *Keep in mind that similar does not mean the same.* Jesus' ministry lasted about three years. What appear to be different versions of the same story or parable may actually be records of two different events.

13. *Recognize that discrepancies can be good.* The fact that all details do not completely line up shows the writers didn't consciously collude to make their stories correlate perfectly.

14. *Blame my agent.* Many stories record questions or statements from one character who may simply have been an intermediary who acted on behalf of someone else.

INTERPRETING THE TEXT RESPONSIBLY

15. *Recognize the difference between a paradox and a contradiction.* Although the Bible teaches many paradoxical principles, it does not contradict itself.

16. *Look for linguistic or translation mix-ups.* Misunderstandings about word meanings can often create the impression of a contradiction.

17. *Look for cultural confusion.* Similarly, we can reach inappropriate conclusions if we don't understand the cultural context of Bible stories and teaching.

18. *Give the Bible the benefit of the doubt.* Like a friend whom you have grown to trust, assume the Bible is reliable while you research the matters you don't fully understand.

At Last, We're Done

I hope you've found that this examination of the Bible and Jesus in a way you may not have previously considered has answered many of your questions.

Many reject Christianity because they consider it intellectually untenable. My first goal has been to erase the notion that anyone who is smart will automatically be a skeptic and anyone who has a strong faith must be a pinhead. My second goal has been to expose the filters people outside the historic Christian faith often employ when critiquing the Bible, to equip you with principles that deal with potential discrepancies, and to demonstrate that there *are* reasonable explanations for many of these challenges.

However, please note that the intellect can only take you so far. It can bring you to the edge of belief, but you yourself have to take that final step of faith. Some would like to call it a "blind leap of faith," implying that we must abandon all reason and, with little evidence to support us, plunge into some vast unknown. I prefer to call it a step of faith, not a blind leap. If you have not yet taken that step, I urge you to do so. I'm sure you, like so many before you, will discover that you are embarking on a life-changing, lifelong relationship with the Unfiltered Jesus of the Gospels.

For the Readers' Guide to this book, go to
www.cookministries.com/GreatQuestion.

Notes

Introduction

1. Michael Weisskopf, "Energized by Pulpit or Passion?" *Washington Post* (February 1, 1993): A1; downloaded October 31, 2003, from http://nl.newsbank.com.
2. Terry Mattingly, "Religion and the Media," *The Quill* (July/August 1993): n.p.; downloaded on January 15, 2003, from http://tmatt.gospelcom.net/tmatt/freelance/Quill93.htm.
3. Daniel C. Dennett, "The Bright Stuff," *New York Times* (July 12, 2003): A11; downloaded on July 22, 2003, from http://query.nytimes.com.
4. Ibid.
5. Nicholas D. Kristof, "Believe It, or Not," *New York Times* (August 15, 2003): n.p.; downloaded August 19, 2003, from http://www.nytimes.com.
6. Walter Scott, "Walter Scott's Personality Parade," *Parade* (New York: Parade Publications, October 19, 2003): 2.
7. Unitarian Universalist Association, "Unitarian Universalist Association Principles and Purposes," downloaded February 22, 2005, from www.uua.org/aboutuua/principles.html.
8. From an e-mail promoting the event generated from the e-mail address "The Hermit IX" generated June 9, 2004, and forwarded to the author on August 6, 2004.

1. Filters

1. Chris Argyris, "Teaching Smart People How to Learn," *Harvard Business Review* (May–June 1991): HBR OnPoint, 9.
2. Dennis W. Organ and W. Clay Hamner, *Organizational Behavior: An Applied Psychological Approach* (Plano, TX: Business Publications, Inc., 1982), 120.
3. J. Sterling Livingston, "Pygmalion in Management," *Harvard Business Review,* September 1, 2002, 3–4. http://harvardbusinessonline.hbsp.harvard.edu.

2. Jesus Unfiltered

1. *The Atlanta Journal Constitution*, "Ideas That Mattered in 2003," December 28, 2003.
2. Charlotte Allen, *The Human Christ: The Search for the Historical Jesus* (New York: The Free Press, 1998), n.p.
3. *The NIV Study Bible*, (Grand Rapids: Zondervan, 2002), footnote on Mark 2:7, 1493.
4. Philip Yancey, *What's So Amazing About Grace?* (Grand Rapids: Zondervan, 1997), 48.
5. Ibid., 41.
6. C. S. Lewis, *Mere Christianity* (New York: Macmillan Publishing Company, Inc., 1978), 55–56.

3. Filters That Add

1. Michael D. Coogan, ed., *The Illustrated Guide to World Religions* (New York: Oxford University Press, 1998), 90.
2. Ibid., 104.
3. Jospeh P. Gudel, "Islam's Worldwide Revival," CRI Statement D1-200-1, The Christian Research Institute, http://www.equip.org/free/DI200-1.htm (downloaded February 9, 2004), 4.
4. All quotes from the Qur'an are cited by R. C. Sproul and Abdul Saleeb, *The Dark Side of Islam* (Wheaton, IL: Crossway Books, 2003), 73.
5. Ibid., 66.
6. Alexander Brooks, "Between Isaac and Ishmael: Jewish and Islamic Animosity toward Christ," cited in Tal Brooke, ed., *The Conspiracy to Silence the Son of God* (Eugene, OR: Harvest House, 1998), 131.
7. Jen Kinney William, *The Mormons* (New York: Franklin Watts, 1996), 19.
8. Keith L. Brooks and Irvine Robertson, *The Spirit of Truth and the Spirit of Error* (Chicago: Moody, 1969).

9. Jerald and Sandra Tanner, *The Changing World of Mormonism* (Chicago: Moody, 1980), 22.

10. Bahá'í Information Center, "Beyond National Sovereignty: World Peace through a New World Order," NTC, 1985. Pamphlet provided by the Bahá'í Information Center.

11. Bahá'í Information Center, "One Common Faith: World Peace through the Oneness of Religion," NTC, 1985. Pamphlet provided by the Bahá'í Information Center.

12. James W. Deardorff, *Celestial Teachings: The Emergence of the True Testament of Jmmanuel (Jesus)* (Tigard, OR: Wild Flower Press, 1990), ix, 19, 32–38, 45–50, 63.

13. Ibid., 3.

14. Lynn Picknett and Clive Prince, *The Templar Revelation* (New York: Touchstone, 1997), 352–53.

4. Filters That Subtract—Atheism

1. R. C. Sproul, *If There's a God, Why Are There Atheists?* (Grand Rapids: Zondervan, 1974), 72.

2. Ibid., 49.

3. Ibid., 39.

4. Paul C. Vitz, *Faith of the Fatherless: The Psychology of Atheism* (Dallas: Spence Publishing Company, 1999), xiv.

5. Ibid., 3.

6. Ibid., 94.

7. Ibid., 145.

8. Ibid., 130.

9. Ibid., 134–36.

10. Ibid., 138.

11. Ibid., 130.

12. Ibid., 26–27.

13. Ibid., 28.

14. Ibid., 27.

15. Bertrand Russell, *Why I Am Not a Christian* (New York: Touchstone, 1957), 16.

16. Ibid., 16.

17. Leon Morris, *The Gospel according to Matthew* (Grand Rapids: Wm. B. Eerdmans Publishing Company, 1992), 257–58.

18. Curtis Vaughan, *The New Testament from 26 Translations* (Grand Rapids: Zondervan, 1967).

19. Alfred Marshall, *The Interlinear Greek-English New Testament* (Grand Rapids: Zondervan, 1974), 72.

20. Russell, 17.

21. Ibid., 18.

22. Allen C. Myers, ed., *The Eerdmans Bible Dictionary* (Grand Rapids: Wm. B. Eerdmans Publishing Company, 1987), 649.

23. Russell, 18–19.

24. Ibid., 19.

5. Filters That Subtract—Antisupernaturalism

1. Michael J. Wilkins and J. P. Moreland, *Jesus Under Fire* (Grand Rapids: Zondervan, 1995), 1–2.

2. Charlotte Allen, *The Human Christ: The Search for the Historical Jesus* (New York: The Free Press, 1998), 5.

3. Robert W. Funk, Roy W. Hoover, and the Jesus Seminar, *The Five Gospels: The Search for the Authentic Words of Jesus* (San Francisco: HarperSanFrancisco, 1993), 36.

4. James R. Edwards, "Who Do Scholars Say That I Am?" *Christianity Today* (March 4, 1996): 15.

5. Craig Blomberg, "Where Do We Start Studying Jesus?" cited in Michael J. Wilkins and J. P. Moreland, *Jesus Under Fire* (Grand Rapids: Zondervan, 1995), 19–20.

6. As quoted in George Arthur Buttrick, ed., *The Interpreter's Bible* (New York: Abingdon Press, 1951), 7:616.

6. Filters That Subtract—Selective Christian Theology

1. Jonathan Yardley, "New Version of 'Huck Finn' Is a Cannibalized

Classic," *The Washington Post* as reported in *Ann Arbor News Advertiser* (December 10, 1985).

2. Ibid.

3. C. S. Lewis, *The Great Divorce* (New York: Simon & Schuster, 1996), 95.

4. Lauren F. Winner, "meetingGod@beliefnet.com," *Christianity Today* (November 12, 2001): 70–74.

5. Ibid., 73–74.

6. Thomas Jefferson, *The Jefferson Bible* (Boston: Beacon Press, 1989) from the introduction by F. Forrester Church, 9–10.

7. Ibid., 12.

8. Ibid., 17.

9. Ibid., 27.

10. Ibid., 28.

11. Ibid., 30.

12. John Shelby Spong, *Rescuing the Bible from Fundamentalism* (San Francisco: HarperSanFrancisco, 1991), back cover.

13. Ibid., x.

14. Ibid.

15. Ibid., 1–4.

16. Ibid., 5–7.

17. Ibid., 18.

18. Ibid.

19. Ibid., 20.

20. Ibid., 21.

21. Ibid.

22. Ibid., 24.

23. Steve Dale, "The smartest animals on the planet," *USA Weekend* (February 20–22, 2004): 10.

24. Philip Yancey, *Reaching for the Invisible* God (Grand Rapids: Zondervan, 2000), 115.

25. Jefferson, 30.

26. Charlotte Allen, *The Human Christ: The Search for the Historical Jesus* (New York: The Free Press, 1988), dust jacket.

7. PRINCIPLES 1–4: APPROACHING THE MATERIAL WITH THE RIGHT PERSPECTIVE

1. Jack Hassard, *Adventures in Geology* (Alexandria, VA: American Geological Institute, 1970), 10–11.
2. Allen C. Myers, ed., *The Eerdmans Bible Dictionary* (Grand Rapids: Wm. B. Eerdmans Publishing Company, 1987), 571.
3. Merrill C. Tenney, *New Testament Survey* (Grand Rapids: Wm. B. Eerdmans Publishing Company, 1961), 96.
4. William P. Barker, *Everyone in the Bible* (Westwood, NJ: Fleming H. Revell Company, 1966), 286–87.
5. Lee Strobel, *The Case for Christ* (Grand Rapids: Zondervan, 1998), 85.
6. David O'Brien, *Today's Handbook for Solving Bible Difficulties* (Minneapolis: Bethany House Publishers, 1990), 60.
7. Barker, 286.
8. Marilyn vos Savant, "The Year's Most Dumbfounding Questions," *Parade* (New York: Parade Publications, December 21, 2003): 14.
9. Randel Helms, *Gospel Fictions* (Amherst, NY: Prometheus Books, 1988).
10. Ibid., 10.
11. Ibid.
12. Ibid., 11.
13. C. S. Lewis, *The Literary Impact of the Authorized Version* (Philadelphia: Fortress Books, 1967), 33.
14. Helms, 63.
15. Ibid., 64
16. Ibid., 65.
17. Robert Young, *Analytical Concordance to the Bible* (Grand Rapids: Wm. B. Eerdmans Publishing Company, 1973), 186.
18. Helms, 64.
19. Strobel, 99.
20. Helms, 64.
21. Frank LoMonte, "A tearful Richard Jewell lashes out," *The Augusta Chronicle* (Augusta, Georgia, October 29, 1996).

8. PRINCIPLES 5–9: UNDERSTANDING THE WRITER'S PURPOSE

1. *The NIV Study Bible* (Grand Rapids: Zondervan, 2002), footnote on Luke 3:23–28: 1541.
2. R. A. Torrey, *Difficulties in the Bible* (New Kensington, PA: Whitaker House, 1996), 151.
3. *The NIV Study Bible*, footnote on Luke 3:23–28: 1541.
4. Walter C. Kaiser, Peter H. Davids, F. F. Bruce, Manfred T. Brauch, *Hard Sayings of the Bible* (Downers Grove, IL: InterVarsity Press, 1996), 455–56.
5. Kaiser, et al., 456.
6. Kaiser, et al., 454–57.
7. Paul Copan, *"That's Just Your Interpretation"* (Grand Rapids: Baker Books, 2001), 186.
8. Downloaded June 24, 2004, from http://lsm.crt.state.la.us/cabildo/cab6.htm.
9. Downloaded June 24, 2004, from http://www.xphomestation.com/frm-history.html.
10. Gleason L. Archer, *Encyclopedia of Bible Difficulties* (Grand Rapids: Zondervan, 1982), 364.
11. Ibid., 335.
12. Kaiser, et al., 455.
13. C. Milo Connick, *Jesus: The Man, the Mission, and the Message* (Englewood Cliffs, NJ: Prentice-Hall, Inc., 1963), 324–26.
14. Ibid., 326.
15. Randel Helms, *Gospel Fictions* (Amherst, NY: Prometheus Books, 1988), 65, emphasis added.
16. David O'Brien, *Today's Handbook for Solving Bible Difficulties* (Minneapolis: Bethany House Publishers, 1990), 410.
17. Jack Kuhatschek, *Applying the Bible* (Grand Rapids: Zondervan, 1990), 143.
18. William L. Lane, *The Gospel according to Mark* (Grand Rapids: Wm. B. Eerdmans Publishing Company, 1974), 365.
19. Ibid., 367.

20. Robert H. Stein, *Difficult Passages in the New Testament* (Grand Rapids: Baker Book House, 1990), 61–62.

21. F. F. Bruce, *Answers to Questions* (Grand Rapids: Zondervan, 1972), 67.

9. PRINCIPLES 10–14: DEALING WITH DISCREPANCIES IN DETAILS

1. R. C. Sproul, *Explaining Inerrancy* (Orlando: Ligonier Ministries, 1996), 39–40.

2. Ian Wilson, *Jesus: The Evidence* (Washington DC: Regnery Publishing, Inc., 2000), 26.

3. David O'Brien, *Today's Handbook for Solving Bible Difficulties* (Minneapolis: Bethany House Publishers, 1990), 407.

4. Ibid., 408

5. F. F. Bruce, *Answers to Questions* (Grand Rapids: Zondervan, 1972), 42.

6. C. Milo Connick, *Jesus: The Man, the Mission, and the Message* (Englewood Cliffs, NJ: Prentice-Hall, Inc., 1963), 181.

7. *The NIV Study Bible*, (Grand Rapids: Zondervan, 2002), 1488, 1734.

8. Leon Morris, *The Gospel according to Matthew* (Grand Rapids: Wm. B. Eerdmans Publishing Company, 1992), 376.

9. William L. Lane, *The Gospel according to Mark* (Grand Rapids: Wm. B. Eerdmans Publishing Company, 1974), 272.

10. Ibid., 272.

11. Ibid.

12. See E. Daniel Orville, *A Harmony of the Four Gospels* (Grand Rapids: Baker Book House, 1986), 286–300; Walter Kaiser, et al., *Hard Sayings of the Bible* (Downers Grove, IL: InterVarsity Press, 1996), 506–8; Josh McDowell and Don Stewart, *Answers to Tough Questions Skeptics Ask about the Christian Faith* (San Bernardino, CA: Here's Life Publishing, Inc., 1980), 52–54; and Gleason Archer, *Encyclopedia of Bible Difficulties* (Grand Rapids: Zondervan, 1982), 347–56.

13. Kaiser, et al., 507.
14. Kaiser, et al., 508.
15. Connick, 382.
16. Ibid., 383.
17. All the charges are from Connick, 383.
18. Kaiser, *et al.*, 459.
19. Leon Morris, *The Gospel according to Matthew* (Grand Rapids: Wm. B. Eerdmans Publishing Comany, 1992), 380.
20. Herbert Lockyer, *All the Miracles of the Bible* (Grand Rapids: Zondervan, 1965), 211.

10. PRINCIPLES 15–18: INTERPRETING THE TEXT RESPONSIBLY

1. Thomas Jefferson, *The Jefferson Bible* (Boston: Beacon Press, 1989) from the introduction by F. Forrester Church, 30.
2. John Shelby Spong, *Rescuing the Bible from Fundamentalism* (San Francisco: HarperSanFrancisco, 1991), 21.
3. F. F. Bruce, *The Gospel and Epistles of John* (Grand Rapids: Wm. B. Eerdmans Publishing Company, 2002), 389.
4. Leon Morris, *The Gospel according to John* (Grand Rapids: Wm. B. Eerdmans Publishing Company, 1987), 841.
5. Gleason Archer, *Encyclopedia of Bible Difficulties* (Grand Rapids: Zondervan, 1982), 346.
6. Leon Morris, *The Gospel according to Matthew* (Grand Rapids: Wm. B. Eerdmans Publishing Company, 1992), 203.
7. Barbara M. Bowen, *Strange Scriptures That Perplex the Western Mind* (Grand Rapids: Wm. B. Eerdmans Publishing Company, 1985), 20.
8. Ibid., 76.
9. Robert H. Stein, *Difficult Passages in the New Testament* (Grand Rapids: Baker Book House, 1990), 45–46.
10. Paul Copan, *"That's Just Your Interpretation"* (Grand Rapids: Baker Books, 2001), 184.